The Company of Critics

BOOKS ALSO BY MICHAEL WALZER

The Revolution of the Saints (1965)

Obligations (1970)

Political Action (1971)

Regicide and Revolution (1974)

Just and Unjust Wars
(1977, second edition 1992, third edition, 2000)

Radical Principles (1977)

Spheres of Justice (1983)

Exodus and Revolution (1985)

Interpretation and Social Criticism (1987)

The Company of Critics (1988, second edition 2002)

What It Means to Be an American (1992)

Thick and Thin: Moral Argument at Home and Abroad (1994)

Pluralism, Justice, and Equality (1995)
(with David Miller)

On Toleration (1997)

The Jewish Political Tradition, Vol. I Authority (2000)
(Edited with Menachem Lorberbaum,
Noam Zohar, and Yair Lorberbaum)

THE COMPANY OF CRITICS

SOCIAL CRITICISM AND POLITICAL COMMITMENT IN THE TWENTIETH CENTURY

Michael Walzer

A Member of the Perseus Books Group

Published by Basic Books,
A Member of the Perseus Books Group

A cataloging-in-publication record for this book is available from the Library of Congress.
ISBN 0-465-09061-3

02 03 04 / 10 9 8 7 6 5 4 3 2 1

for my friends

in Jerusalem

CONTENTS

PREFACE TO THE SECOND EDITION

The subtitle of this book, "Social Criticism and Political Commitment in the Twentieth Century," was meant to be descriptive, not to set temporal limits on the relevance of its subject. Criticism and commitment will be no less necessary in this new century than they were in the last, and they may be more difficult to manage in the absence of those grand ideologies that once guided both critics and activists. On the other hand, the ragged remnants of ideology are no help, as the performance of many American social critics in the aftermath of the September 11 terrorist attack suggests. Driven by "theories" of imperialism, oppression, and third-world virtue, they failed utterly to understand what had happened, or to sympathize with the victims, or to think seriously about the defense of their own country. This book can be read, retrospectively, as an effort to explain how it is that criticism goes wrong in these ways. It is also an argument about the decline of the big ideologies and the need now (but I believe this was always necessary) to base the critical enterprise on a more concrete and intimate knowledge of the world than they provided. If *The Company of Critics* finds a new audience among twenty-first century social critics and political activists, I hope it will give them reasons to seek out that kind of knowledge.

The central argument of *Company* is that criticism is most properly the work of "insiders," men and women mindful of and committed to the society whose policies or practices they call into question—who *care about* what happens to it. This doesn't by any means rule out exiles or expatriots as critics. Just as there are people who stay at home but cut their moral and political ties, so there are people who go abroad but remain connected. I do mean, however, to call into question the critical standing of world-historical ideologists and philosophers-on-the-mountaintop—I mean all those who take radical detachment, absolute impartiality, or a God's eye view of the world to be the prerequisite of criticism. For they have mostly not been caring critics.

Detachment is the issue on which controversy has centered since the first reviews of *The Company of Critics* appeared in American magazines. (Actually, the controversy began before that, as my original preface explains.) How much distance is "critical distance"? What kind of criticism is possible from far away and from up close? My critics have generally defended a distant perspective; I am not convinced, but I will suggest here a somewhat different account of closeness than the book provides. In any case, readers should be forewarned: the field of social criticism is contested territory.

The reason standardly given for distance and detachment is the need for objectivity. Critics are supposed to step back, cut themselves loose, look at their own society as if they were visitors from a faraway planet, and then give us an impartial, objective, and therefore true account of what is wrong. The standard view is that there is only one such account. No doubt, it can be expressed in different idioms and styles—in the staccato language of the political pamphlet, in a satirical novel, in the high poetry of biblical prophecy, in drama and melodrama, and even in the gray prose of an academic treatise. But the message, if it is impartial, objective, and true, is also necessarily singular.

I believe, by contrast, that criticism not only has different expressive forms but also different doctrinal or ideological contents. There are many interesting, provocative, possibly valid critical arguments—and they derive from different experiences and perspectives *within* the society that is being criticized. The ideal critic is part of his or her society, engaged rather than detached. Engagement takes many forms, though there is only one kind of detachment; critics look at society from different perspectives, even if God's eye provides a single view; upbringing, religious belief, and political commitment serve to differentiate critics—and all this guarantees that the critical enterprise, if it is not repressed in the name of ideological correctness, will always be rich and various.

Criticism is a common activity everywhere. But in democracies it is also a public activity. The citizens of a democracy don't have to worry about who is listening; they don't have to avoid controversial or dangerous subjects; they don't have to whisper—hence the critical tumult that Americans know so well. It isn't always easy to tolerate the vociferousness of one's fellow citizens. But democracy requires more than toleration. The democratic rule is: criticize, and pay attention to the criticism of others.

But then how do we judge the many different critiques? Which critics should we listen to? There are no easy answers to questions like these. Some of the critics discussed in this book are more worth listening to than others, but I don't give them grades. There are, of course, critics we have to listen to: the ones who touch our moral nerves (in order to do that, they need to know where the nerves are located) and force us to look at what we would rather avoid, the wrongness in our own society, in our own lives. But even then, there are different views of what's wrong and different accounts of the wrongness: a multitude of critics, all shouting at once, demanding our attention. The reason we are able to sort it all out is that we are critics too, members of the company; we know something about right and wrong; we know what it feels like to touch a nerve.

Amidst all the noise, there is sometimes a voice, perhaps an unexpected voice, that holds us, enlightens us, moves us to action. In this book, I have tried to understand what it is that makes a voice special in that way. I have focused on the standpoint that critics take, the way they relate to their fellow citizens or their comrades in a political movement. Detachment and connection make up the opposition that I explore, and I imagine it, as I have been doing here, in spatial terms: how close? how far? My claim is that critical distance is best measured in inches. Closeness is the crucial quality of the good social critic—I don't mean the successful critic but rather the one whose success we, who are also critics, would wish for.

But I think now that I should describe this closeness in somewhat different terms. For it isn't only a political position that I am after, but also a personal morality. Politics is first of all an adversarial business, and so is social criticism; it is worked out for a political purpose; we judge it from a political standpoint. But we can think of it, secondly and hardly less importantly, as a way of living with others, where what is at issue is not only the critic's rightness but also his goodness. How do we recognize the value of a critic's work? Surely it has to do with what he or she knows, not only about things but also about people. We can best learn about both by looking, as I try to do in this book, at examples drawn from the historical record of our own time. Neither the right political purpose nor the right standpoint guarantee the critic's value. We don't have to look far to find critics committed to an "ideologically correct" position, pressing for reforms that (let's say) you and I strongly endorse, whose criticism nonetheless strikes the wrong note, puts us off, fails to touch our hearts or convince us. What do they lack? I want to suggest that they lack what might be called the critical virtues. Good social criticism is the work of good men and women.

I don't mean "good" simply. People who are cruel to their neighbors and neglectful of their children can still be powerful social critics, even critics of cruelty and neglect. But they do require a specific set of moral virtues. The first of these, and the most obvious, is courage. I have described it in the portraits that make up this book as a political virtue, above all, the ability to sustain a commitment in dark times, to "hang in there" after the failure of a campaign or a movement. But there are obviously other kinds of courage. Sometimes what criticism requires is actual physical courage, to persist in the face of threats, imprisonment, and violence. Many of the East European dissidents of the communist years displayed this kind of courage, often to a remarkable degree, and have since been honored for it. More important for my purposes here, however, is the moral courage necessary to continue a critique of tyranny or oppression when one's fellow citizens are silent or complicit and, what is even harder, to confront and condemn their complicity. It isn't easy to deal with the anger, outrage, and incomprehension that this last kind of criticism, when it comes from someone near and dear, inevitably provokes. "That's what our enemies say about us. How can you also say it?" Critics who hear that question and go on with their criticism are brave human beings—though they are only sometimes honored for their bravery.

Acknowledging that difficult bravery, and honoring it, I also have to say that some people are much too eager to go on with their criticism; they welcome every opportunity to provoke and offend their fellows; they are gleeful critics. *Epater la bourgeoisie* is, after all, a favorite activity of bourgeois intellectuals; I don't think that it requires courage. Or, if it does, the courage in question is what Aristotle would call an excess or distortion of the virtue. Willful provocation, the desire to be outrageous, derives from a kind of moral recklessness. And recklessness doesn't make for good social criticism because it is timely only by accident and rarely accurate in its substance. It severs the link between social critics and the society they are criticizing and frees them from any need to understand the people who live in that society—complacently, perhaps, but sometimes not. These critics know the people's sore points, their moral nerves, and pinch them for effect, without thinking much about where the soreness comes from or what it signifies. Moral consciousness is what it signifies, without which there would be no sensation at all.

The best critics, by contrast, acknowledge that consciousness and respect it. Fearful of criticizing those nearest to them because of the nearness, they make the criticism anyway. Since they regard the nearness not only as a moral tie but as a personal engagement, their critique has the sensitivity, intimacy, and grasp of detail that are features of confessional literature. It is directed outward, toward a society, a group of people, a set of policies or institutions, but it doesn't pretend to distance or detachment. "I have cut myself off. I have nothing to do with those people." Courageous critics, it seems to me, don't usually talk that way (see especially my chapter on the South African poet, Breyten Breytenbach). Their courage lies in criticizing people with whom they have a lot to do, with whom they share a common moral understanding.

The second virtue required for social criticism is compassion. "The need to lend a voice to suffering," wrote Theodor Adorno in *Negative Dialectics*, "is a condition of all truth" (trans. E. B. Ashton [New York: Seabury Press, 1973], pp. 17–18). Well, not of all truth; I would say simply that men and women who don't feel this need are unlikely to recognize the critical truths about their own society.

I thought at first to say that compassion is required for *leftwing* social criticism, which is my subject in most of this book (see especially the chapter on Ignazio Silone), but I am not sure the restriction is accurate. Critics must, however, be able to sympathize with their society's victims, whether these are the victims of political tyranny; racial, religious, or sexist bigotry; ideological fanaticism; economic exploitation; or social or intellectual snobbery. (On these last points, George Orwell is an especially useful example.) And they must sympathize whether the victims are strangers or relatives. Without a generalized compassion of this sort, their criticism will be neither accurate nor timely. They must have some knowledge or sense of the human suffering that their state or their society or (some of) their fellow citizens have caused—first, so that their anger is properly focused, and second, so that it is properly expressed.

But often, in the case of people who think themselves closely connected to the tyrants and bigots among whom they live, compassion for the victims turns into gnawing, devouring guilt. And guilt is as counterproductive as glee for the critical project, for it can produce a radically uncritical acceptance of the perspective of the victims, a surrender—experienced perhaps as a sacrifice—of the critic's own judgement, the faculty most necessary to critical success. Of course, social critics are always accused of "going over to the other side," but even when that is the right thing to do, as it sometimes is, there isn't much point in leaving your critical faculties behind. The other side needs criticism too.

Mostly, however, guilt-ridden critics don't "go over"; they stay where they are. They criticize their own people, but in a wholesale way, without distinction, nuance, or restraint, as if driven by self-hate or by a desire for collective self-erasure. They cannot find or acknowledge the moral strength that exists around them (this is what I found most appalling among some leftist critics of America in the aftermath of September 11); they describe only weakness and corruption. But this is still, or can be, a contribution to the critical project. By contrast, someone who cannot acknowledge the suffering of the victims will have nothing to contribute. The absence of compassion is more dangerous than the distortion of guilt.

What explains this absence in normal human beings who are perfectly capable of feeling the pain of their own children, say, or of their friends? The standard explanation—which is right, I think, in many cases—is that when the victims are people with whom we have no familial, ethnic, or religious relationship, we just don't see them; and so we can't engage emotionally with their suffering. When nationalist intellectuals refuse to criticize their own nation for the suffering it inflicts on ethnic or linguistic minorities, it is because the minorities seem so far away, so radically "other." They don't make a sufficiently concrete appearance on the nationalists' mental screen.

But the failure of compassion may have another source. Sometimes intellectuals can't acknowledge the pain of the victims because their attention is focused elsewhere by some theory about the world. Consider, for example, the role of the theory of totalitarianism in the Vietnam War. Those American intellectuals who were most gripped by the dangers of totalitarian politics were least likely to see what their country was doing in Vietnam. Perhaps they were right about the dangers; the theory of totalitarianism was a pretty good theory, which is why it was so effective in determining what people could and couldn't see. The threat to democracy loomed so large that it was hard to look closely at anything else and, as a result, burning villages were effectively invisible.

The third critically necessary virtue, which doesn't figure much in the literature, is a good eye. I mean a (relatively) unmediated experience of reality or, better, a readiness to have such an experience, an openness to the "real world." Yes, yes, I know that there is no such thing as an unmediated experience of reality, and I know that my parenthetical qualification—"relatively unmediated"—is of little help. We bring all sorts of mental equipment to our everyday experience; our perceptions are always structured by theories of one sort or another. A good eye isn't God's eye, providing the one and only perspective; it can't end all disagreement about what is going on. Still, I persist in believing because it is a feature of my own dealings with politics and society—and probably of yours too—that some people are more ready than others to look at the world and acknowledge what they see. And this readiness seems to me a moral quality, a kind of down-to-earth honesty. "Do you see the war against the totalitarian enemy?" "I see burning villages." Social criticism is well-served by this second kind of seeing. Albert Camus provides an example, which I develop at some length in these pages; he saw the terrorism of the Algerian National Liberation Front and gave it its proper name, while Jean-Paul Sartre, beguiled by some version of third-worldist ideology, quite literally could not recognize the terrorism he "saw."

The idea of a good eye may be clarified through a comparison with a word that Max Weber uses in his well-known essay on political responsibility, "Politics as a Vocation": *augenmass*, which is translated into English by Hans Gerth and C. Wright Mills as "a sense of proportion," a capacity to make "cool" judgements about the relative importance of this or that (*From Max Weber: Essays in Sociology* [London: Routledge & Kegan Paul, 1948], p.115). It is surely a good thing—for social critics as well as political leaders—to have a sense of proportion. But that is not quite what I mean by a good eye. Perhaps the idiom *ein gutes augenmass haben* comes closer: "to have a sure eye," says the dictionary (*New Cassells*, 1958). But that is still an eye for assessment, not simply for seeing. What has to be assessed must already have been seen. I suppose that a critic with a good eye both sees and judges: *This*, he says, must not be overlooked or excused! But the combination requires an immediacy of vision as well as distance and coolness. The immediacy comes first, and its loss is especially disastrous for the critical project.

But I acknowledge the possible excess of this virtue also: the inability or refusal to grasp the larger context or to recognize the value of theory in fixing contextual boundaries. Here, "proportion" plays its critical role. The burning villages aren't, after all, the whole story of the war. The war may be a good one despite the burning villages. And similarly, the bomb in the café wasn't the whole story of the Algerian war; one might "see" the bomb and still come to a different view of the war from Camus'. But without the capacity to recognize and acknowledge what is happening, the larger view is likely to be corrupted.

Perhaps a good eye has to be accompanied by a certain kind of intellectual humility, a willingness to think that one's theories about the world might be wrong or incomplete and that the evidence of one's senses could count against them. It is surprising how many intellectuals who profess to believe in the value of evidence are not humble in this way. Theoretical conviction overrides sensory data. The "big picture" defeats the good eye. But this point is probably best made the other way around: the virtue of a good eye works, when it works, against intellectual arrogance.

Courage, compassion, and a good eye are three virtues that good critics need. They must be brave enough to tell their fellow citizens that they are acting wrongly, when they are acting wrongly, but refuse the temptation of a provocative recklessness. They must sympathize with the victims, whoever the victims are, without becoming their uncritical supporters. They must look at the world in a straightforward way and report what they see. Saying this, I mean only to elaborate on some of the qualities of a good person and to describe (some of) the common virtues. Critics aren't saints, even if one or another of them is virtuous beyond the normal run. Is this an anomaly in my argument? I want social criticism that is accurate and timely, and this will often be, as I argue again and again in the chapters that follow, radical criticism. But I distrust critics who are not men and women of common virtue and ordinary humanity.

I deny the anomaly. What I have offered here is simply a new description of the "connected critic," the hero of this book, who stands in a certain moral relationship to his or her society. The virtues of courage, compassion, and a good eye, properly understood, constitute and sustain the connection. They represent the personal side of a political position—or, perhaps better, they suggest the moral character that makes a decent politics possible.

Michael Walzer
January 2002

PREFACE

I decided to write a book about social criticism for personal as well as political and philosophical reasons. Over a number of years, I have been arguing (most clearly in *Spheres of Justice* [Basic Books, 1983]) against the claim that moral principles are necessarily external to the world of everyday experience, waiting *out there* to be discovered by detached and dispassionate philosophers. In fact, it seems to me, the everyday world is a moral world, and we would do better to study its internal rules, maxims, conventions, and ideals, rather than to detach ourselves from it in search of a universal and transcendent standpoint. But many reviewers and commentators have said that this argument makes social criticism impossible; it binds us tightly, inescapably, to the status quo. Unless we are in sight of the sun, like Plato's philosopher, we can make no judgment about life in the cave. If we are unable to appeal to the outside, critics inside must turn apologist. I take this response seriously, take it to heart, indeed, since I don't mean to turn my own work into an apology for this (or any other) society. And so I have tried to figure out what it is that social critics do and how they go about doing it. Where do they find their critical principles? Where do they stand when they make their critique? How are they connected to, or disconnected from, the men and women whose society they are criticizing?

Questions like these are best answered with reference to the life and work of actual critics. Hence my eleven subjects, all of them intellectuals, publicists, political activists, who have spoken harshly and angrily about their own society. They constitute a small part of the twentieth-century company of social critics, but not, I think, an unrepresentative part; and their lives pose, often in dramatic ways, the question implicit in my title: what further company should critics keep? What is the preferred character of critical accompaniment? Some critics seek only the acquaintance of other critics; they find their peers only outside the cave, in the blaze of Truth. Others find peers and sometimes even comrades inside, in the shadow of contingent and uncertain truths. My own commitment to the cave leads me to prefer the second group. But that preference determines nothing. What is at issue is the cogency and force, the verisimilitude and nuance, of the criticism that results from these different choices.

For it does make a difference where the critic stands, inside the cave or out; and it makes a difference how he relates to the cave-dwellers. I want to explore that difference, in its circumstantial details and its larger meanings, and then point to a way of standing, a way of relating to other people, that warrants imitation: the way of the connected critic. I am not going to suggest a substantive critique of American (or any other) society—though the maxim holds here as elsewhere: Criticize the world; it needs it! My immediate concern is more with the practice of the critic than with his message, and especially with the path he traces over that difficult terrain called "critical distance." Success in criticism probably has more to do with the place and standing of the critic than with his theory of society or political ideology. In that sense, the people who charged me with undermining the critical enterprise by insisting on the internal character of moral principle have at least focused on the right issue. But now we must look at actual critics and ask on what ground they stood when they studied, rehearsed, and proclaimed their critical arguments.

I rehearsed some of my own arguments in *Interpretation and Social Criticism* (Harvard University Press, 1987), and I repeat here an occasional sentence or favorite phrase. But that was more of a philosophical statement; in this book I am concerned with history and politics. That was a general discussion of the critical enterprise; this is a more focused discussion of twentieth-century criticism, of the critic in an age of popular revolt, worked through a series of examples. The examples are crucial; I have tried to choose people who will be familiar to most readers; and I have written about these people at historical junctures, or with reference to political movements, that are also familiar. In different circumstances, my eleven social critics faced similar problems, and so my understanding of their enterprise is developed by repetition rather than by consecutive argument; it has the form of a theme with variations. At the end I attempt a summary statement. But no one who has attended to the examples will have any doubt by then about my view of their meaning.

ACKNOWLEDGMENTS

I worked on this book over a period of seven or eight years, and each of its chapters was read by more friends and colleagues than I can list here. I have benefited from their strictures and their suggestions. Indeed, I have had my own company of critics, at the Institute for Advanced Study in Princeton, at The Hebrew University's Institute for Advanced Studies in Jerusalem, where I spent six months in 1987, and at a number of colleges and universities where I have lectured on social criticism. The chapter on Camus was originally a Yakov Talmon Memorial Lecture in Jerusalem. The chapter on Foucault was first presented at Princeton University. Benda, Camus, and Foucault were the subjects of my Brick Lectures at the University of Missouri. Foucault served again for the Matchette Lecture at Brooklyn College.

A few people provided special help: Adi Ophir with the Buber chapter; Michael Rustin with Gramsci; Franco Ferraresi and James Scott with Silone; Joan Scott, Linda Gordon, Susan Okin, and Jane Mansbridge with de Beauvoir; Clifford Geertz with Foucault; Hermann Gilliomee with Breytenbach.

Irving Howe read every chapter, and though he had and has disagreements with my argument, entered wholeheartedly into my project. His advice was always valuable, both on matters of substance and on matters of style. He is a model social critic, as well as a model literary critic, and this book is in some part his. It is also in some part Judith Walzer's, with whom I have talked endlessly about the relative virtues of connected and disconnected criticism. She is my own most closely connected critic. From my friends in Jerusalem I have learned the meaning of faithfulness in criticism, and that is why this book is dedicated to them.

The Benda chapter is a revision of an essay originally published in *Conflict and Consensus: A Festschrift in Honor of Lewis A. Coser*, edited by Walter W. Powell and Richard Robbins. Copyright © 1984 by The Free Press, a Division of Macmillan, Inc. Used by permission of the publisher. Early versions of the Camus and Foucault chapters appeared in *Dissent*. An exchange with David Bromwich about Camus (also in *Dissent*) helped me to clarify my argument. The quotation from the poem "breyten prays for himself" is taken from *In Africa Even the Flies Are Happy* by Breyten Breytenbach, translated by Denis Hirson, and is reproduced here by kind permission of the author and John Calder (Publishers) Ltd. Copyright © 1976, 1977 by Yolande Breytenbach and Meulenhoff Nederland, Amsterdam, and translation copyright © 1978 by John Calder (Publishers) Ltd.

The staff of Princeton's Institute, Jerusalem's too, was wonderfully helpful. I am especially grateful, again, for the skill and patience of Lynda Emery.

The Company of Critics

1

Introduction: The Practice of Social Criticism

The Ancient and Honorable Company

Social criticism must be as old as society itself. How can men and women ever have lived together without complaining about the circumstances of their common life? Complaint is one of the elementary forms of self-assertion, and the response to complaint is one of the elementary forms of mutual recognition. When what is at issue is not existence itself but social existence, being-for-others, then complaint is proof enough: I complain, therefore I am. We discuss the complaint, therefore we are. And just as Descartes's *Cogito* is not the end of cogitation—as if he had said that having demonstrated his existence by thinking, he could now exist without further thought—but rather the very beginning, so "I complain" is only the beginning of the history of complaint. In the course of social existence, the practice of complaining is steadily elaborated—in satire, polemic, exhortation, indictment, prophecy, and countless other common and specialized ways.

The modern social critic is a specialist in complaint, not the first, certainly not the last. When the specialization first emerged, when intellectuals first claimed the right to castigate their fellows, I shall not try to say. It happened long ago and concerns me here only insofar as past examples shed light on contemporary cases. But it is important to stress that social criticism has a history, for some critics today announce themselves newborn. They are, they say, specialists of a special sort, historically original, the products of a radical break, not only modern but modernist: self-conscious, oppositional, alienated.[1] The argument for newness is so frequently made, by both friends and enemies of the critical enterprise, that there must be something to it. So I shall turn immediately to the claims represented by those resonant adjectives—"self-conscious," "oppositional," and "alienated"—that name the qualities of which twentieth-century intellectuals and social critics are most proud. I mean to deny the novelty of each one, but I will in the end acknowledge that something indeed has changed, not so much in the critic's understanding of himself as in his relations with other people. The problem central to this book—central, it seems to me, to the modern age—is the connection of specialists and commoners, elite and mass. Focusing on that, I shall probably be a little impatient with the insistence of the specialist that his inner life is in itself profoundly interesting.

First claim: that criticism as a self-conscious activity, a chosen role, is a recent phenomenon, the product of enlightenment and romanticism (the activity enlightened, the role romantic). It is difficult, obviously, to judge the self-consciousness of men and women from the distant past, but this cannot be right. Surely the prophets of ancient Israel, to take the most distant example, must have been aware of themselves as social critics, even if they were also, in their own eyes, divine messengers. Though the prophet Amos spoke in God's name when he said, "I hate, I despise your feasts / And I will take no delight in your solemn assemblies," it isn't anachronistic to suggest that he was expressing, and knew himself to be expressing, his own anger and contempt.[2] Again, when Socrates questioned his fellow citizens about their understanding of the good, wasn't he engaged in what we call today "ideological critique"? There cannot be much doubt that he had a fully developed sense of his own critical role:

> It is literally true (even if it sounds rather comical) that God has especially appointed me to this city, as though it were a large thoroughbred horse which because of its great size is inclined to be lazy and needs the stimulation of some

> stinging fly. It seems to me that God has attached me to this city to perform the office of such a fly; and all day long I never cease to settle here, there, and everywhere, rousing, persuading, reproving every one of you.[3]

Many of the sophists must have had similar, if somewhat less extravagant, notions about themselves. And again, the Roman satirists, the preaching friars of the Middle Ages, the humanists of the Renaissance—all these people were, in their different ways, social critics, and they can hardly have failed to reflect on what they were doing, if only because what they were doing was often dangerous. It is a mistake to regard reflexivity as a modern invention. When we cannot recognize self-consciousness in ancient texts, it is probably best to assume it.

Second claim: that all previous critics focused their attention on individual conduct or belief; they did not set themselves in opposition to the social order itself. They were *social* critics only insofar as society is directly constituted by the actions and ideas of its members, without the mediation of ideologies, practices, and institutional arrangements. But this claim involves a misreading of past and present alike. For the past, consider Hosea's angry line, "They have set up kings, but not by me."[4] Or Socrates' claim at his trial that "no man on earth who conscientiously opposes either you [the Athenians] or any other organized democracy . . . can possibly escape with his life."[5] Hosea apparently believed that there was something wrong with monarchy itself, not merely with this or that king; Socrates apparently believed (as Plato certainly did) that there was something wrong with democratic government, not merely with this or that group of citizens. It is true, however, that throughout the Middle Ages and into early modern times, criticism was concerned almost exclusively with individual moral character and intellectual commitment: wicked actions and false doctrines. The medieval and Renaissance "mirror of princes" literature, for example, asks only what the prince should think and do and has nothing to say about the regime over which he presides or the hierarchical order he defends. It censures princes of bad character, never the principality itself. Against this background, the systematic critique of political institutions and social structures can plausibly be called a modern creation.

But even in the present this is not a creation that any of us lives with consistently; structural criticism is rarely sustained for long without being personalized. Modern critics have produced their own "mirror" literature, sometimes for rulers, sometimes for ordinary citizens, sometimes for movement militants. "Here individuals are dealt with only insofar as they are the . . . embodiments of particular class relations and class interests," writes Marx in the preface to *Capital*.[6] One doesn't have to read much further in his work, however, to see that even when this position is adhered to and individual capitalists, say, are exempt from criticism, other individuals—intellectuals and working-class spokesmen who don't endorse Marx's structural analysis and follow his political lead—are not exempt. The critique of intellectual opportunism and working-class "false consciousness" is central to Marxism from its beginnings until the present time. Focused on conduct and belief, this kind of criticism, at least, is very old. I can find nothing in it unique to modernity.

Third claim: that the critic today is alienated, disaffected, and unattached, without a secure social place, a recognized role, or honor among his fellows. *Ill-sorted with the bourgeoisie*—here surely is a modern figure. Maybe. But one can already detect the symptoms of alienation among the radical divinity students and the dissident divines of the Reformation period.[7] Ill-sorted with aristocrats, gentlemen, and merchants alike, many of these divines did, however, find their way to important positions in the universities or within the old parish or new congregational systems. The Protestant ministry incorporated dissidence. Similarly, I suppose, the monastic clergy of the Middle Ages enjoyed, if that is the right word, a kind of institutionalized alienation: ill-sorted outside, its members were secure within. Julien Benda admired monasticism and looked for some contemporary equivalent because he thought that it served the cause of philosophical independence and critical detachment. But is there in fact no contemporary equivalent, no institutional structure within which critics find honor (and economic support)?

Whatever its social location, the class of alienated intellectuals doesn't coincide with the class of social critics, not then and not now. Alienation is most often expressed in political withdrawal, disinterest, or radical escape; and then there is no engagement at all with the critical enterprise. Nineteenth-century "bohemians," for example, despite their disdain for the philistinism of bourgeois society, had only an occasional and intermittent interest in changing that society. They lived on their disdain; they did not produce a serious critique. "The sensibility of bohemia," writes Alasdair MacIntyre, "effectively cuts it off from the vast mass of mankind, on whom the bohemians are in economic fact parasitic."[8] There hardly seems much of a desire to instruct or reform the mass, though there is often a desire to shock its more watchful members. Baudelaire's "cult of multiplied sensation" suggests indeed an alternative to the bourgeois way of life (and to every other way of life) but not one that could possibly be generalized. The bohemian's search for sensation is in psychological fact parasitic on the restraint and frugality of everyone else. Without the dependable dullness of ordinary men and women, his search would cease to be an adventure. Perhaps bohemian artists and intellectuals act out the inner tensions of bourgeois society (between radical individualism and conventional respectability, as Jerrold Seigel has suggested), but the acting out is generally too idiosyncratic to make a critical difference.[9]

Alternatively, alienation gives rise to revolutionary commitment and political activism—or at least to brief fits of commitment and activism. One of the more curious incidents in recent political history is the bolshevization of the cultural avant-garde in the aftermath of the Russian Revolution. Futurists, surrealists, and dadaists hurried to align themselves with the Communist party.[10] Except in a few cases, the alliance did not last long, and its characteristic expression was the manifesto rather than the critical essay or poem. Perhaps the revolutionary movement is too heated an environment for serious critical work. That might explain why, though revolutionary leaders often begin as social critics, most social critics do not end as revolutionaries. Frightened conservatives, indeed, hold criticism itself to be implicitly revolutionary, and the young Marx, from the other side, also argued that the "arm of criticism" only paves the way for the "criticism of arms."[11] But criticism and revolution are two different activities, and alienation is probably more necessary to the second than to the first.

Think, for example, of humanist writers like Erasmus, Thomas More, and John Colet—all of them social critics, none of them alienated, none of them revolutionaries. These people have their more modern equivalents, among whom we should probably count the French *philosophes*, critical, certainly, but also comfortable in the salons of Paris and even, sometimes, in the courts of Europe. And in the twentieth century, didn't a philosopher like Jean-Paul Sartre play a similar part (though he was more likely to be received by Fidel Castro than by the contemporary counterparts of Frederick or Catherine the Great)? Sartre might have wanted to be a revolutionary, but the occasion never presented itself; and it is implausible to give the title "alienated" to the leading light of French intellectual life and the editor of the most influential journal in postwar Europe. Or consider, as easier equivalents of the old humanists, José Ortega y Gasset in Spain or Lionel Trilling in the United States or Jürgen Habermas in Germany—critics, again, but also well-established and much-honored professors. For that matter, does it make any sense to call Herbert Marcuse, who worked for the Office of Strategic Services and moved on to the American professoriat, an alienated intellectual? Or Michel Foucault, who held a chair in the prestigious Collège de France?*

If alienation is a mental state rather than a sociological condition, then it is probably legitimate to apply the term to critics like Marcuse and Foucault. But we must beware of confusing alienation with anger and hostility—with criticism itself. In a sense, every critic is alienated from the society he criticizes, at odds with the complacency and self-satisfaction of (some of) his fellows. This description, however, doesn't help us much in understanding what it means to be a critic or why anyone would bother to claim the title. In any case, the modern academy, like the medieval monastery, institutionalizes this sort of alienation and provides a setting, more or less congenial, for the critical enterprise. So society segregates, while it also protects, the men and women who worry about its legitimacy. Critics who look for a home in (or near) political parties and movements escape the segregation and surrender the protection; they come closer to newness than do their academic fellows; it is harder to find precedents for their experience. But they are hardly aliens in their new environment. Parties and movements are the creations of people very much like themselves. Insofar as they remain critics, critical now of their new comrades, they are not so much alienated as uneasily integrated; their relation to party officials is something like that of medieval religious radicals to the ecclesiastical authorities.

Contemporary social critics, then, are not peculiarly self-conscious; they are not peculiarly hostile to the societies in which they live; they are not peculiarly alienated from those societies. We can best describe them as the most recent members, no doubt with their own rites and symbols, of the Ancient and Honorable Company of Social Critics.

* Foucault's academic position and that of many other contemporary social critics, according to Jacques Bouveresse, constitute an "official marginality" (quoted in J. G. Merquiour, *Foucault* [London: Fontana, 1985], p. 160). The phrase is a good one, but it doesn't apply only to critical intellectuals in modern liberal societies. A surprising number of premodern and preliberal societies have made similar positions available.

Languages of Criticism

Political censure, moral indictment, skeptical question, satiric comment, angry prophecy, utopian speculation—social criticism takes all these forms. The list may include too much, but I expect that it meets the views of the rulers and well-established members of society, who ought to know their critics. Given this list, the practice of criticism is certainly very old. I have stressed its long history in order to draw attention to its normality, its sheer ordinariness. Underlying the different critical specializations is a common activity. That is why the specializations, though various in style and content, are continuous over time. They resemble the specialized practice of medicine: a professional and sometimes scientific overlay on a folk art.

The primary or natural language of criticism is that of the folk; the best critics simply take hold of that language and raise it to a new pitch of intensity and argumentative power—like Luther in his pamphlets or Marx in *The Communist Manifesto*.[12] At the same time, however, more ordinary critics, like doctors, will look for some way to distinguish themselves from their amateur competitors and will find that language is the easiest way. So they are led to imitate the prevailing discourse, sometimes even the technical jargons, of the high culture and the educated elites of their time. Renaissance critics talk like classical historians and philosophers, Reformation critics like theologians, nineteenth-century critics like scientists, twentieth-century critics like modernist poets and novelists. Popular preachers and pamphleteers, journalists and street-corner orators translate the criticism for a larger audience. We can think of a complaining public served at different levels by a series of specialists in complaint. But critics don't commonly specialize in a particular area, the way a doctor might work only on the heart, the brain, or the belly. Until very recently, at least, most social critics were general practitioners. Their specializations were linguistic and methodological rather than substantive. They criticized the political regime in the language of Plato and Aristotle and argued (as Plato and Aristotle had done) that politics encompassed or shaped the whole of society; or they criticized the economy in the language of Adam Smith and David Ricardo and argued that the economy was the foundation of all the rest. One thing leads to another; criticism is a restless and hence a "totalizing" activity.

At its root, however, criticism is always moral in character, whether it is focused on individuals or political and social structures. Its crucial terms are corruption and virtue, oppression and justice, selfishness and the commonweal. When "something is rotten in the state of Denmark," the rot is some wrongful policy or practice or set of relationships. What else could it be? The special role of the critic is to describe what is wrong in ways that suggest a remedy. But he is continually tempted to elevate his description so that it doesn't only supplement but effectively supplants the original perception of rottenness. The perception is too simple, too common, while the critical description can readily be cast in technical or esoteric form. The higher the critic's specialization, the greater the distance between himself and his audience, the more technical or esoteric his criticism is likely to be.

The standard hope of modern radicals is that popular education and democratic politics will bring the critic into a closer relationship with ordinary people so that criticism will be more like common complaint. But there is a problem here: the struggle for democracy seems indeed to bring specialists and commoners together, but the ambiguities of success breed separation. The actually existing popular regimes, more or less democratic, seem to produce a class of critics in flight from their audience. Mass society puts a special kind of pressure on the critic, especially if he claims to speak for the masses. How can he speak authoritatively unless he also speaks differently? Perhaps that is why contemporary "critical theory" is one of the most obscure of all the languages of criticism, and why its practitioners insist that the seriousness of their enterprise is intimately linked to its theoretical difficulty.[13] Curiously, earlier generations of social critics, in predemocratic societies, were far more intimate with their readers and listeners—though the number of these was relatively small. The plain style of the Puritan ministers and the straightforward prose of the eighteenth-century *philosophes* suggest an easy adaptation to a limited and presumably well-known audience. These people were also less driven than contemporary critics are to repress the moral impulse that underlay their work.

But critical obscurity is as old as criticism itself, its inevitable accompaniment, indeed, so long as common complaint gives rise to one specialization or another. The Dead Sea Scrolls provide a nicely ancient example of esoteric criticism—a harsh attack on Judean society, written in a kind of sectarian code, by adepts, for adepts.[14] Christian gnosticism, medieval heretical movements, early modern secret societies—all provide further examples, the critical force of which can't be denied even if the critical doctrine can't readily be understood. Contemporary society has its own gnostics, its own religious, political, even philosphical adepts, masters of some special knowledge around which they build a sectarian order. Consider the example of a fundamentalist preacher expounding the Book of Revelation and denouncing the Babylonian decadence of contemporary civilization: he is undoubtedly a social critic though not, perhaps, immediately recognizable as an intellectual. He articulates common complaints, but he does so in a highly specialized language that obscures, for most of us, what he articulates. A similar description serves well enough for political sectarians who reveal the secrets of capitalism in its final stages or for philosophical sectarians who argue that true knowledge of the good society was delivered to the ancient Greeks and lost forever after. These are critics who work at too great a distance from ordinary life and everyday understanding.

But many more social critics, without sectarian impulses, believe that true knowledge is the source of critical power. That's why they choose to speak in the name of God or Reason (or Reason-in-History) or Empirical Reality. This sort of speech might be decribed as the linguistic clothing of moral argument. The metaphor, however, is not quite right, for clothing merely covers the body while language gives form as well as feature to the ideas it expresses. It is more like binding than clothing, so that moral argument is likely to take on a new shape under its pressure, rather like the feet of Chinese women. Moral arguments can be made more directly, of course, but that may seem, again, too much like common complaint, not special enough, unless the arguments are authoritative, definitive, foundational. And how can they be any of these things without the help of God or Reason or Reality? The choice of a critical language depends, then, on the authority the critic wants to claim or thinks he has to claim in order to be heard. And that will depend in turn on his relation to his audience.

My interest in this book lies mainly with what might be called mainstream criticism, that is, with critics who stand sufficiently close to their audience and are sufficiently confident of their standing so that they are not driven to use highly specialized or esoteric languages. The phrase "mainstream critic" looks, perhaps, like a contradiction in terms: doesn't the critic by definition set himself against the mainstream, "the prevailing direction of opinion"? Criticism in any actually existing society, however, has its own prevailing direction, fixed by the existing norms, aspirations, and ideals. Thus the Afrikaner poet/critic Breyten Breytenbach, reflecting on his own marginality: "Better to talk about the precise ways in which the poet fits, as misfit, in his social environment. . . . Poetry is mainstream."[15] The poet's intuitions have to be more formally elaborated, of course, before they can serve the purposes of a specialized critique. But it is an open question how the elaborated versions connect to the originals, formal criticism to common complaint, theory to intuition. What is the preferred language of social criticism? In trying to answer this question, I shall mostly ignore the more hermetic forms of criticism, though I can hardly provide anything like a demonstration of their disvalue. It is a democratic assumption that the mainstream is better. In any case, the mainstream is sufficiently wide so as to allow me to explore all the difficulties of the critical enterprise. Here, too, critics position themselves differently in relation to their audience, adopt different linguistic strategies, make different claims to authority. They take a stand—that's what criticism requires; but they don't take the same stand; nor do they have the same standing vis-à-vis the society they criticize.

The Critic as Hero

Common complaint is often reduced to muttering; oppression and fear make it inarticulate. The critic, however, speaks out loud, in defiance of the established powers. He is a hero—not just today, under the influence of romantic ideas of heroism, but in ancient times too, before heroes were romantic figures. Indeed, the critic is sometimes doubly heroic: he criticizes the powerful and then he criticizes the others, the members of the complaining public—because they get the complaint wrong or don't complain loudly enough or only complain and never act or act recklessly and ineffectively. The critic challenges friends and enemies alike; he is self-sentenced to intellectual and political solitude.

That, at least, is the standard view of criticism, and it is a view that has been encouraged from earliest times by critics themselves. Amos wants us to know that he was warned by the authorities: "Prophesy not against Israel, and drop not thy word against the house of Isaac." And his response was immediate: "Therefore thus saith the Lord."[16] The prophet stands firm: defiant, outspoken, fearless. It is left to us to discover from other sources (or from a critical reading of his own text) the actual strength of his popular following. Socrates acts out a similar part in front of the Athenian jury and openly claims the honor of a hero, comparing himself to the warrior Achilles, who does not spend his time "weighing up the prospects of life and death. He has only one thing to consider in performing any action; that is, whether he is acting rightly or wrongly, like a good man or a bad one." Socrates too acts rightly and accepts the risk of death; ultimately he accepts death itself. But he does tell us how close the jury's vote was: "It seems that if a mere thirty votes [out of five hundred] had gone the other way, I should have been acquitted."[17] Socrates was not, then, an entirely unpopular figure in Athens; he could never have been accused of corrupting the young had the young not flocked to hear him. He died surrounded by friends. But he is commonly imagined alone, in touch with his *daimon*, proud of his critical mission, facing down the hostility of the people.

Socrates' mission is to question, examine, test, and reprove the people he encounters in the streets of Athens—and to teach them to pursue goodness not only for their own sakes but also for the sake of the city. He speaks to whoever will listen, foreigners as well as citizens, but he is especially concerned with his fellow citizens "inasmuch as you are closer to me in kinship." Amos's concern is similarly focused: "You only have I known of all the families of the earth"—so speaks the God of the Sinai covenant to his people—"therefore I will visit upon you all your iniquities."[18] These are examples, I suppose, of ancient parochialism. Some combination of kinship and consent ties the critic to the people he criticizes; he has a special interest in their virtue or well-being.

But with the expansion and (partial) dissolution of the communities on which this parochialism depended, many would-be critics began to feel the bonds of city and people as an illegitimate constraint on their enterprise. They looked now for a wider arena and a universal warrant. Detachment was added to defiance in the self-portrait of the hero. The impulse was Platonic; later on it was Stoic and Christian. Now the critical enterprise was said to require that one leave the city, imagined for the sake of the departure as a darkened cave, find one's way, alone, outside, to the illumination of Truth, and only then return to examine and reprove the inhabitants. The critic-who-returns doesn't engage the people as kin; he looks at them with a new objectivity; they are strangers to his newfound Truth. The pursuit of Truth at the expense of his own familial or civic connections marks off the critic, and the Truth he discovers through detachment and departure gives to his criticism its special authority. Criticism is different from common complaint because the critic stands, even after his return, outside the city. The return is only physical, the standing moral and intellectual. Critical distance makes a new sort of criticism possible. But the possibility is hard won, for it requires a willful break with the fellowship of the city. The critic's heroism begins even before his criticism begins, when he wrenches himself loose and establishes his distance.

Critical distance is not much in evidence in Amos's prophecy or in Socrates' account in the *Apology* of his Athenian conversations. But perhaps it is implicit in the claim both men make to divine authorization. The critic expresses his sense of distance when he displays his warrants. One can imagine warrants of a democratic sort, but these would authorize anybody; a critic who claims some special authority must also stand apart from the *demos*. At the extreme, he turns himself into an enemy of his own people, at least in their present degraded condition. The model here is Jesus Christ, conceived at once as prophet and savior, who is represented as telling his apostles:

> Think not that I am come to send peace on earth: I come not to send peace but a sword. For I am come to set a man at variance against his father, and the daughter against her mother, and the daughter-in-law against her mother-in-law. And a man's foes shall be they of his own household.[19]

Jesus may or may not be usefully described as a social critic, but these sentences have often been taken (by the Florentine monk Savonarola, for example, or the Genevan reformer John Calvin) to suggest the radical commitment that criticism requires. And then Jesus' death suggests the risks of that commitment. The critic must cut himself loose, but once loose he is also vulnerable. For the sake of religious truth or philosophical objectivity, he invites the hatred of the people with whom he lives: that is his heroism.

In the shaping of this heroic image, the stories of Socrates and Jesus have been oddly confused and conflated. The trial of the philosopher, the passion of the prophet/savior are made to yield a single message: death is the entailed risk of philosophy and prophecy alike whenever these two are critical in character. In fact, however, the two stories are very different. If Jesus' life, as it is conceived in the Gospels, can have only one ending, it is easy to imagine a different end for Socrates. He might have been acquitted. He might even have received what he mockingly asked for, a grant from the city to fund his inquiries, and then spent the rest of his life asking critical questions: a helpful but not a heroic role. But the picture of the critic as hero answers better to the aspiration of most critics—at least in this sense, that it separates them from their fellows, confirms and enhances their specialization, confers upon them the "supreme dignity" of the risk-taker, which is otherwise reserved, as Simone de Beauvoir has noted, for hunters and warriors.[20] Criticism would be a "womanish" business, as common complaint often seems to be, if it involved no danger.*

But the picture is also a response to real dangers. I don't want to minimize these or deny the courage of the detached and defiant critic. Courage is one of the chief virtues of a social critic but so, sometimes, is loyalty and connection. When he stands *here* and cannot do anything else, he isn't always detached. We need to distinguish the three parts of heroism. In the actual experience of the social critic, detachment, defiance, and danger don't necessarily figure together. Socrates, for example, faced the dangers of the critical enterprise without ever breaking the bonds of (civic) kinship. He defied the Athenian jury, but he did not separate himself from his fellow citizens. And there have been many other critics who matched their lives, more or less, to the lines of the heroic image but never found themselves in real danger. Consider, again, the case of the French *philosophes*: their works were often censored, but their lives were not at risk. Critics in their pride, however, are more likely to identify with Socrates than with Voltaire or Helvetius.

The risks of criticism are different, as one might expect, in different social and political settings. Even Jesus might have prophesied without danger were it not for the Roman conquest. Some contemporary critics risk imprisonment and death, while others find criticism virtually risk-free. Nor is it their detachment that determines their danger: they run the greatest risks when they articulate common complaints against a dictatorial regime, as in Argentina under the generals, say, or in Poland in the days of Solidarity or in South Africa under the regime of apartheid. The distance the critic establishes—or, better, the distance he has to establish—also varies a great deal, sometimes with reference to the doctrines he takes to be true, sometimes with reference to the institutions and practices he wants to criticize. Critical distance is contested territory, and the critic's claim to stand apart always has to be examined critically. Not every critic is a hero. Nor does every would-be hero, courting disapproval and even death, who cries out for

* One of the most common forms of complaint is conventionally identified as a womanish business: gossip, writes Patricia Meyer Spacks, "embodies an alternative discourse to that of public life, a discourse potentially challenging to public assumptions; it provides language for an alternative culture." Men gossip as much as women do, of course, but it is chiefly among women that gossip becomes "a resource for the subordinated." This isn't, however, a resource whose use requires much courage; it is designed for those who cannot afford public displays of courage. See Spacks, *Gossip* (Chicago: University of Chicago Press, 1986), pp. 5, 46.

admiration, deserve to be admired. It is one of the discoveries of modern democracy—an advance that we have made over the Greeks—that by not killing the critic, we acquire the right not to admire him.

Under conditions of freedom and toleration, the critical enterprise takes on a character different from the one it had in ancient times (and, for that matter, in most other times). Perhaps it is this fact that leads critical intellectuals today to dwell at length upon their specialization and to imagine themselves more self-conscious or more alienated than critics ever were before. In fact, they are more than ever before like other members of the complaining public: we all study one another's warrants and are always skeptical of one another's heroism. Men and women who retain some sense of criticism as a heroic enterprise worry that the enterprise today is too easy. Liberal culture absorbs criticism, finds it interesting, even titillating; it is a form of entertainment, as Marcuse argues. Socrates appears on a television talk show; Plato, more dignified and detached, gets tenure at a major university. The angry and alienated social critic bangs his head against a rubber wall.[21] He encounters infinite tolerance when what he would like is the respect of resistance. Detachment under these conditions doesn't mean much more than withdrawal; its likely effect is apathy and resignation or bohemian idiosyncrasy. And there is no incentive to return to the cave; or, all the incentives are wrong, having nothing to do with the intrinsic value of the critical enterprise. But I suspect that detachment has always been overrated in the self-portrait of the critic. Criticism is most powerful—so I mean to argue in this book—when it gives voice to the common complaints of the people or elucidates the values that underlie those complaints. And then it is unlikely, even in a liberal society, to be merely titillating. "Sometimes, striving to be just," writes Martin Buber, "I go into the dark, till my head meets the wall and aches, and then I know: Here is the wall and I cannot go further."[22]

Critical Pluralism

Imagine a social critic who breaks his ties with family and country, leaves the cave, discovers True Doctrine, and then returns to measure his former fellows and their common way of life against his new and objective standard.

A hero, certainly (wouldn't we want to kill him?), and entirely sufficient for the purposes of criticism: there would be no point in having more than one such person. If he knew the Truth and judged us without passion, impartially, like a total stranger, we could only listen in silence; his criticism would supercede our complaints. Indeed, not only ours—had he time and energy enough, such a critic could serve the whole world, a Hercules among critics. If his standards were objective, no one could deny him global reach.

But there is no Hercules, no single all-sufficient critic, a fact for which we probably have one another to thank. Though the intellectual thrust of Western culture is undoubtedly monistic in character, so that critics are constantly tempted to think of themselves in Herculean terms, cultural practice is very different. We don't agree on which doctrine is True Doctrine, and so we have many social critics; criticism comes at us from all sides. There is no way to define the critical enterprise so that we will always admire its products. Nor is it easy to describe what social critics do. They do all sorts of things; they measure us by different standards, from different vantage points, in different critical languages, at different levels of specialization, with different ends in view. Most generally, they attend to our faults—our individual as well as institutional faults, as I have already argued, because it is always an individual fault, the failing of particular men and women, to tolerate bad institutions. But since our faults are named and numbered in so many different ways, the critics must compete for our attention, and they do that by criticizing one another. Now there is no reason for the rest of us to listen in silence. We participate in the critical enterprise by supporting one critic or group of critics against the others. Participation is especially extensive and especially important under conditions of modernity. A modern democratic society is a confabulation of critics. But then it makes no sense to look for global reach; each society is its own confabulation.

Perhaps there is one common mark of the critical enterprise. It is founded in hope; it cannot be carried on without some sense of historical possibility. Criticism is oriented toward the future: the critic must believe that the conduct of his fellows can conform more closely to a moral standard than it now does or that their self-understanding can be greater than it now is or that their institutions can be more justly organized than they now are. For all his foretellings of doom, a prophet like Amos must hold open the possibility of repentance and reform, else there would be no reason to prophesy. Socrates' claim that he should be paid to criticize his fellow citizens is similarly optimistic—not because he believes that the claim will be accepted but because he believes that his criticism is a real service: it can make Athens a better city. Even the most savage satire of contemporary minds and mores rests upon some hope, however dim or embittered, that minds and mores might be different in the future. The standard conservative lamentation that things are sliding steadily downhill, despite its undertones of melancholy and despair, is written to arrest the slide or, at least, to slow it down. There is no such thing as a strictly backward-looking social criticism, as if criticism were a kind of retributive punishment for past crimes; the critic may take his standards from the past, but he intends those standards to have some future resonance.

It follows that a strict historical determinism is incompatible with critical argument. Even if the one conceptual possibility that history has determined to be the only actual possibility is also the one the critic has chosen, he has no reason to defend that choice or to find fault with a society in which large numbers of men and women resist it. In a determined universe, the resistance is as blameless as it is pointless. I don't mean to suggest that criticism and determinism have never coexisted in a single person's mind and work. Marxism is the classic example of a doctrine that combines the two. The fact that Marx has been read as if he were a universal social critic, a Hercules among critics, probably has something to do with the combination. If history has only one end, then every temporary stopping point, every social formation short of the end, can be measured and found wanting. But this is, as Marx sometimes says, a scientific and not a moral measurement.[23] It is a measurement made from a great distance, and partly for that reason, it isn't critical in character. There is nothing and nobody to criticize: each stop along the track of history is determined in exactly the same way as the track itself. When Marx writes critically of bourgeois society, he simply forsakes his determinist doctrine. And then, though he is a powerful critic indeed, there is no reason to think him a universal critic: he can no longer claim to be applying an objective and necessary standard. He simply explores some of the possibilities, conceptual and practical, that bourgeois society holds open.

Does it take a theory like Marxism to tell us what those possibilities are? One sort of social criticism is theoretical in this special sense. It works from historical or sociological arguments that stress the inner tensions or long-term tendencies of contemporary institutions. Surrendering determinism, the critic looks for a structuralist version of probable cause—or at least some more or less "scientific" reason to think that his standards don't lie beyond history but are attainable within it. Social criticism, on this view, depends on a critical theory of society.[24] But I don't think that this is an unavoidable dependency. In the long history of criticism, the sense of possibility has more often been assumed than theoretically grounded. Or it has been derived from some theological or philosophical argument about human agency. Men and women must be capable, it is said, of doing what God's covenant commands or what secular morality requires. The truth of that claim depends, of course, on how the critic understands God and morality. The crucial dependency is not theoretical but practical: people are capable of doing only what they believe or can be brought to believe ought to be done. Just as critical theory fails unless it can provide a recognizable account of everyday experience, so criticism generally will fail unless it draws its strength from everyday conceptions of God and morality. The critic starts, say, from the views of justice embedded in the covenantal code or from the bourgeois idea of freedom, on the assumption that what is actual in consciousness is possible in practice, and then he challenges the practices that fall short of these possibilities.

But both the covenantal code and the bourgeois idea of freedom allow for more than one possibility: there are as many possibilities as there are plausible accounts of the code and the idea. And so, again, there are many social critics, many forms of criticism; the orientation to the future is no constraint on critical pluralism. Any given theory of history closes off some possibilities and opens others, but that only means that theories of history will themselves be contested by rival schools of criticism; historical analysis is one possible critical language. Not the only language, for there are critics who dispense with history altogether and there are others who engage it only insofar as they recognize their own historical limits and draw their critical standards from local moralities. There is no plausible way to limit the range and variety of criticism except by repression, which is more likely to be directed at the critical enterprise itself than at the plurality of critics.

The Motives of Criticism

Social critics are driven by a passion for truth or anger at injustice or sympathy for the oppressed or fear of the masses or ambition for power—and underlying any or all of these, by the imitation of heroism: Socrates dressed up as Achilles. But the preferred motive, the one most likely to figure in philosophical accounts of criticism and in the critic's own self-description, is benevolence, a disinterested desire for the well-being of humanity. Criticism may be ruthless and painful, but the critic talks to us like Hamlet to his mother: "I must be cruel only to be kind."[25] Kindness forces his hand, but since what he says doesn't sound kind, he would be happier to be silent. Hence the myth of the reluctant critic, the prophet called by God who would refuse the call if he could or the citizen who grimly waits until the pain of watching some social evil is greater than that of speaking out against it. In fact, there are many critics who aren't at all reluctant to speak out, who, like the Roman Cato, positively enjoy the castigation of others. And it seems priggish to suggest that since castigation is morally necessary, it must never be enjoyable. Misanthropy is also a motive for the critical enterprise. The critic need not feel kindly toward the people he criticizes.

But he ought to acknowledge his connections to those people: if he were a stranger, really disinterested, it is hard to see why he would involve himself in their affairs. The passion for truth will not be a sufficient reason unless it is matched by a passion to tell the truth to *these* men and women (rather than to discover it for oneself or record it for posterity). Connection is a problem, however, if we believe that only the alienated or willfully detached critic is able to recognize the truth, to penetrate the social masquerade and see the moral ugliness underneath. Perhaps he doesn't love his fellows, but so long as he recognizes them as fellows, doesn't he have a powerful motive to join the masquerade? Even the misanthrope, if he is a local misanthrope, may well stop short of the deepest truths. Certainly, many critics have felt that they had to disconnect themselves, to break the bonds of fellowship; it was this act rather than their subsequent critical words that tested their courage. But I am interested now in a rather different argument: that disconnection is not so much chosen as imposed and that the discomfort of disconnected men and women motivates and enables their criticism. This is what drives the critic and makes his penetration and his cruelty possible. He loves truth or truth-telling, or he hates injustice or whatever, because he is alienated.

The argument has been forcefully made by Christopher Lasch in an essay on Lincoln Steffens, one of the original American "muckrakers":

> It is time we began to understand radicals like Lincoln Steffens not as men driven by a vague humanitarian idealism but as men *predisposed* to rebellion as

> the result of an early estrangement from the culture of their own class; as a result, in particular, of the impossibility of pursuing within the framework of established convention the kind of careers they were bent on pursuing. The intellectuals of the early twentieth century were predisposed to rebellion by the very fact of being intellectuals in a society that had not yet learned to define the intellectual's place. . . . [They] were outsiders by necessity: a new class not yet absorbed into the cultural consensus.[26]

This is a sociological version of the contemporary critic's self-description. It has an obvious weakness: how are we to explain why some intellectuals "predisposed" to rebellion actually become rebels while others do not? Why Steffens and Randolph Bourne and John Reed but not Walter Lippmann, who was closely associated with all three? And how are we to explain the earlier generation of rebels and critics to whom twentieth-century intellectuals looked for inspiration—Ralph Waldo Emerson, Henry David Thoreau, Walt Whitman? And what about later rebels and critics who found the career framework (the academic ladder) securely in place, like C. Wright Mills, say, or any of a large number of professorial dissenters, including Lasch himself?

Lasch also notices, perceptively, I think, that alienation can account for the surrender of critical perspective, the "treason" of the intellectuals. It is as useful in explaining the end as the beginning of radical criticism, which makes it too useful by half. "Detachment carried with it a certain defensiveness about the position of intellect (and intellectuals) in American life; and it was this defensiveness . . . which sometimes prompted intellectuals to forsake the role of criticism and to identify themselves with what they imagined to be the laws of historical necessity and the working out of the popular will."[27] But the operative word, again, is "sometimes." Sometimes not, and what is it that makes the difference between those who forsake the critical enterprise and those who stick to it? Perhaps this is a matter of individual psychology, but the use of "forsake" suggests that Lasch is really talking about moral choice. Men and women choose to become critics, and some of those who make the choice are not in any significant sense alienated from the culture of their class (or their city, country, race, or religion)—though they must set themselves in opposition to important aspects of that culture.

Given the general limitations of sociological accounts, the idea of marginality probably does better than Lasch's "estrangement" in explaining the birth and breeding of social critics. They come from some remote and neglected part of the country (Silone), or from an imperial colony (Camus), or from a declining social class (Orwell), or they are members of or choose to identify themselves with a lowborn, oppressed, or pariah group. But this is not alienation or even detachment; it is better described as a kind of antagonistic connection. One of its most common forms is a passionate commitment to cultural values hypocritically defended at the center, cynically disregarded at the margins. Antagonism, not alienation, provides the clearest lead into the critical enterprise. Since criticism derives ultimately from common complaint, it needs to be explained in terms of the ideological contradictions and social conflicts that common complaint reflects, though sometimes only dimly. That explanation may itself require "scientific" detachment. But criticism requires no such thing: a detached critic may well be insufficiently antagonistic, more ready to analyze the contradictions and conflicts than to take a stand within them.

We should probably be no quicker to admire the benevolence than the detachment of the critic. Benevolence itself can be a mask, as Rousseau suggests when he writes caustically of the philosopher who loves humanity only so as more easily to dislike his neighbors.[28] But this is an easy case, since benevolence here is a piece of deception (possibly self-deception). More often it is genuinely problematic: thus the critic whose benevolent feelings are focused on future generations for whose sake he feels that he must be hard on his contemporaries, or the critic who holds lovingly in his mind an idealized picture of his fellow citizens or coreligionists or comrades in the movement (any movement) and then is forced to tell the particular men and women whom he meets that they don't measure up. As this last example suggests, the critic's involvement in social conflict may bring him allies; it doesn't always bring him allies with whom he is content. His fiercest criticism is often aimed at those individuals and groups to whom he feels closest, who are most likely to disappoint him. Christian preachers castigate the faithful, ignore the infidel; Marxist militants worry about working-class, not bourgeois consciousness.

Disappointment is one of the most common motives for criticism. We have an idea about how institutions ought to function or how people ought to behave. And then something happens, the authorities act with unusual brutality; or something doesn't happen, the people are passive and indifferent; and we feel ourselves thrust into the company of social critics. It takes some further motivation, though, actually to join the company and stick to the critical enterprise. Disappointment isn't enough. Nor does a disinterested desire for the well-being of humanity seem a sufficient motive. A moral tie to the agents or the victims of brutality and indifference is more likely to serve. We feel responsible for, we identify with particular men and women. Injustice is done in my name, or it is done to my people, and I must speak out against it. Now criticism follows from connection.

But the moral tie gets considerably more complicated in modern times, when the victims organize themselves, form a movement or party, and defend their interests—often in a language very different from the one the critic has chosen. This is all to the good, certainly, though the critic sometimes finds it hard to surrender his specialized and solitary role. Nor is it clear that he should: movements and parties need criticism as much as societies do. But they also need commitment and support. Would-be critics are warned by movement militants to avoid the sin of pride, urged not to cut themselves off from the political struggle. Imagine the critic pressed by considerations of strategy and tactics—not just ideological movements but practical moves, the political version of feints, ambushes, attacks, and encirclements. Should he stand, ever critical, in the way of success or put aside his scruples and follow orders? If he is alienated and defensive in the ways Lasch describes, he may well bow to party discipline, fall silent, march on command. There are many examples, most of them from the twentieth century; these are not problems commonly faced by ancient, medieval, or early modern intellectuals (though the Catholic Church has long posed analogous problems for its own internal critics).[29]

The same motives that make for criticism at one moment in time make for silence and acquiescence at another. This is most clearly true of the ambition for political power. Contemporary critics especially, because of their engagement with parties and movements, are drawn by the prospect of power—the most dangerous of critical temptations. They imagine the party as the next government, themselves as office-holders (Lenins, not Stalins), able at last to give their criticism practical force. Political power is in two senses the end of criticism, first because the critic aims at the effectiveness that power makes possible, and second because, having attained power, he can no longer be critical of his own effects. Since these effects will undoubtedly require criticism, other men and women will have to take up the task, driven in turn by their own social connections, their own ambitions, and their own imitations of heroism. Every critic who rises to office is succeeded by another critic who claims that office-holding is "selling out." One could write the recent history of social criticism as a series of successions of this sort. But there have always been, and there are today, critics who refuse (and critics who never manage) to rise.

Social Criticism and Popular Revolt

What makes modern criticism both interesting and problematic is not the alienation of the critic but the swelling sound of his accompaniment. Social critics have rarely been solitary or distant figures in this age of popular mobilization, democratic and totalitarian politics, public schooling, and mass communication. It is more likely that wherever they go, they go in crowds; they are alone only in solitary confinement. In the past, critics like the Puritan ministers or the orators of the French Revolution might briefly find a popular following, but most of the time criticism was addressed to a narrow audience, the small elite of literate and powerful men. Whatever the critic talked about, these were the people to whom he talked. His situation was not dissimilar from that of more ordinary members of the complaining public who managed—as petitioners or supplicants or even, occasionally, as rebels—to make themselves heard by the elite. There was no one else to talk to, no one else who mattered. In traditional societies, critics necessarily look up. Today many more people matter, and so critics look around. Popular mobilization, whatever its immediate purpose, poses the old questions about language, specialization, and distance in a new and urgent way. How does the social critic relate to *these* people, who have found a voice, who claim their rights, who trample on the rights of others, who rush to meetings, who march in the streets, who are herded into camps, who feel pain and rage, who throw bombs, who look for a leader, who accept the discipline of a movement or party—and who, some of them, anyway, are waiting to read his books?

According to the conservative philosopher Ortega y Gasset, popular mobilization demands nothing more from the critic than a shift in direction. The select few can no longer argue with one another or aim their criticism at the even more select and fewer, the rulers of the economy and the state; they must criticize the others, the ascendant mob of mediocre men and women, the "vertical barbarians" who come not from outside but from within.[30] Ortega's book, *The Revolt of the Masses*, has been published in cheap editions and assigned for many years in college courses, so presumably it is read by the right people: the most ambitious and aggressive of the barbarians. But Ortega seems never to have felt any genuine tie to these people—the tone of his book is less disappointed than sardonic and disdainful—and so his shift in direction is hardly interesting. A decent man, he was willing enough to provide a cultivated voice for common complaint (or for selected common complaints). He only asked that once the cultivated had spoken, the uncultivated should keep quiet. What happens, however, when they are anything but quiet, when the noise level steadily rises, when politics suddenly seems all crudeness and clamor? Now detachment and distance may well be prudent, the conventionally better part of wisdom. Are they also the better part of criticism?

This question is faced most directly by critics who find much to admire or much to hope for in popular politics and culture. Soon enough, some of them will be disappointed, and we will begin to find traces of Ortegan disdain in their writings (Herbert Marcuse provides the clearest example). But I am interested now in the early encounters of critical intellectuals and the "people" (the working class, the nation, blacks, women, and so on). Of course, intellectuals are people too, but they are the ones who draw the line between the two groups—and then set out to cross it. Sometimes the way they draw the line merely anticipates their failure. Thus the Russian radical Dmitry Ivanovich Pisarev, writing in the 1860s:

> Only some sort of material catastrophe . . . jolts [the] mass into uneasy movement, into the destruction of its customary, dreamily tranquil, vegetative existence. . . . The mass does not make discoveries or commit crimes; other people think and suffer, search and find, struggle and err on its behalf—other people eternally alien to it, eternally regarding it with contempt, and at the same time eternally working to increase the amenities of its life.[31]

Here the "uneasy movement" of the mass serves no social purpose; only the elite of radical critics and revolutionaries acts purposefully; the people are nothing more than the objects of its benevolent activity. But there are two alternative possibilities, both of them sketched in Marx's writing. The first possibility is that the people are the instruments of social criticism or, in Marx's organic image, that critical philosophy is the head and the proletariat the body of the revolution.[32] The philosophical "negativity" of the critic shapes and directs the rebelliousness of oppressed men and women.

It was left to Lenin to argue that the head itself had to be embodied (in the vanguard or party) before it could exercise directive force. One might say that this argument also anticipates failure, whether or not the instrument is "used" successfully. Human instruments are notoriously recalcitrant, rebellious, ungrateful.

The second possibility is that the people are the subjects of criticism: the revolt of the masses is the mobilization of common complaint.* Now the critic participates in an enterprise that is no longer his alone; he agitates, teaches, counsels, challenges, protests *from within*. This is my own view of the proper location and appropriate work of contemporary social critics. I don't mean to suggest that they must bow to the weight of noise and numbers. They have their own voice; they defend their independence; they are still associates of the Ancient and Honorable Company whose trans-historical existence I have tried to evoke in this introduction. There is only this that is different about them, given the existence of the people as critical subjects: they are newly connected to popular movements and aspirations. Their criticism is auxiliary as well as independent. They can't just criticize, they must also offer advice, write programs, take stands, make political choices, frequently in the harshest circumstances. Alert to the defeats, often self-inflicted, of the mobilized people, they are nonetheless not ready to call for a return to traditional passivity. Critics of this sort must look for a way of talking in tune with but also against their new accompaniment. They need to find a place to stand, close to but not engulfed by their company.

This is the shared dilemma of the subjects of my book. They are all of them men and women of the left, otherwise it would not be their dilemma. I shall not focus here on writers like Ortega or, more generally, on the conservative literature of lamentation—which is not to say that this isn't often an impressive and moving literature nor to deny that lamentation has its place in the critical enterprise. Indeed, I begin with Julien Benda, who provides a classic defense of the old idea of intellectual detachment and critical solitude and who laments the eagerness of contemporary intellectuals to attach themselves to mass movements. But Benda writes more in anger than in sorrow; his is a lament from the left, jeremiad rather than dirge. (The movements he has in mind are nationalist and fascist.) He believes

* This is the standard Marxist view, though how many Marxist intellectuals have actually held it I cannot say. It is the argument of the *Manifesto*: that capitalism teaches the workers who experience it to be social critics and revolutionaries. Intellectuals have little more to do than to elaborate on the meaning of that experience.

that the intellectual best serves the people from a distance—but he still wants the intellectual to serve. Nor is he opposed, as we shall see, to a kind of emergency enlistment in particular struggles against tyranny and oppression. Benda sets the terms of the twentieth-century argument. All the other writers with whom I deal are enlisted in one way or another, engaged, committed, but they have been forewarned and now must confront the dangers of their position. Despite these dangers, it is a new reason for lamentation when enlistment no longer seems possible.

After Benda, I have simply looked for representative figures, whose work is touched by the triumphs and catastrophes of our time: the two world wars, the struggles of the working class, national liberation, feminism, totalitarian politics. The selection is my own but not entirely personal or arbitrary. I have chosen to write about working social critics rather than philosophers of criticism,* and about critics by vocation rather than political activists on their way to power and office. And I have chosen mainstream critics rather than sectarians. My subjects are well known; mostly, they knew or knew of one another; they refer, sometimes directly, sometimes indirectly, to each other's work; for all their disagreements, they have much in common. They are all, to use a phrase of Michel Foucault, "general intellectuals"—including Foucault himself, who argued that the age of the general intellectual was over. They all have something to say about the whole of society and also about the critical enterprise itself. Though they confront new problems, with a new urgency, they address the issues that have always been central to the Ancient and Honorable Company. How does the critic stand vis-à-vis the others? What sort of authority can he claim? How much distance does he require? Where does he find his standards? What language does he speak? What motives set him to work?

It may be that my list of critics, arranged in rough chronological order, tells a story: of the rise and fall, the making and unmaking, of critical connection. The revolt of the masses opened certain possibilities, seized upon in exemplary fashion, it might be said, by writers like Ignazio Silone and George Orwell. But a long series of defeats has closed off those possibilities. The critic is alone again or, at least, he is deprived of any close relation to an audience, driven to recover authority by establishing his distance. Silone

* Hence the omission of Jean-Paul Sartre, who is nevertheless a major presence in these pages. Sartre's is one of the most important theories of social criticism in the twentieth century, and I devote quite a bit of space to an account of its faults. But he was not a first-rate practitioner. Though he disliked the everyday life of his contemporaries, he was not really interested in it; he held with great consistency a highly stereotyped view of the institutions and practices that gave it shape.

and Orwell look now like figures from a faraway past—modern figures seen from a postmodern age. Maybe. I want to argue that they are still exemplary and that connected criticism is still possible. But I shall wait to make that argument until I have told the story to the end and confronted the most advanced forms of critical disconnection.

2

Julien Benda and Intellectual Treason

His other books are long forgotten; his life, which spanned nine decades, is today only a historical footnote; but Julien Benda's *The Betrayal of the Intellectuals* will be read as long as there are intellectuals capable of treason.[1] Eventually, perhaps, we will need the help of a scholarly apparatus to understand it, for its examples and references derive mostly from the ideological controversies of the late 1920s. But the book is written with a passion, eloquence, and lucidity that lift it above those controversies—or, better, that turn the controversies into common stuff, that make them ours. It remains the best single statement of the critical intellectual's creed and the most vivid account of the temptations and dangers of intellectual politics. And so it is the necessary starting point for any discussion of twentieth-century social criticism. Its arguments have often been repeated; many men and women have aspired to play the part of Benda's "true intellectual." But that is not an easy part to play, not, at least, if one takes the script literally; nor did Benda himself play it with any consistency. A few people, sensing the difficulties, have tried to rewrite the script, and that is what I want to do also. I shall look closely at Benda's theoretical arguments and at his practical politics, and then suggest a somewhat different (though similarly normative) account of intellectual treason and fidelity.

Benda's Radical Dualism

Benda locates his "clerks," or intellectuals, in moral, not sociological, space. He has ideas about what we might think of as the sociological requirements—the material underpinnings and institutional boundaries—of that location, but these are not his central interest. He is a moralist from the beginning; his purpose is simply to tell intellectuals where they should stand and how they should conduct themselves. And he would have said that the effort to locate a class of intellectuals without regard to moral standing and conduct is simply a mistake. Either the members of such a class act in accordance with certain principles and are in fact intellectuals, or they don't and aren't. Benda's dramatic title suggests that those who fail to act properly are traitors; they have gone over to the other side. But many of the people Benda describes are really pretenders; they were always on the other side. In any case, he sets out to study the effects of intellectual pretense and betrayal in the Europe of his own time. What happens on the other side, above all in the world of everyday politics, when it is invaded by false intellectuals?

Benda is a dualist and a functionalist. His Gaul is divided into two parts: a distant and ideal realm inhabited by (true) intellectuals and a realm of reality, near and immediate, inhabited most importantly by politicians and soldiers. Both are necessary to the wholeness of civilized life, and the distinction between them is necessary too. Intellectuals uphold the eternal values of truth and justice. Politicians and soldiers do what must be done for the survival and enhancement of their communities. Curiosity, playfulness, skepticism, and critical discrimination sustain the "clerk"; loyalty, pragmatism, and worldly interest sustain the "layman." Civilization, writes Benda, is possible "only if humanity consents to [this] division of functions, if side by side with those who carry out the lay passions and extol the virtues serviceable to them, there exists a class of men who depreciate these passions, and glorify the advantages which are beyond the material."[2]

Benda's argument is characteristically emphatic and radical; he was never one to hold back. There is no useful labor by either clerks or laymen without the division of labor. His functionalism hangs on his dualism. Here he is faithful to the tradition that lies behind his religious imagery, Augustinian and Lutheran rather than Catholic, despite Benda's great admiration for medieval Catholicism. The intellectual's kingdom is not of this world. It follows then that the world should not be ruled by intellectuals. "I entirely dissociate myself from those who want the 'clerk' to govern the world . . . for it seems to me that human affairs can only adopt the religion of the true 'clerk' under penalty of becoming divine, i.e., of perishing as human."[3] I will want to argue that this is not an entirely accurate statement of Benda's ultimate stand, but he does not shrink from its political application. Caesar's morality, he insists, is "the right morality" for the prosperity of worldly kingdoms. His argument is very close to Luther's equally emphatic and radical injunction to the Protestant saints: "You have the kingdom of heaven, therefore you should leave the kingdom of earth to anyone who wants to take it."[4] This is an odd argument for a man who joined up with the Dreyfusards in the 1890s and again with the antifascists in the 1930s and 1940s. But Benda comes to it honestly and abandons it only with difficulty, for it is the entailment of his dualism.

I shall consider first the nearer side of the dualism, Benda's own side, the realm of the intellectuals. Here Benda is a moral and emotional ascetic. He has little to say about the material life of his clerks; though he assumes that they won't concern themselves overmuch with the pursuit of wealth, he imposes no vow of poverty. It is the affective richness of the everyday world that worries him. The true intellectual must be indifferent to the passions and attachments, far more than to the physical comforts, of ordinary men and women: "he *plays* human passions instead of living them." He is "purely disinterested," "guided by the desire for truth alone, apart from any concern with the demands of society."[5] Benda is not afraid of the charge of "rootlessness" frequently leveled against writers like himself, for he believes with Plutarch that "man is not a plant created to be immobile and to have his roots fixed in the soil where he was born."[6] It is, indeed, dangerous for an intellectual to have a country, for the temptations of nationalism are the strongest temptations of all. He must judge his own country as if he were the citizen of another.[7] Benda's philosopher never returns to the cave; he just looks in, occasionally, to criticize the inhabitants. Philosophy is a hard discipline, unlikely to bring worldly rewards—not the wealth of nations, not the warmth of a particular nation.

The clerk's first task is to pursue the truth; his second task is to publish it to the world. He tells truths that laymen don't want to hear, and then he pays the price. Once again, Benda is drawn to a radical statement. The intellectual who "condemns the realism of the State," he writes, "does really harm that State. Hence it follows that the State, in the name of its practical interests, to defend which is its function, has a right—perhaps a duty—to punish him."[8] Both Socrates and the Athenian jury acted rightly. We know an intellectual by his heroic readiness to "drink the hemlock." It seems to me, though, that an intellectual tutored by Benda would not refuse, as Socrates did, to flee the *polis*; he would have no local attachment.

On the other side of the dualism one finds the precise reversal of moral asceticism, a politics as free of morality as morality is free of interest and affection. Here Benda's model is the Machiavellian prince, who teaches himself, with a stern devotion worthy of a better end, "how not to be good." This world must be ruled by statesmen mentally prepared to poison philosophers. Not eager to do that, not wantonly cruel: if they are really statesmen, they make a cool calculation, and then they administer the poison, or not. But coolness can't be their only attribute. They must be capable of expressing, as well as controlling, the political passions. Here too Benda has the courage of his dualist convictions. Though he hated the nationalists of his time and thought Auguste Barrès and Charles Maurras the greatest of contemporary traitors, he could still write, thinking of their work, "Every Frenchman attached to the continuance of his nation must rejoice that in the last century France has possessed a fanatically nationalist literature."[9] The Germans had made nationalist history and poetry into a worldly necessity, and the world must be served.

But not by clerks, or not by true clerks—for their service blurs the line between the two realms. Ideally, politicians and soldiers do what they have to do here and now, and intellectuals from their distant perspective denounce them when what they do is wrong. Intellectuals can't prevent politicians and soldiers "from filling all history with the noise of their hatred and their slaughters," but they can prevent them "from thinking themselves great men as they [carry] out these activities."[10] This is what the survival of civilization requires: not that evil is forbidden or forgone but that it is known to be evil, so that even when morality is violated, "moral notions remain intact." It is a good thing when princes are hypocrites, as Machiavelli taught them to be, for "they at least acknowledge the standards they transgress." Machiavelli may well have been a teacher of evil—in certain circumstances and, as Benda notes, "not without melancholy"—but for him and for the princes he taught, "evil, even if it aids politics, still remains evil."[11] Benda returns to this point again and again, for it is here that clerkly betrayal has its starting point.

False intellectuals are "the moralists of realism."[12] They locate themselves within the real world; they share in its passions; and they invest those passions with the authority of mind and spirit. They moralize politics, not in the sense of making it moral but rather in the sense in which we speak of someone rationalizing his actions or his interests, that is, justifying them with a show of reason. So false intellectuals lend to politics the aura of morality and teach politicians not so much to do evil (for the necessity of that they understand well enough) as to think it good. And then the evil they do is so much worse, for it is entered into with enthusiasm and pursued systematically— pursued with a clear conscience, without the doubts, hesitations, and sleepless nights that are the only useful contributions that intellectuals make to the men and women who inhabit the realm of the real.

Nationalism is Benda's chief example of a moralized politics. The medieval clerks and early modern philosophers whom he admires so much were not citizens; national patriotism was one more of the passions they didn't feel. And even today the true intellectual renders unto Caesar the things that are Caesar's, "that is, his life perhaps, *but nothing more*." He is never diverted "from single-hearted adoration of the Beautiful and the Divine." In this sense, though not in some others, Hegel set a perfect clerkly example when, after the national defeat at Jena, his only thought "was to find a corner in which to philosophize."[13] Later in the century, however, writers calling themselves intellectuals adopted an entirely different position. They made the nation into a cult; they sought morality in national traditions, exalting only what was distinct, particular, peculiar to the history of their own country; they gave up their grip on eternal and universal values; they justified whatever seemed necessary for the aggrandizement of the state. The new nation-state had indeed an authentically "real" history, but treasonous intellectuals joined to this history an inauthentic idealism: a creed, an argument, "a whole network of strongly woven doctrines." And so they transformed the natural antagonism of nations into a sustained, coherent, systematic hatred, which was bound to be expressed, eventually, in war.

The same process, Benda believes, has been at work with regard to race and class—and with similar results. "The intellectual organization of political hatreds" produces at one and the same time anti-Semitism, authoritarianism, and nationalism; the three together are embodied in National Socialism, the ultimate union of passion and ideology, the ultimate surrender of "abstract principle" and "disinterested activity."[14] Benda sensed earlier than most the danger of Nazism, and he provided the first of many accounts of its intellectual sources in Hegel and Treitschke, Nietzsche and Sorel, Barrès and Maurras. I am not concerned here to defend or criticize this genealogy. It was in any case a plausible list of enemies for a man committed to "look for the notion of good in the heart of eternal and disinterested man."[15]

Commitment and Solitude

But the deep distinction on which Benda's argument rests is less plausible, and he can hardly assert it without immediately qualifying it. From the beginning, in the 1920s when he wrote the *Betrayal* and not only later on when he joined the antifascist struggle, his argument is subject to an intricate process of internal revision. This is so for two reasons: first, because many of Benda's greatest heroes were by no means as detached and disinterested as his doctrine seemed to require; and second, because he himself, the old Dreyfusard, was unprepared to leave the world to his enemies. One can read the *Betrayal* as if it were a palimpsest, the image of the detached clerk obscuring, but never entirely blocking out, the image of the engaged intellectual. Benda senses the theoretical difficulties and keeps coming back to them, but he never brings the images into focus. He is both committed to his dualism and unable to live within its terms.

Benda's difficulties are nicely illustrated by his references to the theory of the just war. He was a great admirer of the Catholic Scholastics; he thought their social position (defined by the standing of the Church vis-à-vis the secular powers and then by the standing of the monastery and the university vis-à-vis the Church) conducive to critical detachment and their doctrines exemplary of it. The romantic admiration for war seemed to him one of the crucial signs of intellectual betrayal—as indeed it is—and he quoted with approval the standard Catholic condemnations of military aggression. Benda had been outraged by the German invasion of neutral Belgium in 1914, and he had strongly supported the French war effort—not out of any national feeling, he insisted, but out of a recognition that in this case the cause of his own nation "coincided . . . with the cause of abstract justice."[16] But the theory of the just war doesn't merely define that cause, it also represents a clerkly effort to make it effective, to shape and influence behavior in the "real" world, to replace Caesar's morality with something else. So Benda blurs his dualism and seems to acknowledge that there is a legitimate way to "moralize" reality. At the same time he tries to reestablish the dualism by claiming that intellectuals can say nothing about the conduct of a just war. Their writ reaches to *jus ad bellum*, not to the more immediate problems of *jus in bello*. Once the fighting has begun, realism prevails, and Caesar does whatever he thinks necessary. The use of poison gas, Benda writes, is a matter for technical, not moral, judgment.[17] That had not, however, been the view of the Scholastics, who consistently included "just means" in their list of criteria for a just war. I suspect that if the Germans had been alone in their use of gas, Benda would have been more open to arguments about just and unjust means of warfare. When it came to the French and the Germans, he was never a disinterested clerk. But this, perhaps, reflects only a weakness in the man, while the incomplete account of the just war is important because it reflects a weakness in the argument.

How far can the intellectual venture into the realm of reality? "When the clerk descends to the market place I only consider that he is failing to perform his functions [if] he does so . . . for the purpose of securing the triumph of a realist passion." This is rather like giving a license to good intellectuals, not to bad ones. We could all provide lists of the two kinds. Thus Benda:

> When Gerson entered the pulpit of Notre Dame to denounce the murderers of Louis d'Orleans; when Spinoza . . . went and wrote the words "Ultimi barbarorum" on the gate of those who had murdered the de Witts; when Voltaire fought for the Calas family; when Zola and Duclaux came forward to take part in a celebrated lawsuit [Dreyfus affair]; all those clerks were carrying out their functions as clerks in the fullest and noblest manner.[18]

But, to pursue only one of these examples, it was not Voltaire's purpose merely to be a witness to the cause of justice; he aimed actually to vindicate Calas and to sustain his family, and one could hardly say of his arguments what Benda says later in the *Betrayal* about the true intellectual, that "the grandeur of his teaching lies precisely in [the] absence of practical value."[19] Nor were Voltaire's arguments of practical value only to the Calas family. He would surely have said that France as a whole would be better off if the Huguenots were accorded full religious freedom. Indeed, Benda himself praises Spinoza for arguing that states that respect the rights of their citizens are more likely to endure than states that violate those rights.[20] But then he also says that intellectuals who claim practical value for their arguments inevitably are defeated "for the very good reason that it is impossible to preach the spiritual and the universal without undermining the institutions" of the real world—which is just what Spinoza's and Voltaire's opponents would probably have argued and what the anti-Dreyfusards did in fact argue.

T. S. Eliot wrote of Benda that he had "a romantic view of critical detachment."[21] The image of the heroic intellectual, who speaks the truth and drinks the hemlock, certainly had an extraordinary appeal for Benda. And yet there is ample evidence that he preferred victory to defeat and the triumph of justice to the martyrdom of its advocates. There is a wonderful passage in the *Betrayal* where Benda condemns those intellectuals who equate justice with defeat, who make a "cult of misfortune." They are moved, he suggests, by "the thought that the just person must inevitably be weak and suffer, that he must be a victim. If the just man becomes strong and comes to possess the means of enforcing justice towards himself, then he ceases to be just to these thinkers." Perhaps they are unwilling to identify with strength for fear of being thought corrupt. In exactly the same way, Benda goes on, some intellectuals insist that, in any international quarrel, their own country is always in the wrong—lest they be thought to have surrendered to nationalist feelings. Thus "the frenzy of impartiality, like any other frenzy, leads to injustice."[22]

The cult of misfortune and the frenzy of impartiality are not properly understood as features of "*la trahison des clercs*." They don't arise among the nationalist intellectuals whom Benda loathed so deeply. They are, one might say, the characteristic vices of left-wing social critics, of the true intellectuals, "the officiants of justice." I don't mean to deny that there have been leftists enough who have surrendered to national egotism or abased themselves before the idols of the state. I only want to suggest that the effort to avoid these forms of betrayal breeds the "romantic view of critical detachment," and then the view of oneself as a hero of detachment, that Eliot found in Benda's own writings. One can indeed take an unseemly pride in standing apart and in standing alone: "*le vrai intellectuel,*" Benda wrote, "*est un solitaire.*"[23] Some intellectuals glory in this solitude and seek out every opportunity to distinguish themselves from those nearest to them. They are heated in their denials of affinity. Benda struggles to avoid this kind of romanticism, not always successfully, taking refuge in "coolness of mind" and "intellectual discipline." Here he is true to the austere classicism that is probably his deepest commitment. Reading these passages, however, one longs for a more commonsensical account of intellectual life, an account that might go farther than Benda's book does in explaining his own politics.

Before attempting such an account, however, I want to turn briefly to a more particular effort at self-explanation from Benda's later work. In a little book of reflections, *Exercice d'un enterré vif*, that he wrote while in hiding during World War II, Benda describes his Jewishness as a possible key to his intellectual politics. Jewish intellectuals in the modern world, he suggests, are rather like the Catholic clerks of the Middle Ages. They are universal men cut off from particularist loyalties: "Connected for the most part to the nations they adopt by intellectual rather than fleshly bonds, they escape the prejudices of nationalism and treat certain problems with a liberty achieved only by the most emancipated non-Jews."[24] This is, of course, a conventional view, but one that Benda applied to himself only under the impetus of Nazi anti-Semitism. One might carry the application a step further and suggest that his own peculiar view of critical detachment derives not only from being a Jew cut off from other nations but also from being an assimilated Jew cut off from other Jews. For Benda never identified himself with the community of French Jews; in this regard he was indeed *un solitaire*. And in the case of his own "race," as he called it, Benda seems readily to fall into the cult of misfortune, believing that Jewishness makes for justice only when the Jews are homeless and persecuted. Zionism is the first nationalism he condemns, almost as if to establish his credentials, in his grand attack on intellectual treason.[25]

And yet one of Benda's greatest heroes was a committed Zionist. The case of Albert Einstein is instructive, for he conforms in almost every respect to the model of a true intellectual. It was *almost* true of him, as Benda wrote in the *Betrayal*, that "he felt no passion but the passion for thought."[26] "Politics is for the moment," Einstein is reported to have said, "but an equation is for eternity." It is a line that Benda would certainly have quoted had he known it. He had every reason to admire Einstein, for the two of them shared a deep dislike for every kind of collective egotism and a deep belief in eternal and immutable values. Isaiah Berlin's account of Einstein's convictions would fit Benda just as well:

> He was neither a subjectivist nor a skeptic. . . . Moral and aesthetic values, rules, standards, principles cannot be derived from the sciences . . . but neither are they, for Einstein, generated or conditioned by differences of class or culture or race. No less than the laws of nature . . . they are universal, true for all men at all times, discovered by moral or aesthetic insight common to all men at all times, and embodied in the basic principles (not the mythology) of the great world religions.[27]

Like Benda, Einstein thought that the Jews, because of their history, had come to embody the crucial ideals of intellectual life: "knowledge for its own sake, an almost fanatical love of justice, desire for personal independence." But Einstein chose to identify not only with those ideals but also with the people whose ideals they were. For the ideals by themselves did not make a life; by themselves, indeed, they made for "moral instability" as often as for heroism. "Man can flourish," Einstein wrote, "only when he loses himself in a community."[28] That is probably too strong. The goal that Einstein set for his own life was not the loss of self but the establishment of a "spiritual equilibrium"—and this he thought possible only through the shared life of a nation. A critic like Benda might say of Einstein that though he always thought himself homeless (a good sign), he had nevertheless succumbed to the temptations of belonging. But within the Zionist movement Einstein was a maverick and a dissenter, a frequent critic of leaders and policies. He was never an easy man to satisfy, though "his loyalties remained unimpaired." A man of passion and detachment, he found his own equilibrium in a balance of the two.

Against Dualism

So in his own way did Benda, not with the Jews but with the French. The *Betrayal* is full of naive expressions of his love for France, a love that went far beyond the "affection . . . based on reason" that is all he permitted to true intellectuals. Even in the 1930s, when he was preaching the "idea of Europe" and calling for a real unity of European states, he could not refrain from suggesting that since Latin was no longer available as a common language, French, because of its "rationality," would be the best substitute.[29] Upon reflection, he decided in the 1940s that the deepest cause of his own detachment was not the fact that he was Jewish but that he spoke "the language of Descartes" (but so did Barrès and Maurras).[30] I suspect that there is more sentiment than insight here, but the passage does reflect a deep truth about Benda's personal situation: he was, if not "lost," then to use another phrase of Einstein's, "wholly absorbed" in the life of France, an engaged, even if often a critical, intellectual. He spanned his own dualism in a way that he never fully admitted or explored.

But it may make the argument too easy to see intellectual engagement only in the context of nation, language, homeland, and so on, for these are—except for homeless peoples—inevitable backgrounds as much as they are willful commitments. Consider instead the cause, the movement, and the party, where the intellectual is invited to sign up "for the duration" of a particular political struggle or, since some struggles are unending, forever. This Benda consistently refused to do. He seems to have conceived of the intellectual's "descent into the market place" as an occasional foray by some heroic individual (Emile Zola in the Dreyfus case, for example). Down and back, a quick thrust in defense of ideal values and a return to the only realm where those values have a sustained existence. Benda's intellectual is rather like the hero of the American Western, the lone gunman who rides into town, clears the villains out, and then rides away into the hills or the endless plains: two solitary romantics who can never settle down among the citizens. But figures of this sort can be effective only if the basic structures of justice already exist in the "market place" and the town. They vindicate standards to which ordinary men and women are already committed and defend institutions that are already in place, though under attack. If Caesar's morality were in fact the morality of the real world, neither the intellectual nor the gunman would stand a chance. Or, insofar as Caesar's morality *is* the morality of the real world, they can't just come and go; they have to stay and fight.

This, in essence, is the argument of Paul Nizan, who published in 1932 a savage attack (appropriately titled *The Watchdog*) upon French academic philosophers—among whom he took Benda to be "the shrewdest" (perhaps because Benda was never an academic).[31] His vaunted detachment, Nizan claimed, was a fraud; it merely upheld the "established order," the pattern of bourgeois domination. When one leaves the world to Caesar, one doesn't serve the ideal; one serves Caesar. Everything else—universal values, critical detachment, the pursuit of truth—is mere hypocrisy. The only alternative is to join the class struggle, to attach oneself to the working class. In practice, since Benda could never become what Antonio Gramsci called an "organic" proletarian intellectual, this meant submitting to the discipline of the Communist party. Writing in France in 1932, Nizan could hardly have understood what that submission entailed.

Benda himself had a livelier understanding; here his basic theory served him well. He responded to Nizan (in 1935) by saying flatly that if he had to choose between the maintenance of oppression and the loss of intellectual independence, he would "resign [himself] to maintaining oppression."[32] He didn't think that such resignation was necessary, but how, on his terms, could it be avoided? The dilemma was real enough. The intellectual's readiness "to drink the hemlock" may count for more than Nizan thought, but it isn't the same thing as the readiness to fight a sustained battle against oppression. In 1937, when he had been engaged for some time in the antifascist struggle, Benda offered a compromise position: "I admit the secular clerk, the clerk military, the clerk who, to obtain something for human nature, resigns himself to the relative. But I hold that alongside this secular man there must be *reguliers*, men of pure speculation, who maintain the ideal in its absolute form."[33] So the parish priest engaged in his pastoral tasks is sustained by the thought of the monk (*le regulier*) who dwells alone with God. Perhaps; though I am more inclined to think that God is sustained by the work of the parish priest. In the long battle against Nazism, Benda may well have taken comfort in the idea of absolute intellectuality. I doubt that he was comforted by those absolutist intellectuals who refused even then to join the battle.

All the difficulties and improbabilities of Benda's argument derive from its radical dualism. The world can be divided in all sorts of ways, but these two realms just don't exist. There is no realm of absolute intellectuality, at least not one inhabited by human beings. We can pretend that the monastery or the academy is such a place, but then the men and women who live there, uplifted by the pretense, would be unlikely to imitate Benda's own political modesty. Benda ought to have been forewarned by the arguments of Plato on behalf of his philosophers and by the political aggrandizement of medieval monks. Philosophers and clerks in touch with eternity are all too likely to seize the present moment. So are intellectuals who think they know the ends of history. Such men are dangerous. But there is no reason to accept the pretense. The knowledge of truth is always incomplete, and the passion for truth is always impure. Truth itself may be universal and immutable, as Benda thought, but every practical embodiment of it in philosophical doctrine or poetic vision is partial and ideological, a parochial mix of insight and myopia. Every one of these embodiments is disputed, and in every dispute not only truth but also reputation, prestige, and glory are at stake. To say this is not to play the cynic or to embrace some anti-intellectual doctrine. The purpose of questioning one side of Benda's dualism is to redeem the other.

For there is also no realm of reality such as Benda describes, where Caesar reigns supreme and where justice is always a threat to worldly interest. It is indeed a threat to some worldly interests, but it is also deeply implicated in the structures and practices of everyday existence. Justice is embodied not only in doctrines and visions but also in conventions, customs, beliefs, rituals, and institutions. The mark of the intellectual is not that he is necessarily detached from these forms of "real life" and critical of them—for sometimes surely he must defend them—but that he is never blindly bound and wholly uncritical. He stands somewhat to the side; he establishes a critical distance. But this is a distance that can be measured in inches. It's not a matter of living (spiritually) somewhere else, across a chasm, in a distinct and separate world; it's a matter of living *here*—and drawing a line. Most often, as we shall see, critical intellectuals live by the moral standards of their own time and place; they speak the language of their fellows. But they refuse, or they ought to refuse, the easy hypocrisies that make day-to-day relationships more comfortable. They tell hard truths, first to themselves, then to others. Hard but familiar truths, else no one would understand them. Homelessness isn't their natural condition, only their occasional one, and if it sometimes breeds a specially acute knowledge, it also has, as Einstein saw, its own pathologies. Similarly, it's not the natural destiny of intellectuals, but only their occasional destiny, to drink the hemlock. Nor are the only heroes of intellectual life those who renounce their homes or accept the poison.

I don't mean to argue that Benda's standards are too high, but that they are the wrong standards. At least, they are the wrong standards so far as justice is concerned. Pure science, art for art's sake, the contemplation of God—these may well carry their votaries, not into another realm, but out of the reach of the rest of us. Where exactly they come to rest is not my concern here. But the love of justice is very different. It brings the intellectual back into reach, forces him to stand among his fellows. Here the proper model is not the medieval monk but the biblical prophet.

It is an interesting sidelight on Benda's life that he never read the prophetic books until the early 1940s (he was in his middle seventies), when he was hiding from the Nazis. Persecution forced upon him "a feeling I had never known before, that of a veneration for my race in the person of its Prophets, who hurled into the world [*jetèrent dans le monde*], at the cost of their repose, the idea of morality."[34] In one sense, Benda captures the precise character of biblical prophecy when he writes that the prophets "never ceased to denounce the immorality of their own people (not, however, in order to oppose to it the morality of other peoples)." But the phrase "hurled into the world" is wrong, and wrong in a characteristic way. It suggests that the prophets stood outside the social and political world. They didn't. They withdrew from it and then returned to it; they spoke in the marketplace and in the courts of power; they comforted as well as denounced their people. Above all, they identified themselves as members of the community, and the morality they defended was only a strong version of the morality that the people themselves claimed to live by.

A certain degree of detachment is, as Lewis Coser has written, the very precondition of intellectual life. But this may go along with—at some level, it *must* go along with—"a deeply felt commitment to the ideals and central values" of one's own society.[35] And if to the ideals and values, then also to the people who embody them (as with Einstein and the Jews). Benda often writes about truth and justice as if they were disembodied concepts. But they are merely abstracted from real though imperfect experience. It is no part of the intellectual's duty to abandon the experience for the sake of the abstraction. His duty is to submit the experience to critical judgment. And that he can do, indeed can only do, while still acknowledging it as his own experience, the common life of his own people.

The Intellectual in the World

Benda believed that the major source of intellectual treason was "the national passion" and all the related passions of identification and belonging. Certainly, such feelings can easily lead to deception and self-deception, apology and rationalization. The *Betrayal* is full of sobering examples. On the other hand, as Coser says, "we are likely to be especially critical of the things we love," in which case love itself can hardly be responsible for the surrender of critical judgment. I would suggest that surrender is a yielding more often to power than to passion. Or, better, it is a yielding to the passion for power, not to the passion for membership and solidarity. This is the only asceticism that the intellectual must practice: he cannot rule over others, not because rulers are never just, but because they are never perfectly just, and the task of the intellectual is to point his finger at the inevitable gap between their pretensions and their achievements. Justice is a judgment on power, not on love.

The treason of the intellectuals is the failure to make that judgment. It has its beginnings most often in a sneaking admiration for those worldly activists, princes and soldiers, who do what the intellectual can never do and who seem, therefore, strong and effective in ways he cannot be. Machiavelli writing about Cesare Borgia provides an example that modern intellectuals have often imitated, preening themselves in the mirror of their minds not as powerful political leaders but as men and women with access to power—who happily whisper in the ear of the prince. Benda understands that the treasonous intellectual admires strength and power, but he thinks this comes about only indirectly. The "traitor" loves his nation and wants it to be strong, and then, convinced that strength depends upon authority, he defends "autocratic systems, arbitrary government . . . reason of State, the religions which teach blind obedient submission."[36] But the connection is not usually so indirect. When intellectuals become defenders of tyranny, it is because they hope to become tyrants—or at least advisers to tyrants. And this is not because they have first become citizens (and parents, husbands, and so on) and lost their sense of distance. Tyrannical ambition is more likely bred than banished by the sense of distance, that is, by the conviction of superior knowledge and the disdain for ordinary people.

The crucial moral principle of the true intellectual has the form of a self-denying ordinance. It was perfectly expressed many centuries ago by a Jewish sage giving advice to other sages and would-be sages: "Love work, do not domineer over others, and never seek the intimacy of public officials."[37] Julien Benda, though he did not know the maxim, lived by it. But he never understood its moral and sociological basis. He thought that one of the chief causes of "the great betrayal" was that the intellectual had come to resemble everyone else. Unlike the medieval clerk, he is subjected to all the responsibilities of citizenship: "His nation claps a soldier's pack on his back . . . and crushes him with taxes . . . the day of enlightened patronage is over . . . he has to earn a living" and so on.[38] Benda can, though he doesn't often, fall into what I have called conservative lamentation. And, conceivably, all this does make the survival of "nonpractical values" more problematic than it once was: Marcuse, some forty years later, makes a similar suggestion. On the other hand, the citizenship of the intellectual may also generate new barriers to treason. For treason is the betrayal not only of the abstract ideal of justice but also of the concrete human interests that the ideal is supposed to protect. In our own time (Benda's too) intellectuals have too often claimed to defend the ideal while losing all sense of the importance of the interests. And so they have set themselves in opposition to ordinary men and women, sought out the intimacy of public officials, and learned in their turn to domineer over others. The democratization of political and intellectual life makes this sort of thing harder to defend. And it suggests what may well be the most attractive picture of the true intellectual: not as the inhabitant of a separate world, the knower of esoteric truths, but as a fellow member of this world who devotes himself, but with a passion, to the truths we all know.

3

The War and Randolph Bourne

Bourne of Bloomfield

Born some twenty years after Julien Benda, Randolph Bourne published his own attack on the betrayal of the intellectuals in the midst of World War I, a decade before Benda's *Betrayal* appeared. He was a clerk *avant la lettre*, who played the part with splendid vehemence and political recklessness. Benda himself supported the French war effort in 1914 and still justified it in 1927, and this must have made his critique of nationalism a little easier for his fellow citizens to accept. Bourne took a more radical line. Along with a tiny minority of American intellectuals and a small group of American socialists, he defied the war hysteria of 1917 and stood up for the "ideal." Not, however, for Benda's ideal: Bourne was an explicit, if peculiar, nationalist and in longing, if not in fact, a member of what he called a "beloved community." His own romanticism focused more on involvement than detachment. When he denounced the American war, he thought he was defending the "American promise."

It is true, nonetheless, that if one were to search for an American embodiment of Benda's "true intellectual," there is no more likely candidate than Randolph Bourne. Few Americans have set themselves so passionately to be intellectuals, and few have been so faithful to that calling. This description of Bourne is common in the critical literature, and it is commonly made to seem overdetermined—as if the role of "true intellectual" had been physically and socially assigned, even before it was morally chosen. With his twisted face and hunched back, Bourne, on this view, was marked out from infancy as an outsider. Alienated in small-town New Jersey, he went to New York so as to be alienated at large. And there he drifted into what Christopher Lasch has described as the creation of the age, the new class of classless intellectuals. Disconnected from church and sect, without any clear professional standing, living in a social void, Bourne was one of those lonely and alienated figures "predisposed" to criticism and rebellion.[1] Detachment and distance sought him out. Bourne's self-descriptions match the terms of this account: he was "a lonely spectator," he wrote in a letter to a friend (July 1915), "reserved from action for contemplation. . . . I have unsuspected powers of incompatibility with the real world."[2] If Lasch is right, the powers need not have been entirely unsuspected, for Bourne's incompatibility was shared with many others, a collective fate rendered more intense and poignant in his case by what Theodore Dreiser called "the fumbling hand of nature."

Even a collective fate, however, can be differently experienced, differently constructed, by the person whose fate it is. Bourne often presents a more complicated view of his own life. Here, from an earlier letter (March 1913), is an account of ambition and foreboding that adds a second and more interesting dualism to the familiar set-off of action and contemplation:

> I want to be a prophet, if only a minor one. I can almost see now that my path in life will be on the outside of things, poking holes in the holy, criticizing the established, satirizing the self-respecting and contented. Never being competent to direct and manage any of the affairs of the world myself, I will be forced to sit . . . in the wilderness howling like a coyote that everything is being run wrong. . . . Between an Ezekiel and an Ishmael, it is a little hard to draw the line; I mean, one can start out to be the first and end only by becoming the latter.[3]

Ezekiel or Ishmael, prophet or outcast: an easy choice, really, if one is free to choose. One can't choose to prophesy in the wilderness, however, for a prophet requires an audience; he must be heard, whether or not he is honored, in his own country; he can't just howl, he must speak the local language. If he was really isolated and alone, if he really inhabited a social void, only divine intercession could rescue him (as it rescued Ishmael) from oblivion.

But social voids, like black holes, are hypothetical phenomena, and we know enough about Bourne's early life to exclude the hypothesis. His detachment and his involvement have a history—which begins in Bloomfield, New Jersey, where he lived until he was twenty-three. I want to focus on Bourne's response to the war, but it is his response to Bloomfield that establishes him as a social critic. He is first of all a critic of his own local society, plausibly taken to represent contemporary America; he learned his critical principles at home. No one is born critically detached. Bourne's early life is more familiar and more conventional than one might expect, given his physical appearance. Elected president of his senior class, editor of the school paper, active in his church (the First Presbyterian), assiduous reader in Bloomfield's free library, he doesn't seem "predisposed" to rebellion. Perhaps the financial circumstances that prevented his early entrance into college—he had been admitted to Princeton in 1903 but was unable to continue his studies until he won a scholarship at Columbia in 1909—pressed him toward what he called "irony," his own name for critical-mindedness. For six years, he worked to earn a living, and this experience provided a certain material basis for his later commitment to social democracy. In the beginning, though, "socialism was really applied Christianity." He learned it, or he first heard himself expounding it, in his Young Men's Bible Class.[4]

In similar fashion, his earliest social criticism is an exposure of small-town hypocrisy. It begins, that is, from the acknowledged principles of the local elite—principles that Bourne never wholly abandoned though he came to interpret them in ways that outraged Bloomfield's Presbyterian elders. "The social spirit of [the] ruling class," he wrote in a study of Bloomfield published in the *Atlantic Monthly* in 1913, "seems to consist in the delusion that its own personal interests are identical with those of the community at large."[5] A common delusion, and Bourne's attack upon it has much in common with other attacks written at roughly the same time by other children of the ruling class. His elders claim to serve the community, and the Christian ideal of service is central to their self-understanding. But this ideal is really ideology: the service of the elders is "utterly selfish," Bourne wrote in another *Atlantic Monthly* article and went on to explain to the respectable readers of that eminently respectable magazine the radical critique of "doing good":

> What of the person who is done good to? If the feelings of sacrifice and service were in any sense altruistic, the moral enhancement of the receiver would be the object sought. But can it not be said that for every . . . merit secured by an act of sacrifice or service on the part of the doer, there is a corresponding depression on the part of the receiver?[6]

A morally serious philanthropy would aim to create a society where philanthropy was unnecessary: "a freely cooperating, freely reciprocating society of equals." But the ideology of service requires inequality and the practice confirms and upholds it. The ruling class battens off the men and women it serves; its self-respect is swollen at their expense. Bourne isn't writing here from any great distance. What he sees, he sees close up:

> How well we know the type of man . . . who has been doing good all his life! How his personality has thriven on it! How he has ceaselessly been storing away moral fat in every cranny of his soul! His goodness has been meat to him. The need and depression of other people has been, all unconsciously, the air which he has breathed.[7]

This is indeed the prophetic style, Ezekiel's, not Ishmael's (with more than a touch of Nietzsche). Despite the moral anger signaled by those exclamation points, however, Bourne never intended to repudiate the ideal of "service." In July 1916, writing in *The New Republic* and worried by the agitation for a warlike "preparedness," he proposed a "moral equivalent" for military conscription. William James had made a similar argument years before, recognizing the value of collective effort and personal sacrifice. Now Bourne sets the question, "How can we all together serve America by really enhancing her life?" and works out in response the idea of a domestic Peace Corps. I am less interested in the details of the proposal—which reveal Bourne's commitment to feminism as well as his sensitivity to the concerns of the labor movement—than in the spirit that animates it. The writer now is Randolph Bourne of Greenwich Village, American bohemian and radical, but the spirit belongs to an earlier Bourne, Bourne of Bloomfield and the First Presbyterian Church: "I have a picture of a host of eager youth missionaries swarming over the land." This is service transformed, because it is genuinely universal and egalitarian, but it is service still: "food inspection, factory inspection, organized relief, the care of dependents, playground service, nursing in hospitals."[8]

"Eager youth missionaries": if Bourne had ever written about the revolutionary vanguard, that is probably the way he would have described it. He divides the world by generations before he divides it by classes, and he tends to write about generations and classes in the style of a secular evangelism. Since the style is authentic, it is not unattractive. Bourne is the advocate of *lift* and *stir* (two of his favorite words, which he regularly uses as nouns)—not conventional Christian uplift but something close enough to that, forward movement, radical agitation, for the sake of a richer culture and a more "experimental" life. He speaks for a new "American newness," the work of his own generation, which seems in Bourne's essays to have invented both youthful enthusiasm and radical politics. "It is the glory of the present age that in it one can be young."[9] His own America is always young, and his early death at thirty-one saved him from having to construct a picture of himself in middle age. As it was, middle age and middle class were conditions that always invited criticism. The two together were represented by Bloomfield's elders, "the private club of comfortable middle-class families" that was also the "older generation." How had these people gone wrong? In 1917, Bourne would write about intellectual betrayal; in the years before 1917, he wrote repeatedly about the betrayal of the elders. They had turned their backs on the American promise, chosen privilege over passionate commitment. Ambitious intellectuals have no monopoly on treason.

"The town changes from a village to an industrial center . . . the world widens, society expands, formidable crises appear," and the older generation—the businessmen, lawyers, ministers, and teachers of Bloomfield and a thousand similar places—are "weary, complacent, evasive."[10] Bourne reads the changes as so many opportunities to realize the American promise. Immigrants arrive, the workers mobilize, women claim their rights. The social classes (generational or economic) to which Bourne's parents and grandparents belong can only recoil in fear and dislike. It's not so much that they are cruel; except perhaps at the very top of the social hierarchy, they lack the energy for that. They are willfully ignorant, closed off in their minds from both the misery and the hope around them. Bourne appeals to an earlier America, the world of the great-grandfathers—Emerson, Thoreau, and Whitman—and to a future America created by his own contemporaries in the image of the promise: open, vivid, democratic, cooperative.

Bourne's "beloved community" was not Bloomfield, but neither was it Greenwich Village; he wasn't a real bohemian. The community he longed for was unrealized but immanent somehow in American life. The sense of this immanence gave his criticism its concreteness and force. He was detached from Bloomfield respectability, but not simply detached, for the promise is available only to participants. In an early essay, "The Life of Irony," he provided an account of himself as participant, contrasting his own critical style with that of an unnamed opposite, almost certainly H. L. Mencken. Both are judges of their society, but Mencken judges from a distance; he is mocking, satirical, brutal, overbearing. Bourne's ideal critic is very different; "judge" is probably not the right word for him:

> If the idea of the ironist as judge implies that his attitude is wholly detached, wholly objective, it is an unfortunate metaphor. For he is as much part and parcel of the human show as any of the people he studies. The world is no stage, with the ironist as audience. His own personal reactions with the people about him form all the stuff of his thoughts and judgments. *He has a personal interest in the case*. . . . If the ironist is destructive, it is his own world that he is destroying; if he is critical, it is his own world that he is criticizing.[11]

Bourne sometimes thought of himself as a "lonely spectator," but that was not what he meant to be. Distance, he argued, made for cynicism and sourness, and neither of these sat well with his youthful evangelism. "The ironist is a person who counts in the world. . . . His is an insistent personality; he is as troublesome as a missionary." Like "judge," "missionary" isn't quite the right word, for a missionary carries his gospel to foreign lands, while irony, as a critical style, works only at home. Bourne did think of himself as a man with a mission—to interpret and defend the newness of America. But he had no gospel to proclaim, at least not in the usual sense of that word. When he left Bloomfield and the First Presbyterian Church, he also gave up the idea of eternal truth. Irony is exposition of another sort. "We may not know much, and can never know the most," he wrote in a letter of 1913, "but at least we have the positive material of our human experience to interpret . . . it is only when we try to interpret the world in terms of pure thought that we get into trouble."[12]

Cultural Nationalism

Bourne is a clerk, then, of a special kind. I suspect that it is his commitment to the "positive material" of everyday experience that explains his nationalism. When he traveled in Europe in the year before the war, he found much to admire (especially on the Continent: he seems to have recognized too much of Bloomfield in Britain), but he came home committed to "decolonization." America must stand on its own, tap its own resources, reclaim its democratic destiny. Like the other young men of *The New Republic*, he declared himself a cultural nationalist. That didn't mean that he was prepared to defend the national culture as he found it. What he found at home reeked of sweetness and light, that is to say, of hypocrisy. The surface was too genteel; everything interesting and vital was repressed. The actuality of America was rougher, livelier, more obstreperous than the elders could admit.

So the content of cultural nationalism had still to be determined, and Bourne hoped to have—and briefly did have—a voice in that determination. The literary criticism that he wrote for *The New Republic* and later for *Dial* should be read in terms of his commitment to a cultural war—in which his central strategy is to outrage his audience and his greatest enemy is an audience too genteel to be outraged. "The literary artist needs protection from the liberal audience that will accept him though he shock them . . . that subtly tame him even while they appreciate."[13] Bourne championed writers whom he thought untamable, like Theodore Dreiser, "the product of the uncouth forces of small-town life and the vast disorganization of the wider American world." Dreiser himself is always on display in his novels, Bourne wrote, and the display "is a revelation of the American soul." Part of the revelation is sexual: "[Dreiser] feels a holy mission to slay the American literary superstition that men and women are not sensual beings." (Sex, like service, had its evangelists in early twentieth-century America—and has had them ever since.) Part of the revelation is more broadly cultural: "His emphases are those of a new America . . . latently expressive. . . . For Dreiser is a true hyphenate, a product of that conglomerate Americanism that springs from other roots than the English tradition."[14] Bourne claims the hyphen for himself too, and so makes cultural nationalism into a defense of a "conglomerate" culture and, as he wrote in one of his finest essays, a "transnational" nation.

Despite his socialist convictions, he was not a nationalist on behalf of the working class or a literary critic in search of proletarian literature. His prophetic message is not some updated version of the Abbé Sieyès's "The third estate is France!" His adherence to the revolt of the masses takes the form of a defense of the great immigration. Bourne's message is that the "hyphenates," all of them, are Americans.[15] The generational categories in which he commonly expressed himself fit immigrants better than workers: here were new Americans for the new America. And each group of immigrants brought its own culture, high as well as low, and produced its own intellectuals. Bourne was especially sympathetic to the Jews—not because he had any special feeling for the people of the Lower East Side, rather because he recognized and valued the "clarity of expression . . . radical philosophy . . . masterly fiber of thought" of the Jewish intellectuals he knew: Walter Lippmann, Felix Frankfurter, Horace Kallen, Morris Cohen.[16] These were the first American products of the great immigration; there would be many others like them so long as the new Americans were not forcibly cast in the mold of the elders. It was not the factory system that Bourne feared most; it was, in the standard metaphor of his age, the melting pot.

What would America become? Bourne professed not to know. He knew only that it would not become a nation on the European model, with a dominant race imposing its own culture upon minority peoples. His own English-Americans were only one more minority, and they acted against their own deepest values when they urged assimilation upon the other minorities—"as if we wanted Americanization to take place only on our terms, and not by the consent of the governed."[17] Consent would generate something radically new, a pattern of conflict and coexistence whose richness could only be intimated. Repress the variety, break up the integral culture of the hyphenated groups, and the result would be "tasteless, colorless . . . insipid." The real alternative to what Kallen called "a nation of nationalities" was a nation without any national character at all. Bourne anticipated later descriptions of mass society when he wrote about the fate of "assimilated" Americans:

> They become the flotsam and jetsam of American life, the downward undertow of our civilization with its leering cheapness and falseness of taste and spiritual outlook, the absence of mind and sincere feeling, which we see in our slovenly towns, our vapid moving pictures, our popular novels, and in the vacuous faces of the crowds on the city street . . . the cultural wreckage of our time.[18]

This sounds rather like an aristocratic critic of the modern "horde," until we remember that Bourne was writing on behalf of men and women with foreign-sounding names, strange customs, and uncouth ways. He was afraid of such people only when they lost their pride, their sense of self and collective integrity. If he was an aristocrat, he was more than willing to tolerate rival aristocracies; he was not looking for submission.

An immigrant society, so long as it avoids the melting pot, will internalize cosmopolitanism. That was Bourne's vision of America: a great cultural variousness, each immigrant group remaining separate but interacting with the others, the individual members at once Swedes, Italians, Slavs, or Jews—and also Americans. The vision may lack sociological coherence, but it is large, generous, welcoming—and this in an age when many American defenders of "community" were calling for the restraint of immigration and the rapid, if necessary the coercive, assimilation of the immigrants to a uniform Americanism. Bourne, by contrast, never doubted that uniformity was un-American. "Transnational America" was not for him a transcendent ideal; it arose out of our national history and our democratic faith. He defended it against his own English-Americans (who did not, he pointed out, adopt the culture of the Indians) as an American democrat.

Service and Solidarity

But what kind of a democrat was it who wrote so harshly about "the flotsam and jetsam of American life . . . the vacuous faces of the crowds"? Bourne was also, even in his earliest essays, a self-conscious intellectual, and he was not unwilling to allow himself "a certain tentative superciliousness towards [the] Demos."[19] He didn't stand aloof and apart; he was involved in the life he criticized; he had a personal interest; but his interest was in improvement and not only in connection. Despite his communitarian faith, his style was never sentimental.

Raymond Williams, the British socialist and social critic, has distinguished two different sorts of criticism: one founded on the ideal of service, the other on the ideal of solidarity. The first starts from hierarchy and authority, the second from "mutual responsibility" ("a freely reciprocating society of equals").[20] Williams prefers solidarity; so does Bourne. But the alternatives are too simply drawn. It isn't difficult to conceive of social critics loyal to a culture or a country or a religion or a class and still forced by the circumstances of their birth and education to work within a hierarchical world. That was Bourne's fate, as it has been the fate of every one of the critics discussed in this book. Concern, commitment, connection, fellow-feeling—all these are possible in one degree or another. But the demand for a strict solidarity is often an invitation to dishonesty. What could Bourne do? The "orthodox elders of the socialist church"—not entirely unlike the elders of the Presbyterian Church—urged him to put aside his "university knowledge" and to hide his "intellectualism." "Go down into the labor unions and the socialist locals," they told him, "and learn of the workingman." He was not in principle unwilling; he had learned a great deal during his own wage-earning years. But now he believed that he had something to teach. "The labor movement in this country needs a philosophy, a literature, a constructive socialist analysis and criticism of industrial relations." And "the only way by which middle-class radicalism can serve is by being fiercely and concentratedly intellectual."[21]

Bourne wanted to be a critical servant of the labor movement, the new immigrants, the country, and the culture generally. The only legitimate aim of service, however, is to make service superfluous. The good servant aims at a future solidarity. This is his heroism: he deliberately sets out to transform the conditions that give value to his work and importance to himself. Such heroism is not uncommon among twentieth-century radicals, though its sincerity is always in doubt. "The aim of the intelligentsia," Lenin once wrote, "is to make special leaders from among the intelligentsia unnecessary."[22] Maybe; but Lenin's stronger and more controversial point is that leaders from the intelligentsia are necessary now. "Labor," Bourne argued in a similar vein in 1916, "will scarcely do this thinking [socialist analysis and criticism] for itself." But Bourne never aspired to "special leadership" in anything like Lenin's sense. He marched with the cultural avant-garde, not the political vanguard; he made no claim to state power. His view of the intellectual's vocation was suggested by his evangelical vocabulary: prophet, missionary, apostle—"Do we not want minds with a touch of the apostolic about them?"[23] There is presumption enough in sentences like that, but it isn't a Leninist presumption. It justifies intellectual intolerance and radical criticism, but not rulership or repression.

The critic is a person "who counts in the world." But he counts because what he says moves the world in certain ways; since he is insistent, questioning, troublesome, involved, he has effects on other people—though sometimes, Bourne acknowledged, "unexpected effects."[24] Even this acknowledgment represents what I think of as the up side of Bourne's self-understanding, the apostolic buoyancy that marks most of his published work until the war years. His letters suggest the down side: not counting in the world but howling in the wilderness, not Ezekiel but Ishmael. (This second view, it seems to me, involves more pretension than the first.) The shifting placement of the self, first in the world, then in the wilderness, may well reflect the "classlessness" of Bourne and his friends—"the fact of being intellectuals," as Lasch says, "in a society that had not yet learned to define the intellectual's place."[25] But don't intellectuals characteristically resist such definition? Certainly Bourne would have resisted: what else could it mean to live an "experimental life"? At the same time, experimentation, evangelism too, was in the 1910s a distinctly middle-class activity; its sociological location is no problem at all. Bourne was a middle-class radical and never pretended to be anything else. Superciliousness did not come naturally; it was a pose adopted for the sake of his mission, the critic's protective coloration. His more natural style combined diffidence with an intense romanticism. He seems never to have felt, in any case, that nervous defensiveness about his own mental powers, that anxiety with intellectuality, that drove other intellectuals into extreme forms of isolation or commitment. For all the fears that his letters express, Bourne had a remarkably straightforward sense of what he was about. His mission was to oppose the hypocrisies of the elders and the passivity of the people—and his sense of himself, up or down, reflected the relative standing of the opposition in American life (also, obviously, the course of his own career-in-opposition). It was only the war that drove him definitively into the wilderness.

War

At first, though, opposition to the war was the health of Randolph Bourne. Never was his prose so charged, his tone so taut, his arguments so strong, as in the essays that he wrote for *Seven Arts* between June and October 1917. It is hard to believe that he was as unhappy as he says he was during those months; a man must glow, writing like that. But he wasn't only writing against the war; he was also, and more importantly, writing against the intellectuals who supported the war—and these were his friends and teachers. So the pride of opposition was clouded by the sense of loss and betrayal.

"A war made deliberately by the intellectuals!" That was Bourne's ironic comment on a *New Republic* editorial of April 1917 boasting that the "influence" of a "numerically insignificant class" had brought about American participation in the war: "college professors, physicians, lawyers, clergymen, and [who else?] writers on magazines and newspapers."[26] Bourne opposed both American participation and the "influence" of this intellectual class, and it seems clear that he was as outraged by the second as by the first. He sometimes called himself a pacifist, and he has been claimed as a comrade or at least a sympathizer by pacifists ever since, but I can find no evidence in his essays that he was committed to either a religious or a political pacifism. He was never unwilling to contemplate the use of force. His proposal for an "American strategy" in response to German submarine warfare included "the immediate guarantee of food and ships to the menaced nations and . . . the destruction of the attacking submarines."[27] That sounds like a program for limited naval war; it is certainly not a program for neutrality or isolation or nonviolence. But the war that America entered in 1917 was not limited; nor did the American entry impose limits on the Allied war effort. If anything, it added a new grandiosity, a set of ultimate aims far beyond anything that military force might accomplish—and for this Bourne blamed the intellectuals. In Benda's terminology, they "moralized" the war; they made the fight against Germany into a cause, hoping to achieve in the maelstrom of global warfare what they had failed to achieve in time of domestic peace. And this improbable hope justified in turn a rush for office that was especially unseemly: for even if the war had been a good one it would still have required a sustained and systematic intellectual critique.

It is interesting to see how the key concepts of Bourne's earlier essays reappeared in his wartime writing. The culture of prophecy and service, he now argued, had been an insubstantial culture, lacking, for most prophets and servants, both emotional depth and intellectual rigor. It was neither vividly conceived nor concretely enacted. The very superficiality of its American commitments made it available for global adventures. "Never having felt responsibility for labor wars and oppressed masses and excluded races at home, they [the intellectuals] had a large fund of idle emotional capital to invest." Or again: "Too many of these prophets are men who have lived rather briskly among the cruelties and thinnesses of American civilization. . . . Their moral sense has been stirred by what they saw in France and Belgium, but it was a moral sense relatively unpracticed by deep concern and reflection over the inadequacies of American democracy."[28] Bourne never argued that the intellectuals were insufficiently detached. They were insufficiently engaged. They hardly knew the workers or immigrants they pretended to serve. They were not seriously involved in or absorbed by the struggle for democracy; they had, consequently, no clear sense of what democracy means. Eager to act, but without any experience of collective action, they made easy recruits to the discipline of war. "They have . . . no clear philosophy of life except that of intelligent service, the admirable adaptation of means to ends. They are vague about what kind of society they want . . . but they are equipped with all the administrative attitudes and talents necessary to attain it." Above all, they wanted, as Bourne also wanted, to count in the wider world—and once the war had begun, "the only way one can count is as a cog in the great wheel."[29]

The focus of Bourne's anger was narrower than his third person plural pronouns suggest. He meant to include a lot of people, but he spoke directly to a few, his *New Republic* colleagues and his teachers at Columbia—especially Walter Lippmann and John Dewey. Lippmann had gone off to Washington; Dewey had written what were for Bourne the most important defenses of the war effort. Lippmann was the chief of those young men "trained up in the pragmatic dispensation," of whom Bourne wrote that it was "as if the war and they had been waiting for each other." Dewey was the chief pragmatist. Both Lippmann and Dewey saw in the war an opportunity not only to make the world safe for democracy but also to enhance democracy at home: to turn the federal government into an instrument of democratic transformation and to back up the government with a newly socialized people. Wasn't this service in the cause of solidarity?

I suspect that Bourne would have supported a genuinely defensive war, fought to protect a threatened community. But a war fought to create a community? This was a desperate act, a naive and willful politics, for war was not a machine that a few intellectuals could control. Its technology was not designed for social service; it answered to different purposes; it produced different effects. In those first months of fighting, Bourne saw with remarkable prescience what those effects were likely to be. He wrote now as a true prophet—though his growing insistence on the inevitability of everything he foresaw tended to undercut his reason for writing:

> War determines its own end—victory, and government crushes out automatically all forces that deflect, or threaten to deflect, energy from the path of organization to that end. All governments will act in this way, the most democratic as well as the most autocratic. It is only "liberal" naïveté that is shocked at arbitrary coercion and suppression. Willing war means willing all the evils that are organically bound up with it.[30]

This may not be right in general, but it was right enough in 1917. President Wilson took a divided country into an unnecessary war, and the result was an odd combination of popular apathy and national hysteria, democratic propaganda and brutal repression—a "psychic complex of panic, hatred, rage, class arrogance, and patriotic swagger" that could only issue, in the end, in disillusion and spiritual impoverishment. It was "a war made deliberately by the intellectuals" (that was part of the class arrogance) in the face of "the hesitation and dim perceptions of the American democratic masses."[31] The search for social solidarity by way of military mobilization was doomed to failure.

The intellectuals had betrayed their true service. In the most powerful of his essays, "Twilight of Idols," an attack on John Dewey, Bourne blamed the betrayal on "the pragmatic dispensation." He didn't offer a philosophical critique of pragmatism; he was himself a philosophical pragmatist, committed to the experimental life, sharing the sense of openness, process, participation that pragmatism at its best still stimulates. But this is a sense that needs to be cultivated, tested "inch by inch," shaped and controlled by intelligence. The mere eagerness for action and effectiveness, the realist's search for "influence," is a vulgar pragmatism, a doctrine for bureaucrats and "special leaders." Even Dewey, Bourne perceptively charged, "somehow retains his sense of being in the controlling class." (But what does he control?) His disciples were "immensely ready for the executive ordering of events, pitifully unprepared for the intellectual interpretation or the idealistic focusing of ends."[32]

The task of intellectuals is to address the question of ends or values. To be sure, values are not given or known in advance; they have to be worked out, as Dewey taught, experimentally. But the relevant experiments are mental before they are practical: "interpretation" and "focusing" precede action, else how would we know what to do? Dewey, Bourne argued, had failed to make this necessary precedence clear; he good-naturedly tended to assume that other people had hopes, intentions, political goals, very much like his own. What else could they possibly want? "There was always that unhappy ambiguity in his doctrine as to just how values were created."[33] Bourne himself had little to say about the creation of values; his own argument began, like all such arguments, sometime after creation, *in media res*. The point was to attend critically to the values we already have. "Our intellectual class might have been occupied, during the last two years of war, in studying and clarifying the ideals and aspirations of . . . American democracy." That is from the first of the antiwar essays, published in June 1917; by the time he wrote "Twilight of Idols," in October, Bourne seemed to feel that clarification was not enough. Intellectuals now must "rage and struggle until new values come out of the travail, and we can see some glimmering of our democratic way."[34] Even here, however, the commitment to find a *democratic* way is simply assumed, and the way is still *ours*, that is, it represented for Bourne a shared vision of the future. So long as he could say "our way," he believed that he was still serving, for all his rage, the cause of solidarity. He also (still) believed that that cause required a fierce and concentrated intelligence. It wasn't served by practical service, "a cheerful and brisk setting to work," unless practical service was intellectually focused on its proper ends.

Liberal intellectuals had enlisted in the war effort, in part, out of fear of being cut off from a great national struggle. To oppose the war meant to howl uselessly in the wilderness. Unprepared for that, they were ready to believe that the long-term effects of the fighting would be good—almost as if they thought that "a war patronized by *The New Republic* could not but turn out to be a better war than anyone had hoped."[35] In any case, they did not want to exclude themselves from its management. How could they serve if they had no hold on the agencies and instruments of service? "We were constantly told by our friends," wrote Jane Addams years later, "that to stand aside from the war mood of the country was to surrender all possibility of future influence, that we were committing intellectual suicide."[36] In response, Bourne charged that the intellectuals had already committed suicide by enlisting in a struggle they could never control. Their claim to political effectiveness was pitiful; it was "the least democratic forces in American life" that actually controlled the course of the war, while the intellectuals, from the inside, could not even sustain a liberal critique. Their influence hardly extended to the government's propaganda, let alone to its conduct of the war. They had even lost the capacity to deplore the domestic repression they once promised to prevent. "Their thought," Bourne wrote, had become "little more than a description and justification of what is going on."[37] All that was true enough, as Lippmann and Dewey, the best of the enlisted intellectuals, later admitted. But Bourne's opposition, like their involvement, had its own costs. Though most of the time he wrote like Ezekiel, he felt more and more like Ishmael, and his last pieces, unpublished at his death, show the marks of his growing desperation.

Distance and Despair

Power may or may not be personally corrupting; sometimes it is and sometimes it isn't. But the pursuit and exercise of power certainly corrupt intellectual life, at least as Bourne conceived intellectual life: a life of irony and criticism, lived fiercely and with concentration. Given their mission, intellectuals have no choice but to stand aside from official positions and official doctrines. So Bourne argued, years before Julien Benda, for a division of labor between value "creators," "interpreters," and "emphasizers," on the one hand, and those other men and women who are in fact "ready" for the executive ordering of events, on the other. But Bourne insisted at the same time that values ought to shape the executive orders: it is the task of American intellectuals to focus political action on democratic ends. They point the way for political leaders—and then they dog their tracks, hunting, not heeling, critical of every false move. Here Bourne was true to his Protestant evangelism; he did not believe that the values of the clerk are different from those of the layman. There is only one set of values, captured (for us) in the idea of the American promise. But there are two sets of people: the first interprets the promise; the second enacts it.

One promise, just as there is one promised land: intellectuals do not inhabit, either ideally or in practice, a separate realm. "It is his own world that he is criticizing." The same men and women who stand aside from office seeking must also sustain their democratic connections. But the pressures of the war made this complex positioning increasingly difficult. Pragmatic intellectuals, who tended now to call themselves "realists," found it hard to stand aside; radicals like Bourne found it hard to sustain the connection. Had he been more closely tied to the Socialist party, he might have found some support for his own fierceness. But though his sympathies lay with the socialists, his personal ties were with reformers, liberal nationalists, progressives, Greenwich Village bohemians—not, with rare exceptions, a crowd given to fierceness. In the *Seven Arts* essays of 1917, Bourne resisted even the thought of his own alienation. He was a "thorough malcontent," he wrote in "Twilight of Idols," but not one of that old tribe of malcontents who went off to Europe before the war. He won't become an expatriate, even when that is possible again; he and his friends "are too much entangled emotionally in the possibilities of American life to leave it."[38] Those were brave words, and the bravest one was "possibilities." Bourne still believed—or professed to believe—that the intellectual's mission made sense and for all the bloodiness of the war might give shape and purpose to a life. "The war—or the American promise: one must choose."[39] But there was still the promise.

The tone of Bourne's writing changed in 1918, though how definitive the change was remains unclear. Perhaps he preserved some sense of his mission; he did, after all, keep on writing. But he was also increasingly skeptical about the "possibilities" of American life—and increasingly bitter in his skepticism. Now, even in his published work, the placement of the intellectual was more and more extreme: he is a "spiritual vagabond," a "declassed mind," an "outlaw," even an "exile" from American life. And in a letter to Van Wyck Brooks (March 1918), Bourne seemed to despair of democracy itself and of the prophet's commitment to speak to the people: "Why let your voice cry in the wilderness, when a healthy, lusty, and unanimous democracy not only will not hear but is almost as ready to spill your blood as it is to destroy the enemy abroad?"[40] From the wilderness, indeed, things look different, uglier, more forbidding, than they do when one is standing in settled territory. In Bourne's last writings, the world he criticized was no longer his own.

The most important of these writings is the unfinished essay-treatise, "The State." Only the beginning of a political theory, "The State" is almost the end of Bourne's politics. In time of war, he argued, there is nothing that citizens can do. The state at war is the "inexorable arbiter and determinant of men's businesses and attitudes and opinions." And this is the *telos* of state power: the permanent goal of office-holders is just this "inexorable" determination of their subjects' lives, fully possibly only when mobilization begins. "War is the health of the state." Nor do the subjects resist, for war feels like their health too. "The purpose and desire of the collective community live in each person who throws himself wholeheartedly into the cause of war. . . . He achieves a superb self-assurance, an intuition of the rightness of all his ideas and emotions, so that in the suppression of opponents or heretics he is invincibly strong."[41] His personal strength, however, serves only to enhance the power of the state, from which his ideas and emotions alike derive.

Bourne carefully distinguished between the nation and the state—he was still a nationalist—and assigned to the nation all the "life-enhancing forces" that make for industry and culture. But the nation is a complex community, "not a group . . . [but] a network of myriads of groups representing the cooperation and similar feeling of men on all sorts of planes and in all sorts of human interests and enterprises." It doesn't provide for its members the immediate reassurance of state power. The nation arises through the "disaggregation of the herd"—a long and difficult social process—while the state, especially the state-at-war, re-creates the herd. Only autonomous adults, individuals capable of moral choice and rational cooperation, can sustain the nation, while the state sustains itself by exploiting, as it were, the latent childishness of its subjects—who become in war real children, "obedient, respectful, trustful . . . full of that naive faith in the all-wisdom and all-power of the adult who takes care of them . . . in whom they lose their responsibility and anxieties."[42] War is the health of the state, but it is the moral death of the people. And yet the people rush headlong to their death, and the intellectuals (so Bourne had already argued), for all their pride and aloofness, join the rush. The psyche craves security; "the intellect craves certitude." War, or at least the idea of war, provides for both.

Bourne's theory of the disaggregated nation and the herd-state was cobbled together to fit the immediate occasion. The idea of the state as an agency inherently opposed to social differentiation anticipates, perhaps, later theories of totalitarian politics (in which the ideological party/movement plays a similar part). But it is barely developed and virtually without historical reference. The idea of the herd is less interesting and even less developed. Bourne took it over from the popular sociology of his time and used it to castigate a democratic public that had yielded to the hysteria of chauvinism and repression. It is the opposite term to his "beloved community" and appears as immanent now in American life as the other did before the war. What had happened to the world of the great-grandfathers, the democratic promise, transnational America? It hardly seems the case anymore that these have been betrayed by the intellectual "realist"; they no longer constitute a presence sufficient for betrayal. The national or transnational community is so dimly seen behind the grandeur of the state-at-war that it can no longer serve as a political ideal or a rallying point. And there was more (and worse) to come. In what must have been the last essay Bourne wrote, scribbled in pencil on the back of the manuscript pages of "The State," he described a wholly determined social world in which individuals are, in peace as much as in war, "entirely helpless," the weapons of criticism entirely impotent. Most men and women "live a life which is little more than a series of quasi-official acts," while the occasional rebel is immediately crushed. What we take to be our personal choices and decisions merely enact "the codes and institutions of society."[43] The essay that his editors named "Old Tyrannies" makes "The State" seem wonderfully robust. It is as if Bourne wrote, a month or so before his final illness, a theoretical obituary: an account of the death, not of the man, but of the mission.

These last writings suggest a connection, to which I drew attention in chapter 1, between distance and determinism. It is only the connected critic who believes in the effectiveness of the critical enterprise—who believes in himself as someone "who counts in the world." Seen from far enough away, the world simply is what it is, and the lonely spectator doesn't count at all. Perhaps Bourne thought that he had achieved a kind of scientific detachment at the end, but this is a detachment born of despair. Or should the description be reversed: a despair born of detachment? It doesn't matter; the circle is complete and wholly vicious; there is no escape. "We all enter as individuals into an organized herd-whole in which we are as significant as a drop of water in the ocean, and against which we can about as much prevail."[44]

But this isn't the authentic Bourne, the man who wrote the savage essays of 1917 and obviously meant to prevail if he possibly could. His detached science is a wartime hallucination. When the armistice was celebrated in New York, he wrote to his mother: "Now that the war is over, people can speak freely again and we can dare to think. It's like coming out of a nightmare."[45] He died of influenza a few weeks later.

4

Martin Buber's Search for Zion

Philosophy and Criticism

I don't have an I–Thou relationship with Martin Buber. His philosophical theology or religious philosophy has always seemed to me obscure and portentous. The life of dialogue is too heavily weighted with significance ever to have been lived by mere mortals; angels, intimate by nature, might manage it. But perhaps we should think of Buberian dialogue as an early version of what contemporary critical theorists call ideal communication: in Buber's case not so much face-to-face as soul-to-soul, a "pure" exchange from which all traces of vanity and self-interest have been eliminated. His emphasis is on personal intensity, absolute openness, the gift of the self to the other.[1] The theoretical structure of the exchange, the effort to derive from it a systematic ethics—all this comes later. But Buber is already able to criticize instrumental and manipulative exchanges. Without intimacy or (genuine) intensity, they are weighted with negative significance: I–It. The polarities of I–Thou and I–It exhaust the universe; there isn't much room for an ordinary good talk or nasty argument. But I suspect Buber of a sneaky realism about such matters and more common sense than he sometimes displays. Concealed by the overheated prose of his major works, realism and common sense are the surprising marks of his occasional writings.

"Occasional writings" is not quite the right phrase. Buber was an extraordinarily prolific writer; he seems to have been writing all the time, turning easily from big projects to smaller ones. He became famous for his philosophical books, his Hasidic tales, his speeches on Judaism, his biblical translations and exegeses. None of this was occasional. He is less well known as a participant in and critic of Zionist politics. This interest was not occasional either; indeed, there is nothing in his life and work so pervasive, so continuously present, as his Zionist commitment. But the writing here is different: short essays, newspaper articles, public statements, open letters—all in a direct, forceful, and relatively simple prose. When Buber gave his inaugural lecture at Hebrew University in 1938, one of his listeners said, "Clearly, he has learned our language: now he is as obscure in Hebrew as in German."[2] His Zionist pieces were written in German during much of his life, later on in Hebrew, and they are rarely obscure. A large number of them have recently been collected in a single volume by Paul Mendes-Flohr. Read in sequence they reveal the extent of Buber's achievement: almost half a century of sustained and courageous criticism.[3] It's not dialogue exactly; Buber was often involved in controversy, but he rarely elicited the responses he hoped for. Still, the work is a model of its kind, and Buber the philosopher-theologian must also be recognized as a powerful social and political critic.*

I suppose that his criticism is nourished by his philosophy (though philosophical reference is largely absent); his understanding of Zionism and his theory of criticism are obviously connected to his more general, more fully elaborated doctrine. But they also stand independently and are readily expressed in the language of twentieth-century political engagement. This is my own language, and I shall not search for its deeper ground. In Buber's case, the ground is muddy, even if it is also sustaining. It may well be that Buber was driven all his life by a passionate desire that Zionist Jews establish

* It is worth noting that Buber's work was known and admired by two of the other critics with whom I shall be dealing: Albert Camus thought highly of his books, *I and Thou* especially, and corresponded with him. (Buber returned the admiration and arranged to have *The Rebel* translated into Hebrew.) Ignazio Silone wrote a letter in 1961 nominating Buber for the Nobel Prize in Literature—probably for his Hasidic tales, which have some resemblance to the kind of storytelling at which Silone himself excelled.

an I–Thou relation with Palestinian Arabs. Fortunately for his critical enterprise, he also defended a less extravagant program, more intimately tied to, even if it was also in sharp tension with, the ordinary understanding of Zionist politics.

Interpretation and Reiteration

Writing to Buber on his eightieth birthday, David Ben-Gurion praised his "faithful participation in the work of the rebirth of Israel from your youth to the present day."[4] In his youth, for a few years, Buber had edited the theoretical journal of the Zionist movement. Since that time, he had held no office and done no official or even unofficial work for the movement. His "faithful participation" consisted of constant criticism, often directed at Ben-Gurion himself. But he remained a committed Zionist from 1898 until his death in 1965. Asked in 1962 to write an article on Jewish-Arab relations for the American Council on Judaism, an anti-Zionist group, he sent a brisk refusal, arguing that his own "criticism of the Israeli government's Arab policies comes from within, yours from without. Our program for Jewish-Arab cooperation is not inferior to what is called official Zionism; rather it is a greater [that is, a better] Zionism."[5] Buber is a nationalist critic of nationalist politics, a position that Julien Benda thought impossible. This internal critique was first worked out in an essay written in 1921; Buber defended it more explicitly in a speech in Antwerp in 1932 responding directly to Benda's *The Betrayal of the Intellectuals*.

Buber's argument in the essay "Nationalism" displays two of the most important devices of internal criticism, and so I shall consider it in some detail. The argument begins by distinguishing peoplehood, nationality, and nationalism, the first a matter of common experience, "a unity of fate"; the second a collective awareness of this unity; the third a heightened or "overemphasized" awareness in the face of division or oppression. Peoplehood is an impulse, nationality an idea, nationalism a program.[6] The program is conceived in difficulty; it aims to mobilize the nation so as to overcome some deficiency in its common life. The mobilization is legitimate, Buber believes, but the strains to which it responds and the enthusiasm it requires combine, very often, to produce presumption and extremism. Nationalism tends to exceed its limits. But how does one recognize and affirm the limits? Buber rejects the conventional philosophical response to this question, which is, he writes, "to limit this expanding group egoism from without, to humanize it on the basis of abstract moral or social postulates."[7] His own alternative is twofold in character. First, group egoism is limited, as we might expect, from within the group by "the character of the people itself," its common experiences and shared values. Peoplehood and nationality together constrain programmatic nationalism. For the Jews this means that the understanding of justice first affirmed in the Exodus code, reaffirmed by the prophets, and then reinforced by centuries of exile and persecution must determine what Zionists do and don't do. Jewish nationalism is legitimate only insofar as its activities are shaped by the adjective, not the noun; its terms derived not from the category "nation" but from the category "Judaism." The derivation won't have the results Buber hopes for, obviously, unless his own account of Judaism is accepted, but this is an account that many Zionists, though not many religious Jews, have probably found congenial.

The second limit to expanding group egoism is found in the process of expansion itself. Programmatic nationalists encounter other nations with programs of their own. Here political movements may be compared to individuals: "A genuine person also likes to affirm himself in the face of the world, but in doing so he also affirms the power with which the world confronts him. This requires constant demarcation of one's own right from the rights of others."[8] The recognition that the other person has rights follows, Buber believes, from the nature of the encounter itself. "It is only common sense," as the Talmud says. "Who knows that your blood is redder [than his]? Perhaps his blood is redder."[9] The same argument holds with regard to the group: "There is no scale of values for the function of peoples. One cannot be ranked above another."[10] It is not by comparison and classification that we acquire moral knowledge of other people; rather, we understand others by reiterating our self-understanding. Thus Buber argued in 1929, responding to those of his fellow Zionists who thought Arab nationalism an "artificial" creation: "We know that . . . we have genuine national unity and a real nationalist movement; why should we assume that these do not exist among the Arabs?"[11]

The moral value of stepping into the other person's shoes is a commonplace of philosophical and practical ethics: we must try to see the world from the perspective of the other. It is important to stress, however, that this is the very opposite of another commonplace, which enjoins us to step back from every particular perspective, to detach ourselves, to take a God's-eye view of the world. The first mode, stepping into rather than stepping back from, is the more modest enterprise. Indeed, we can never fully understand the world view of the other by stepping into his shoes, for what he sees, hopes for, resents, and loves is shaped more by where his shoes have been than by where they are now. But we can grasp the simple moral fact that he exists, that he has hopes, resentments, loves like ours—as legitimate as ours.* Imagine, writes Buber, that "we were the residents of Palestine and the others were the immigrants who were coming into the country in increasing numbers, year by year, taking it away from us. How would we react to events?"[12] Our imaginations don't, in fact, reach to true or certain knowledge of the other person's reaction. We don't enter into his head when we step into his shoes. To think that we do is a characteristic mistake of philosophers who believe that heads have no histories. We don't, because we can't, reproduce other people's ideas; instead, we reiterate our own. If we want to go beyond this and find out what other people think, we have to ask them. But the recognition that the others have experiences and ideas similar to ours is already a significant moral achievement. It is, Buber writes in "Nationalism," the prophet Amos's achievement when he tells his people that the God who brought them out of Egypt also brought the Philistines out of Caphtor and Aram out of Kir. Instead of imagining a universal exodus, Amos imagines a series; and the fact that he can specify the details of only one of the series does not deter him from acknowledging the moral value of the others.[13]

Buber's first limit on nationalist excess is interpretive in character: it requires him to tell a story about Jewish experience and understanding. His second limit is reiterative in character: it requires him to recognize that a similar story could be told about the others. Similar but different—there is no ideal story, no single correct account of nationalist aspiration that, in the best of worlds, we and they might simultaneously recite. But if legitimate nationalism takes many forms in Buber's account, illegitimate nationalism seems to take only one, its terms dictated by the abstract conceptions of

* Buber sometimes goes further than this, as when he writes (under the impetus of the Arab revolt of 1929) that "we need . . . the ability to put ourselves in the place of the other . . . the stranger, and to make his soul ours" (*A Land of Two Peoples: Martin Buber on Jews and Arabs*, ed. Paul R. Mendes-Flohr [Oxford: Oxford University Press, 1983], p. 79). This is the language of *I and Thou*, and it suggests a good deal more than we need to do (or can do). Morality requires that we recognize, not that we possess, the soul of the stranger.

political realism. What the realist sees is a world of nation-states, each one conceived apart from its own history and culture, hence identical with all the others in aim and action, having no purpose save that of preserving and asserting itself. Interpretation gets no start here, and reiteration yields only an endless series of nations as frightened and aggressive as we are. Zionists who aspire to "normality," who want the Jews to become a nation like other nations, really mean, writes Buber, to join the series. He denies the legitimacy of that goal: "The activities which we have begun in Palestine are not directed toward creating just another small nation in the family of nations . . . another creature to jump and intervene in world disputes."[14] Zionism must create a nation different from all the others, true to what Buber calls its "eternal mission." That is an ominous phrase, like "manifest destiny" in American ideology, full of evil omens; but the evil is avoided by reiteration. Then we acknowledge that every nation has its mission, and what remains is to work out the "line of demarcation" between one mission and another. "No nation in the world has [self-preservation and self-assertion] as its only task, for just as an individual who wishes only to preserve and assert himself leads an unjustified and meaningless existence, so a nation with no other aim deserves to pass away."[15]

If there is no single correct nationalist program, no universal version of a mission, we might still hope for a single correct rule with which to draw the line of demarcation. But Buber denies that any such rule exists. There are indeed rules, against murder and expropriation, for example, but these do not draw the line. The line can only be negotiated; it comes into being as a result of "a thousand small decisions."[16] Here politics takes precedence over philosophy, though this must always be a politics guided by interpretation and reiteration. "There are no formulas: for truly responsible conduct there is only an orientation, but no formulas." Morality cannot work at a distance. This is Buber's explicit response to Julien Benda. Certainly intellectuals have betrayed their calling by becoming apologists for this or that nationalist program, "manufacturing words," Buber writes, for every new demand. But this betrayal "cannot be atoned for by the intellect retreating into itself . . . only by its proferring to reality true service in place of false."[17] "True service" is both critical and worldly, critical in and of the world. Buber's defense of worldliness is sometimes matter-of-fact and sometimes high-flown, sometimes prosaic and sometimes poetic, as if he is a little unsure about the nature of the world to which he is committed. "If work is to be done in public life," he wrote in 1930, "it must be accomplished not above the fray but in it." And, in the same piece: "The Word is not victorious in its purity but in its corruption—it bears fruit in the *corruptio seminis*."[18] For Buber, indeed, the Word was not victorious in any form, but he stuck nevertheless to his worldly commitment, "true to the spirit . . . on the plane of reality." Against the realism of *raison d'état*, he struggled to work out a realistic politics of his own. I want to turn now to the substantive character of that politics.

Binationalism

The central theme of Buber's criticism from 1918 until 1965 was the failure of Zionist leaders to work hard enough, inventively enough, for Arab-Jewish cooperation in Palestine. Buber's opponents in the movement insisted that the word "enough" was meaningless here, for Arab-Jewish cooperation was simply impossible. What motive could the Arabs have to cooperate with these Jewish interlopers? One had only to perform Buber's thought experiment—imagine the Jews as the residents, the Arabs as the immigrants, "coming into the country in increasing numbers . . . taking it away from us"—to see that the problem had no solution. For many Zionist leaders, the encounter with the Arabs took the form, almost from the beginning, of a historic tragedy. The Jews had to come, for they had no other place; the Arabs were already in place and had what Buber called an "inalienable right" to remain. Once the tragedy was recognized, what could one do but play it out? Soon enough the looming danger of catastrophe in Europe made the tragic encounter with Palestine's Arabs seem a minor price to pay for a place of one's own. But Buber all his life rejected the tragic view. His rejection works on two planes, and on the second, it seems to me, more successfully than on the first. The first is higher: Buber proposes to resolve the tragedy by establishing a binational state. The second is lower: Buber tries to resist the tragedy at the level of the "thousand small decisions," setting himself against every particular act of provocation or terrorism, looking for but not waiting for signs of reciprocity from the Arab side: the interlopers, he thought, had to take the initiative in creating some degree of mutual trust. The binational state was the centerpiece of what might be called

Buber's macrocriticism, but he was also, with admirable persistence, a Zionist microcritic.

I do not believe that binationalism was ever a plausible politics; the trust that it required could not have been won except by the surrender and departure of the Jewish settlers—in which case trust would have been unnecessary. Then ordinary nationalism would have sufficed for the Arabs. In fact, ordinary nationalism sufficed in any case; it was sufficient to their purposes, since they never proposed to share political power with the Jews; they were the majority and demanded their democratic as well as their national rights. Ordinary nationalism sufficed for the Jews too, given their most essential purpose, which Buber shared, at least early on: to establish "the right of free Jewish immigration to the land."[19] He rejected the standard nationalist goal, the sovereign nation-state, but it is hard to see how the right of immigration could ever have been vindicated short of sovereignty. Buber argued throughout the twenties and thirties that the Arabs would accept Jewish immigrants if only the Zionist leadership committed itself to economic cooperation and political compromise. But immigration was not an issue that lent itself to compromise. What was at stake wasn't just the institutional arrangements or the practical policies of the binational state but its very population. Who would be present and counted among its citizens? How many of each nation? In the event Buber was driven by his commitment to binationalism to deny or at least to hedge the Jewish right to come into the land.

Mass immigration, obviously, would frighten the Arabs and generate an increasingly fierce nationalist politics among them. But Buber had another and, to my mind, less honorable worry. The immigrants would be frightened Jews, refugees rather than pioneers, whose desperation, he sensed, would blind them to the justice of a binational state. They were not likely supporters of a Buberian program. This was indeed a realistic view but not a sympathetic or generous one. The formula Buber eventually adopted called for the "greatest possible number" of Jewish immigrants, where "possible" was (or seemed to be—his language here was never explicit) a complex function of the absorptive capacity of the Jewish community in Palestine and the agreement of the Arab community.[20] But this was an impossible position within the Zionist movement—for Buber adopted it at the very moment when the urgency of Jewish need was overwhelming.

Binationalism in the late 1930s and early 1940s looks like a peculiarly doctrinaire position, the triumph of moral principle over moral reality. Faced with a steadily intensifying Nazi persecution and a growing stream of refugees, the Jews of Palestine could hardly do anything else than fight for "free Jewish immigration"—a necessity whether or not it was a "right." But Buber could never quite bring himself to acknowledge the necessity. The horror of Nazism is largely missing from his published writings during these crucial years. Only in 1959 did he try to explain how the extremity of the situation and the urgent need of the refugees had overwhelmed binational rectitude. "The principle of selective, organic development" could not stand, he acknowledges, against "the most frightful happening of modern history, the extermination of millions of Jews by Adolf Hitler. The harassed, tormented masses crowded into Palestine. . . . Who would have taken it on himself to obstruct this onrush of the homeless in the name of the selective method! The masses came and with them came the necessity for political security."[21]* Here Buber says the obligatory things: that the refugees had to be taken in and that the community that took them in had to protect them against further onslaughts ("the necessity of political security" is Buber's belated bow to statehood and sovereignty). But he clearly regards the arrival of the refugees as a disappointment of his theoretical hopes, and that is not, in human terms, an adequate response to their experience.

This, it seems to me, was Buber's worst time. And yet his dogged, resolute opposition to Jewish statehood was consistent with his position from his earliest years in the movement and represented, indeed, an important strand of Zionist thinking. It addressed the moral reality of life in Palestine, the need to find some *modus vivendi* with the Arabs. And it gave expression to a sensibility born of centuries of statelessness and, as Arnold Zweig wrote to Buber in 1918, ill-disposed to the paraphernalia of power: "canons, flags, and military decorations."[22] A certain sort of socioeconomic normality was much sought after by Zionist leaders: Jewish farmers, dockhands, engineers, even policemen. But political normality—"another creature to jump and intervene in world disputes"—remained a highly controversial subject into the 1940s. Only Jewish helplessness in the face of Nazism made normality

* Compare to these lines the speech of Berl Katznelson, the moral leader of Labor Zionism, twenty years earlier, at the Twenty-first Zionist Congress in 1939. Katznelson had also favored a policy of selection; now, recognizing the Nazi threat, he called for mass immigration. "We may ask why it is that history did not choose free . . . and well-behaved Jews to be the bearers of its mission and preferred instead the Jewish refugees, the most wretched of all humankind, cast adrift on the seas. But we cannot change the fact. That is what history has determined, and it is left to us to accept its choice. . . . What, after all, is Zionism all about? Summer camps? Sabbath eve gatherings? Hasn't it always been its aim . . . to provide a true salvation to the Jewish people?" (Berl Katznelson, *Collected Writings*, vol. 9 [Tel Aviv, 1948], p. 75 [in Hebrew]. I owe this reference to Dahlia Ofer.)

in all its forms look more and more attractive. Given that helplessness, anyone who opposed "normal" sovereignty had to explain how he would cope with the immediate and overwhelming problems of the Jewish people. So far as I can tell, Buber never did that, and so when he wrote angrily in May 1948, just after the proclamation of Israel's independence, that "today the Jews are succeeding at [normality] to a frightening degree," the outburst did not carry the critical force that he intended.[23] What was the alternative to this frightening success?

Buber's microcriticism worked against the background of his binationalist convictions, but it served at the same time another purpose: not to avoid or resolve the tragedy of Jewish-Arab conflict but to minimize the injustices done by the Jews. "We cannot refrain from doing injustice altogether," he wrote in 1945, "but we are given the grace of not having to do more injustice than absolutely necessary." Settlement itself was unjust, for it encroached upon Arab living space, "if not in the present generation, at any rate for future generations."[24] But this injustice Buber was prepared to defend. What he opposed, consistently, year after year, was every use of force by the settlers that was not literally and narrowly defensive. Writing against Jewish terrorism in 1938 and 1939, for example, he drew the essential "line of demarcation" with clarity and force: "If a man enters the room where his child is playing, and sees a stranger point his rifle through the window, it is his right and duty to fire the first shot." But if the attacker makes his escape, "right and justice will not admit of the victim waylaying [another] stranger only because he is of the same blood as the criminal."[25] This short essay with its reiterated refrain, "faith has been broken," was followed by another—the two together are eminently reprintable—denouncing the "pseudo-Samsons" of the Jewish right. Again and again, without ever adopting a pacifist position, Buber denied the efficacy of violence; only compromise would open the way to everyday coexistence and cooperation between Jew and Arab. After independence, his larger politics shattered, Buber maintained this critical posture, rejecting expropriations and reprisals, searching out local opportunities for cooperative work. His microcriticism sustained him in those years, and it also did him honor. I want to come back to Buber's life as an Israeli citizen, opposing many of the policies of the state from within the state. But first I need to say something more about his own understanding of this internal standpoint.

"This Place, This People"

In 1945 a group of right-wing Jewish militants, led by Menachem Begin, attacked the *Ichud* (Union), the organization that was Buber's political home for the last twenty-three years of his life. The members of *Ichud*, Begin wrote, were professors from Mount Scopus (where the Hebrew University was located—the Hebrew name means "hill of observation"), and they were "indeed observers . . . not party to what takes place below, they reside above on the heights of a moral Olympus."[26] This is a fairly standard critique of critical intellectuals, but it had a special force, it cut especially deep, in 1945 because what had just taken place "below" was the Holocaust. Buber could not avoid a response, though these were not opponents to whom he usually responded. He insisted that the "quiet, refined, reproachful" tone (the adjectives are Begin's) in which he and his friends wrote did not mean that they had not wept for the Jews of Europe but only that they had stopped weeping in order to address the hard choices that the Jews of Palestine now faced. "Those who have been in hell, and have returned to the light of day again, have learned to speak quietly and clearly." The reference here is to Plato's well-known metaphor, but with an important difference. Hell is not the cave; it is someplace far worse; and the light of day is ordinary light. Buber's claim is not that the philosopher must leave the cave but that he must leave the concentration camps. He cannot speak calmly and rationally unless he distances himself from the Holocaust. I have already suggested that Buber may have exaggerated the necessary distance. But he did sense, very early on, some of the pathologies of a politics shaped entirely by the Holocaust experience: the belief that one must fight "against the whole world" and the identification of heroism with a refusal of every compromise. This, he wrote, "is not the heroism of Prometheus, but that of Don Quixote . . . a tragic Don Quixote, tragic in every sense of the word."[27]

If not from hell, however, then not from heaven either: the critical philosopher stands on the ground—stands, in fact, on a particular piece of ground. Buber's example is the ancient Hebrew prophet (better understood here than by Benda) who "does not confront man with a generally valid image of perfection, with a Pantopia or a Utopia. Neither has he the choice between his native land and some other country 'more suitable to him.' In his work of realization, he is bound to the *topos*, to this place, to this people, because it is the people who must make the *beginning*."[28] That is, I assume, a self-description as well as a historical portrait. Buber's prophetic presence—face bearded, voice resonant, language too often straining for poetic power—must have annoyed many people in Palestine and then in Israel, who, despite their *topos*, did not look for prophecy in their everyday politics. But he was tied to those same people nonetheless, and in exactly the way he describes. The claim that the prophet was just one of the people, however, was never part of his description. Buber's politics is elitist as well as prophetic, "equally free," he wrote in 1947, "from the megalomania of the leaders and from the giddiness of the masses."[29] His attitude toward mass immigration was governed by this same elitism (he preferred "the principle of selective development"), even though, as he acknowledged years later, "the tradition of the Messianic promise still lived on" among the mass of refugees.[30] And if it didn't live on, what else could the prophet do but remind the people of the promise? He could hardly go looking for a more "suitable" people. Commitment, if it is serious and sustained, moderates the presumption of the "spiritual elite."

Standing on solid ground, Buber managed some startlingly prescient prophecies. He always called himself a realist, and his critical writings display an admirable grasp of the concrete and an unblinking sobriety. We often imagine that political leaders must be realistic and sober, while social critics must be idealists, fierce but distant, out of touch with the complexities of real life. The social division of labor, like a very clever personnel manager, supposedly sorts us out to match these ancient stereotypes. But the stereotypes are almost certainly wrong. Without what Buber called the megalomania of the Zionist leaders, there would never have been a Jewish state. I don't mean to suggest that they were not realists in their own way. Megalomania is, in fact, the wrong word to describe them: they were mad with hope, not with power or glory, and without this madness they could not have done what they did. But Buber saw a reality that they mostly missed. He saw, first, that the partition of Palestine and the establishment of Israel meant not one war, but a series of wars, for the international standing of the new state could not make up for what was absent at home, that is, an agreement between Palestinian Jews and Arabs. Hence, Israel would have to "apply its best forces to military activity."[31] And he saw, second, that sovereignty for the Jews, political power piled on top of their existing economic superiority, meant the reduction of the Arabs "to the status of second-class citizens"—which could only make the necessary local agreement harder to obtain.[32]

Under the conditions of the middle and late 1940s, these may not have been satisfactory arguments against statehood. Buber was simply describing, it might have been said, risks that had to be taken. And if they were to be taken, they probably had to be discounted, even denied. I suspect that Ben-Gurion really believed that the war for Israel's independence would be followed by some sort of peace. Buber did not believe it, and in the early weeks of the war he must have reached the nadir of his commitment "to this place, to this people." The binational state was lost, so it seemed, forever: Arabs and Jews were cooperating only in mutual slaughter; and the massacre of Arab villagers at Deir Yasin confirmed the breach of faith that Buber had already discerned in the response of right-wing Jewish groups to Arab terrorism in 1939. He insisted nevertheless upon his connection: "Often in earlier times, Arab hordes had committed outrages of this kind and my soul bled with the sacrifice; but here it was a matter of our own, or my own crime, of the crime of Jews against the spirit."[33] But it wasn't, in fact, his own crime; if ever a man was innocent he was; and people with his political views must have been tempted to turn innocence into escape, to cut their ties and set out in search of some "more suitable" country. Some of Buber's friends and followers left Palestine at this point; Buber chose to remain. "Against my will," he wrote in May 1948, "I participate in [the war] . . . and my heart trembles like that of any other Jew."[34]

After 1948, Buber made his peace with the new Jewish state, though the Arabs did not. This may be taken as a great betrayal of political principle, but what is striking to me is Buber's absolutely unchanged position at the level of the "thousand small decisions." Here is a model moment in the history of social criticism, when a critic is forced to respond to the failure of his largest hopes. It is not that Israel's victory in its war of independence was a defeat for *Ichud*; the war itself was the defeat (the loss of the war would have been a greater defeat, as Buber recognized when his "heart trembled"). When the fighting was over, a sympathetic Jerusalem shopkeeper greeted Buber with a line that has many echoes in the lives of twentieth-century critics: "Oh! An utter political rout like the one your circle suffered is no common thing. It looks as if you'll have to face the facts and resign yourselves to total silence for the time being."[35] Buber did not resign himself; he seems to have been no less active and outspoken after the war than before, at least until age and illness began to limit his activity (he was seventy-two in 1949 but still politically engaged and wonderfully busy). In fact, the defeat was not an "utter rout," for the people to whom Buber was committed were intact and free, possessed, indeed, of a new capacity not only to "jump and intervene" in world politics but also, if its leaders possessed the necessary moral imagination, to seek peace with its Arab neighbors. So Buber accommodated himself to statehood and remained a critic of the state—the actuality now rather than the idea, policy rather than program.

The announcement of his accommodation has that oracular tone that annoyed, and still annoys, many of his readers. "I have accepted as mine the State of Israel, the form of the new Jewish community that has arisen from the war. I have nothing in common with those Jews who imagine that they may contest the factual shape which Jewish independence has taken. The command to serve the spirit is to be fulfilled by us today in this state, starting from it." But not ending with it: that simple statement rather than the high-sounding "I have accepted" makes the crucial point. Buber called upon his political friends to work on the new ground of the state "to make good all that was once missed . . . to free the blocked path to an understanding with the Arab peoples."[36] Binationalism soon reappeared in his writing as federation: if he could not associate nations in a single state, he would seek to bring states together in a larger association. But at the very end of his life, in his last published essay, he called only for a "confederative union" of Israel and the nearer Arab states, which would allow, he wrote, "a considerably larger national autonomy" than would federation.[37] He came gradually, I think, not only to accept the state but also to value sovereignty—never, to be sure, as a good in itself but as a necessary instrument for doing good. Ours is the first generation of Jews in two thousand years, he wrote in 1957, that has the prerequisite for fulfilling the Jewish "mission," that is, "the independence of a strong nucleus . . . the power to determine for itself in no small measure its institutions, its modes of life, and its relations with other nations."[38]

Buber set very high standards for the use of this power, and, of course, the new state did not live up to them. His critical writings after 1948 are a litany of protest; most often they take the form of open letters, public statements, memoranda addressed to state officials, for now there are Jewish officials who need to be reminded of their larger responsibilities. These indeed are breathtaking in their scope. If the new state is to be a "Jewish state," Buber writes, it must subject "its whole social life to [God's] rule, which means the realization of justice and truth both in its internal and external . . . relationships."[39]* What is most attractive in Buber's post-1948 writing is his readiness to attend to the details of this extravagant subjection. Binationalism had been for him a kind of theoretical guarantee of peace and justice; federation and confederation represent something less in his mind; and statehood is entirely open-ended, power and possibility, nothing more. We have reached a goal, he wrote in 1949, but it is not called Zion. "We have full independence, a state, and all that appertains to it, but where is the nation in the state? And where is that nation's spirit?"[40] He is still a Zionist, that is, still in search of Zion, but the search, at least as it is revealed in his published writings, seems less programmatic than it once was, conceptually underdetermined. It is more a matter of one thing after another; "the realization of justice" means acting justly in this instance and the next one. It means taking the initiative in resettling Arab refugees, ending martial law in Arab areas, rejecting reprisals against Arab civilians, opening opportunities for Arabs in the professions and the Israeli civil sevice, and so on. These demands don't add up to a resolution of the Arab-Jewish conflict. What lies behind them is more an "orientation" than a blueprint or a theory. If Buber still denies the idea of tragedy, he does so now almost entirely on what I called earlier the "lower plane," the plane of everyday decision making.

He was no more successful, as the world measures success, on the lower plane than on the higher. His earlier stands on immigration and independence robbed him of whatever popular support he might have had. A few ministers in the early Labor governments were sympathetic but not so sympathetic as to risk their political careers on the hard ground of Arab-Jewish cooperation. They gave in, Buber thought, to the eternal temptation of statehood and political realism: "To see in the demands dictated by transient interests . . . the decisive and indeed the ultimate demands."[41] He did not give in to the opposite (and equally eternal) temptation of critical philosophy: to refuse altogether to recognize the value of "transient interests" and the moral standing of the men and women who assert those interests. "I have no warrant whatever," he wrote in 1953, "to declare that under all circumstances the interest of the group is to be sacrificed to the moral demand."

* An account of what Buber meant by justice in internal relationships can be found in his *Paths in Utopia*, trans. R. F. C. Hull (Boston: Beacon Press, 1958), first published in 1949, a year after Israel's war of independence. This is Buber's most important work of political theory, a strikingly secular defense of communitarian socialism, with an epilogue on the kibbutz. Curiously, its arguments play little part in his Zionist criticism.

He only wondered about public officials who did not bear the scars of "this inner conflict." The moral demand comes from within: "Were we not refugees in the diaspora?" The political interests are immediate and pressing and, it is commonly said, irreconcilable with the morality. So where are the scars?[42]

Success as the world measures it is not the measure of social criticism. The critic is measured by the scars his listeners and readers bear, by the conflicts he forces them to live through, not only in the present but also in the future, and by the memories those conflicts leave behind. He doesn't succeed by winning people over—for sometimes it just isn't possible to do that—but by sustaining the critical argument. Often enough Buber felt like a prophet in the wilderness, but the right response to this feeling, he wrote, is not "to withdraw to the role of silent spectator, as Plato did." Instead, the prophet must keep talking. "He must speak his message. The message will be misunderstood, misinterpreted, misused; it will even confirm and harden the people in their faithlessness. But its sting will rankle within them for all time."[43] Those lines have a certain romantic élan, and while I am inclined to resist romanticism in social critics, the élan is irresistible. Mendes-Flohr's collection of Buber's critical "messages" suggests that his work still carries a sting. And if there are readers in whom that sting rankles, the people can't be entirely faithless.

5

Antonio Gramsci's Commitment

Questions

His is one of those lives that invites counterfactual questions. A founder of the Italian Communist party, a brilliant writer and devoted militant, Antonio Gramsci was imprisoned by the fascists in 1926 when he was only thirty-five and died in a prison hospital eleven years later, in 1937, the middle year of the Moscow trials. In his *Prison Notebooks*—thousands of pages, to which thousands more pages of scholarly and political exegesis have now been added—Gramsci's focus was historical, his style reflective; he knew virtually nothing about what was happening outside his prison cell during the last decade of his life. The steady degeneration of international communism occurred, as it were, behind his back. Did Mussolini save him from Stalinist orthodoxy or deprive the left of a brave and supremely intelligent opponent of Stalinism? Had Gramsci been free in the thirties, alive in the forties and fifties, what would he have said? Where would he have stood when Ignazio Silone rejected party discipline and communist orthodoxy in 1929? Whom would he have supported in 1946 when Elio Vittorini defended the intellectual freedom of communist militants against Gramsci's old friend and political successor Palmiro Togliatti? In more immediate terms, is Gramsci the secret ancestor, the silenced theorist of Eurocommunism (or even of Eurosocialism)? Or was he always a loyal Leninist, committed and likely to have remained committed to the dictatorship of the Central Committee?

Questions of this sort are obviously unanswerable, and yet they underlie and probably motivate the extraordinary outpouring of books and articles about Gramsci, not only in Italy but also, more recently, in Britain and France and even in the United States (though the interest here is more academic than political). Writers on the left seek, no doubt, to understand Gramsci; but they also seek to appropriate him. For he is a rare bird in the twentieth century—an *innocent communist*—and he didn't have to leave the party but had only to be found guilty in a fascist court to preserve his innocence. Mostly, the appropriation of his work serves a good cause; it helps to legitimate democratic politics in a communist or far left setting. Gramsci's years of antifascist struggle and then his prison years add up to a small piece of usable past, a countertradition to set against the long line of Leninist precedents.[1] But is Gramsci in fact rather than counterfact a democratic communist—as one might say of someone that he is a democratic socialist, meaning that he would not establish a socialist regime except with the consent of the people? I think that he isn't; his view of the role of the party and of the place of intellectuals like himself in political life is so profoundly ambiguous, so painfully unresolved, that it can't be given such an agreeable label. Gramsci is not committed to some such "ideal" as Benda describes, like freedom or justice or self-determination; he is committed to a doctrine, an integrated set of "scientific" arguments. And then he is committed to a group of people who figure in the arguments, whom he claims to understand scientifically and hopes to engage politically. All the problems of his work derive from the tense relation between the claim and the hope, understanding and engagement, Marxist science and working-class politics.

Intellectuals and the War of Position

The committed intellectual is the central figure in Gramsci's version of Marxist doctrine. And it is specifically the intellectual's *intellectual* activity, his work as a philosopher and critic, that Gramsci values. Ever since Marx, every Marxist leader has had to prove himself as a theorist—for without a correct theory, how is it possible to act correctly in political life? The sole purpose of theory, the only reason to get it right, is political action, and action of a narrowly specific sort: the organization of the proletariat for the seizure of power. Gramsci must have held this Marxist view of intellectual purposefulness, at least during the brief years when he led the Italian Communists. Writing in prison, however, after the terrible defeats of the early twenties, he argued for a significant shift in priorities. In the West, the seizure of power would come only after the creation of a new proletarian culture, and then it would come with relative ease, a short political or military engagement confirming the outcome of a long cultural struggle. Hence the task of the intellectual was not merely to act from a correct theory but to elaborate and expound a new view of the world.

Gramsci's great discovery was the density and complexity, the sheer sturdiness, of bourgeois civil society. In the developed capitalist countries, he argues, the state is the creation of the leading groups in civil society, the instrumental appendage of a hegemonic class and its immediate allies. State and class stand to one another in what Marxists have always regarded as the "proper relation." (Gramsci hardly seems interested in any further Marxist proprieties: the economic base, the relations of production, and so on.) Only in countries like Russia is the state "everything" and civil society "primordial and gelatinous," its classes underdeveloped, politically disorganized, incapable of controlling state power. In such conditions, a Leninist coup d'état is possible.[2] But nothing like that is possible in Italy (even less so in Britain or France) where the state is protected by what it is ostensibly designed to protect. The real bastion of bourgeois power is ordinary life. It is in everyday actions and relations, and even more importantly in the ideas and attitudes that lie behind these, that the hegemony of a social class is revealed. The state cannot be seized until that hegemony has been decisively overcome.

Gramsci distinguishes between a "war of maneuver" such as Lenin had fought in Russia and a "war of position," necessary in the more developed countries of the West. The first of these is literally and simply the seizure of state power—buildings, communications, police. The second is the "seizure" of civil society, which is neither literal nor simple, more like infiltration than takeover, a long and arduous cultural struggle, with the new world slowly, painfully, displacing the old. The argument points toward a kind of communist Fabianism—focused more on the radio, the printing press, and the school, however, than on the municipal waterworks. And Gramsci has, sometimes, a Fabian optimism: "In politics the 'war of position,' once won, is decisive definitively."[3] So the French Revolution was won in the years of enlightenment, not in the more exciting days of insurrection. The process was crucial, not the "events."

Gramsci does not, however, take a passive or complacent view of this process. Here he marks himself off from (his own reading of) German and Austrian social democracy; he is a Leninist of the cultural struggle. The long process of enlightenment is indeed a war; it requires discipline, organization, constant militancy; it requires a structure of command and obedience; it requires a vanguard of intellectuals like himself, a Communist party. But if this military imagery testifies to Gramsci's radicalism, it doesn't quite do justice to his practical intentions. Nor is his comparison of the party to Machiavelli's prince immediately comprehensible: what is the life of the prince but an endless war of maneuver? Gramsci has something else in mind. "The modern prince must be and cannot but be the proclaimer and organizer of an intellectual and moral reform . . . creating the terrain for a subsequent development of the national-popular . . . will towards the realization of a superior, total form of modern civilization."[4] It is an awkward sentence because of the multiplication of forward-looking prepositions, adjectives, and nouns—as if Gramsci, sitting helplessly in Mussolini's prison, recognizes that a "superior" civilization is very far away. He seems to describe three stages in its development: (1) the party creates the terrain for (2) the development of a national-popular (not merely proletarian) will, which is not yet the achievement of but is only directed toward (3) the realization of a new way of life. In the *Notebooks*, Gramsci focuses mostly on the problems of the first stage. What did it mean, exactly, to create the terrain of a new popular willfulness? And why did this require a disciplined political party? Why not, as in eighteenth-century France, a band of *philosophes*? Perhaps Gramsci confused these two, imagining a utopian vanguard, a disciplined army of free intellectuals.

The Problem of Common Sense

The task of the party is "intellectual and moral reform," where reform does not refer to an incremental politics in the style of Central European social democracy but to something more like a religious reformation or a cultural revolution. Gramsci's Marxism requires him to believe that the content of this reform, its socialist or communist character, is historically given. The civilization of the future is carried—though not consciously carried, not carried aloft—by the industrial working class. It is revealed in the practical activity of the workers (cooperation in the factory, union solidarity) but not yet in their understanding of the world, not yet in what Gramsci calls their "common sense." So the party's reformation aims at raising the workers to the level of their own activity, "fitting culture to the sphere of practice."[5]

Common sense is, I suppose, Gramsci's version of false consciousness. But it is far more subtle than the standard Marxist account, repeated with hardly any embarrassment after every revolutionary failure. The standard account blames the victims: if only the workers knew their own interests! Gramsci falls easily enough into this style of reasoning, and Frank Parkin is not entirely unfair when he describes "a succession of Marxist theorists, from Lukacs and Gramsci to the Althusserian and Frankfurt schools," whose diagnosis of revolutionary failure implies "in the most oblique and scholarly manner that the proletariat [is] suffering from a kind of collective brain damage."[6] Hence the need for the party, the undamaged brain of the working class, which defends the "real" interests of the workers with or without their participation. It has to be added, however, that Gramsci is not entirely content with this account. In the *Notebooks*, common sense is never a matter of interests alone; it includes ideas that are true as well as ideas that are false—and also ideas to which these predicates just don't apply, as they clearly don't apply to consciousness as a whole. What is at issue in the war of position is culture itself, from philosophy and religion down to the most ordinary understandings of health and sickness, love, marriage, work, exchange, honor, and solidarity. It is not so easy, then, for the party to impose its "correct" line and lead the political struggle. If it is an agent of intellectual and moral reform, it is an agent that can only work through, not behind the backs or over the heads of, the workers: it must change their understanding of the world before it can change the world. Or, more democratically—and Gramsci sometimes writes in this style too—it must help the workers educate and change themselves.

Gramsci's argument begins with the firmly egalitarian assertion that "all men are intellectuals. . . . There is no human activity from which every form of intellectual participation can be excluded: *homo faber* cannot be separated from *homo sapiens*."[7] Men and women cannot live, work, love, or raise children without coming to hold a view of the world, adopting and defending a line of moral conduct, sustaining or modifying a set of received ideas. *Received* ideas, for not even the most brilliant philosophers among us start out *ab novo*, with pure intuitions of Morality and Truth. Nor are our minds blank tablets on which the ruling class—or the party, if only it could get there first—writes out its instructions, the marks of a dominant ideology. Our consciousness is instead a historical composition, the product of a process that has "deposited" in us (this is Gramsci's best phrase) "an infinity of traces, without . . . an inventory."[8] The sign of a hegemonic class is that its professional intellectuals are able to refine and reshape this composition, or at least to overlay it with a new "deposit," and to do so not only for their immediate students and readers but for society as a whole. They provide a high philosophy that is reiterated, though with much distortion, at every level of social and intellectual life. One gets then a strange break in the culture of subordinate classes. Their thinking does not reflect their practical activity; consciousness does not follow existence. This break, Gramsci argues in an important passage in the *Prison Notebooks*,

> signifies that the social group in question may indeed have its own conception of the world, even if only embryonic; a conception that manifests itself in action, but occasionally and in flashes. . . . But this same group has, for reasons of submission and intellectual subordination, adopted a conception which is not its own but is borrowed from another group, and it confirms this conception verbally and believes itself to be following it.[9]

And does follow it, Gramsci goes on, in "normal times." In fact, however, the borrowing is incomplete; the borrowed ideas are combined with the fragments of earlier ideologies and like them are adapted to the needs of a subordinate social setting. On the one hand, a practical activity that can't be articulated; on the other, the partial and disjointed articulation of inherited and borrowed ideas: this is what Gramsci means by common sense, the ordinary wisdom with which ordinary people negotiate their way in the world. "Common sense is the folklore of philosophy."[10]

So Gramsci adapts and complicates Marx's dictum: "The ideas of the ruling class are in every epoch the ruling ideas."[11] But his understanding of these "ruling ideas" is developed in political and cultural directions that few Marxists—until very recently anyway—have been willing to follow. He himself does not always pursue the hints and intimations of his own arguments, which point toward the replacement of political economy by a kind of cultural anthropology. These same arguments force upon the Marxist intellectual, face to face with the workers, struggling to understand and reform working-class common sense, the standard anthropological dilemma: should he make a virtue of his distance from the workers or should he engage himself more immediately in their everyday life? Should he stand outside or should he accept the risks of "going native"?

The intellectual must choose distance or nearness, and in making this choice, two Gramscian arguments are crucial; unhappily, they point in different directions. The first of them is suggested but never worked out by Marx himself. Ruling ideas are always something more than rationalizations of class interest. "For each new class which puts itself in the place of the one ruling before it, is compelled, merely in order to carry through its aim, to represent its interest as the common interest of all the members of society."[12] Gramsci elaborates on this suggestion: ideas don't come to rule, he says, unless they are expressed in "universal" rather than "corporate" terms—and universality is never a mere pretense. Every hegemony is "national-popular" in character, even though its deepest values and organizing principles are determined by the way of life of a particular class.[13] The visible organization of hegemony and the range of values it expresses are worked out through a complex political process; the result is something close to a common culture. Ruling intellectuals are armed with pens, not swords; they have to make a case for the ideas they are defending among men and women who have ideas of their own, who are intellectuals-of-everyday-life. Coercion has its place in (or alongside of) hegemony, but the power of ideas lies elsewhere, and hegemony is not possible without ideas. When a ruling class has to rely on force alone, it has reached a point of crisis in its rule. If it is to avoid that crisis it has to compromise: "The fact of hegemony presupposes that one takes into account the interests and tendencies of the groups over which hegemony will be exercised, and it also presupposes a certain equilibrium, that is to say that the hegemonic groups will make some sacrifices of a corporate nature."[14]

Parkin's joke about brain damage, then, misses Gramsci's most interesting point: when subordinate classes accept a view of the world that is at odds with their practical activity, they do so only because that view does allow, if only in a concessionary way, some scope for practical activity (if not for a full class consciousness). Ruling ideas internalize contradictions. It would seem to follow that Marxist intellectuals don't have to stand outside the world of culture and common sense in order to see the "real" interests of the working class. These interests have, if only in a partial way, been incorporated into the structures of hegemony. The workers have a place within the old society, subordinate but not entirely negative—not a mere absence of status and entitlement—and opposition properly starts from where they are.

Gramsci's second, and rather different, point derives from his general view of consciousness. Like common sense, ruling ideas extend well beyond "interests and tendencies." The ideas elaborated by bourgeois intellectuals embody not only the most powerful but also the most nearly true understanding of social reality (and, not insignificantly, of natural science). They reach to the most beautiful conceptions of art and literature; they incorporate classical humanism as well as bourgeois liberalism. They are, quite simply, the best ideas of the epoch (and of all previous epochs), and Marxism itself is continuous with them, the "consummation" of German philosophy, English economics, and French political science.[15] The new civilization carried by the working class can be articulated only through the medium of these ideas. At this point, no sacrifices or concessions are called for. It is indeed a matter of some anxiety that cultural dominance is so radically incomplete. Ruling ideas rule directly and fully only among the rulers and the intellectuals. Among subordinate classes these ideas are nothing more than the last of the "infinity of traces," overlaying all the others but not displacing them. The common sense of the masses remains, to some significant if undetermined degree (there is no inventory), prebourgeois, a less than coherent amalgam of old prejudices, superstitions, and "utopias," which derive in their turn from previous ruling ideas, themselves never wholly understood or absorbed.[16] And alongside all this, embryonically, there exist intimations of something radically new.

Or perhaps not so radically new: for these intimations also appear as "traces" in the ruling ideas. Because of the concessionary character of hegemony or because of its scientific and "advanced" character, the civilization of the future can be anticipated by intellectuals like Marx or Gramsci, who grow up among, share the culture of, and then set themselves in opposition to the ruling class. Unfortunately, they must also set themselves in opposition to the working class, at least insofar as the working class is shaped by its common sense. Though they hope for a new civilization, communist intellectuals are carriers of the old hegemony.

The Party and the Workers

This, then, is Gramsci's dilemma: his task is social criticism, but not a criticism aimed most importantly at the dominant groups or the prevailing injustices of the society in which he lives. He must take aim instead at the consciousness, the culture and way of life, of the very people he hopes to lead. He must criticize them without alienating himself from them; he must reform their "moral and intellectual life" without coercively imposing his own. He must make himself, Gramsci says, into a "new type of philosopher . . . a 'democratic philosopher' "—that is, one whose philosophy "is an active social relationship of modification of the cultural environment."[17] A relationship, presumably, with other men and women whose practical activity (since they belong to a progressive social class) is already modifying the environment and who, at least dimly, know this to be so. But this is not by any means an easy democracy, for the knowledge of the people is indeed dim—not because *they* are dim but because their cultural life is broken and out of joint—while that of the party intellectual is scientific and precise. The two stand to one another as master and pupils, by no means a relation of equality. Supposedly, the master takes his lead from his pupils, for his teaching is implicit in their lives. He is likely, nonetheless, to appear to them very much as an outsider, the bearer of a new and alien truth.

He appears as an outsider first of all because he is an outsider—in class terms, a stranger, unlikely to have grown up in a factory town or ever to have worked in a factory. "The proletariat as a class," Gramsci wrote in 1926, just before his arrest, "is poor in organizing elements, does not have and cannot form its own stratum of intellectuals except very slowly, very laboriously, and only after the conquest of State power."[18] A grim view, especially in that last phrase, which suggests that throughout the long war of position the proletariat will be led by outsiders. Gramsci had argued differently some six or seven years earlier when the factory councils, Italy's soviets, were active in Turin and he was active in defense of the councils (by 1926, his politics consisted mostly of intraparty intrigue). He suggested then that the councils were little models of the proletarian state within which the creation of a new culture was already far advanced. Throughout his life he looked back to the councils as the characteristic form of working-class organization and the crucial arena of working-class education. In the councils, he wrote in 1919, the working class could "educate itself, gather experience, and acquire a responsible awareness of the duties incumbent upon classes that hold the power of the State."[19] It is less clear in the *Prison Notebooks* that he still believes in self-education. Perhaps he never really believed; there was always something schoolmasterish about Gramsci, and he seems to have held throughout his life both a stern conception of the tasks of the proletariat (those "incumbent" duties) and a low estimate of its members. They were not brain damaged, but they were culturally retarded; backwardness was the practical consequence of subordination. Briefly, in 1919, in a moment of enthusiasm, he repudiated the role of "tutor."[20] The *Notebooks*, it seems to me, are a sustained defense of exactly that role, reflecting the lessons Gramsci learned from the defeat of the councils and the triumph of fascism.

But the defense is not without its complexities: Gramsci wanted a tutorial party but also a party prepared to give way (not too soon!) to its own pupils. He too believed that "the role of the intelligentsia is to make special leaders from among the intelligentsia unnecessary."[21] For the moment, however, nothing was more necessary than "special leaders":

> Critical self-consciousness means, historically and politically, the creation of an elite of intellectuals. A human mass does not "distinguish" itself, does not become independent in its own right without, in the widest sense, organizing itself; and there is no organization without intellectuals . . . without the theoretical aspect of the theory-practice nexus being distinguished concretely by the existence of a group of people "specialized" in [the] conceptual and philosophical elaboration of ideas.[22]

Since the working class doesn't produce such people from its own midst, they can only come from the body of "traditional intellectuals," recruited largely, like Gramsci himself, from the petty bourgeoisie. But the orientation of these intellectuals toward the proletariat is awkward and unstable, and the philosophical elaboration of ideas appropriate to the proletariat is a process "full of contradictions, advances and retreats, dispersals and regroupings, in which the loyalty of the masses is often sorely tried." And yet, in the long war of position, the masses can only be loyal: "Loyalty and discipline are the ways in which [they] participate . . . in the development of the cultural movement as a whole."[23] For them, the war of position is a war *in* position. Like schoolchildren, they must learn to sit still while a somewhat unruly (and unreliable) group of teachers struggle to work out a proper curriculum.[24]

The English editors of the *Prison Notebooks* assure us that when he uses the word "elite," Gramsci does not mean to associate himself with the reactionary school of "elitists," the followers of Vilfredo Pareto and Gaetano Mosca. No doubt; but what exactly does he mean? "The process of development is tied," he writes, "to a dialectic between the intellectuals and the masses."[25] This is the style of someone who isn't sure, or who means to avoid saying, exactly what he means. In fact, Gramsci faces real difficulties. The party intellectual must not get too close to the workers, lest he lose his ability to criticize their common sense. Romantic identification is a failure of nerve, and the support of proletarian spontaneity is bad politics, very much like preferring folklore and superstition to modern science. On the other hand, rejecting proletarian spontaneity is also bad politics, for every spontaneous movement "contains rudimentary elements of conscious leadership."[26] And a refusal of identification is dangerous too for reasons that I have already suggested: it is the proletariat, after all, and not the bourgeois intelligentsia, in whose practical activity the civilization of the future is somehow implicit. "The socialist state already exists potentially in the institutions of social life characteristic of the exploited laboring class."[27]

So the intellectual hovers uncertainly between the high culture of the old society, of which modern science and Marxism itself are the most advanced products, and the common sense of the people, the internalized form of their subordination (and their resistance to subordination), which simultaneously holds within itself intimations of a still higher culture. He wants to be a missionary and a comrade. As a missionary, he aims to bring art and science and "the philosophy of praxis" to the masses. His task is like that of the Gramscian teacher, who must commit himself to uproot "folklorist" conceptions of the world "and replace them with conceptions that are deemed superior."[28] As a comrade, he aims at an active union with the people, perhaps even at a "unity of manual and intellectual work" (something Gramsci himself never attempted and, given his health, probably could not have done), and then a transformation from within of working-class common sense.[29]

It is the purpose of the Communist party, of course, to mediate between these two conceptions. Ideally, the party brings together an elite of intellectuals and the "most advanced" sections of the proletariat in everyday political struggle. Education and action go hand in hand; the protagonists of the two learn from one another. The intellectual elite, governed by an egalitarian ethic, works closely with the intellectuals-of-everyday-life. Its members are critics of common sense, but they don't merely proclaim their own scientific truths. "Initially," at least, they base themselves "on common sense [itself] in order to demonstrate that 'everyone' is a philosopher and that it is not a question of introducing from scratch a scientific mode of thought . . . but of renovating and making 'critical' an already existing activity."[30] Gramsci suggests a surprising model: the preaching friars of the Middle Ages, organized in religious orders that imposed an "iron discipline" on their members, not for conspiratorial purposes, but "so that they [would] not exceed certain limits of differentiation between themselves and the 'simple.'" When they move beyond such limits, intellectuals "become a caste or a priesthood."[31]

But if Gramsci recognizes this danger—the lines just quoted may be intended as self-criticism—it is not clear what he means to do about it. In practice, the positions that his own party adopted in this or that political struggle were more often determined by external instructions from the popes and bishops of the Comintern than by the internal "dialectic" of theory and common sense. Nor was that dialectic ever as fruitful as Gramsci hoped it would be—and for reasons about which he was always brutally frank. The proletariat was terribly slow in producing suitably advanced elements. With few exceptions, the intellectuals of the party were not "organic intellectuals" of the working class. They neither emerged from the class nor (except briefly, perhaps, at critical moments like the Turin strikes) integrated themselves within it. The party remained throughout the 1920s largely a missionary organization, whose members called one another comrades but were radically alienated from the workers whose comrades they hoped to be. The socialists achieved a much closer integration with the workers but only, Gramsci believed, opportunistically, by surrendering theory to common sense.

Perhaps the communist and socialist experiences exhaust the real possibilities: either missionary work from the outside by an elite of intellectuals or the creation of a mass party without a missionary elite and, soon enough, without a mission. There is an inexact but suggestive correspondence here to Julien Benda's radical dualism. The communist intellectuals are the "clerks," committed to truth or, at least, to the "correct ideological position," while the socialists are "laymen" acting, if mostly ineffectively, in the real world, adapting to circumstances and seeking allies through compromise (rather than conversion). Gramsci's persistent use of military and Machiavellian metaphors suggests how fiercely he wished to transcend this dualism—to be, as a good Marxist is supposed to be, at once a critical theorist and a tactician, a revolutionary leader and a preaching friar, a *clerk militant.* Given the war of position, however, tactics recede in importance (and in prison they cease entirely to be interesting). What is important now are the larger strategies of cultural criticism. Where is that criticism to come from?

If the workers really represent the culture of the future, then the socialists were right to think that it could only come from within, from the slow development of working-class institutions, the slow elaboration of practical activity into a new culture.* The deepest argument for communist politics is the (Leninist) claim that this internal criticism and inner-class transformation are simply not possible. Hegemony can only be overthrown by expatriate bourgeois intellectuals, equipped with hegemonic knowledge. "Only after the creation of a new state does the cultural problem . . . tend toward a coherent solution."[32] This argument from the *Notebooks* parallels the passage from 1926 that I have already discussed. Gramsci's meaning is clear: the working class won't produce its own organic intellectuals or its own culture until the work of the communist missionaries is backed up by the power of the state, until the party controls the media and the educational system. I have been using pedagogy as a metaphor for Gramscian politics. But Gramsci takes the metaphor seriously; he has a direct, personal as well as theoretical, interest in the school and the curriculum. Here he draws

* Or, alternatively, the slow elaboration of cultural activity into a new practice: this is the line taken by contemporary followers of Gramsci who have broken decisively, as he never did, with vanguard politics and who tend to assign a greater value to popular culture.

most explicitly upon his own experience and gives us, briefly, a glimpse of the inner life of a communist militant.

Communist Schooling

Some of Gramsci's earliest articles focused on educational issues, but his most systematic discussion comes in the *Prison Notebooks* where he criticizes a reform proposal drafted by the idealist philosopher Giovanni Gentile, Mussolini's minister of education. The details of the proposal need not concern us here; it was ostensibly "progressive," emphasizing something called "active education" as against mere "instruction," which was taken to be dry, formal, repetitive, and incapable of engaging the interests of the young. Gramsci's response is remarkably conservative:

> Latin and Greek were learnt through their grammar, mechanically; but the accusation of formalism and aridity is very unjust and inappropriate. In education one is dealing with children in whom one has to inculcate certain habits of diligence, precision, poise (even physical poise), ability to concentrate on specific subjects, which cannot be acquired without the mechanical repetition of disciplined and methodical acts.[33]

An education of this sort has, apparently, no specific class character; it is neither bourgeois nor (Gramsci's word) "oligarchic." The old schools in which Greek and Latin were taught were oligarchic only because of the exclusion of working-class children. Admit such children and the character of the school will change. Gramsci is an advocate of the "common" or "comprehensive" school—and at the same time of the traditional curriculum. Reluctantly, he agrees that it might be necessary to dispense with ancient languages, though he can muster no enthusiasm for this reform, widely advocated on the left. "It will not be easy to deploy new . . . subjects in a didactic form which gives equivalent results in terms of education and general personality formation."[34]

The challenge of a genuinely progressive education is not to produce a new curriculum but to bring working-class children (and peasant children too) into touch with what is best in literature and science. The school, like the party, has to stand in tension with the common sense of the people. Communists should not attempt to relieve this tension; they should insist upon it, live with it, fight it through until the defeat of common sense. The teacher, writes Gramsci, "must be aware of the contrast between the type of culture and society which he represents and the type of culture and society represented by his pupils, and [he must be] conscious of his obligation to accelerate and regulate the child's formation in conformity with the former and *in conflict with the latter*."[35] Education is always hard work; no one is born with diligence, precision, and poise. But given the character of the cultural conflict (the war of position) and the relative preparation of the two sides, it is much harder for the children of factory workers than for the children of "gentlemen." So be it, then—on this point Gramsci is uncompromising: "In the future these questions may become extremely acute, and it will be necessary to resist the tendency to render easy that which cannot become easy without being distorted."[36]

It had not been easy for Gramsci himself, the son and grandson of provincial officials; it would be harder still for students from lower social strata. And yet it was the schools, the old curriculum, rote learning, and even the occasional assistance of largely incompetent teachers, he believed, that had carried him from the remote and backward province of Sardinia to modern Turin. Physically weak, often ill, a hunchback and near-dwarf, he had made his way, not without help. "Expect nothing from anyone," he wrote to his brother Carlo in 1927, "and you will avoid delusions."[37] And yet his notes on education (his letters from prison, too, where he worries about the education of his son) are full of expectations. The school is, of course, an agent of hegemony, that is, it teaches "a responsible awareness of the duties incumbent upon classes that hold the power of the State." But it can do this as well for workers as for gentlemen—if only the workers were admitted to the schools. They won't be admitted, Gramsci argues, under the conditions of bourgeois rule, except to schools whose curriculum has been adapted to their supposed capacities and interests. And there they won't confront the hegemonic culture and learn the "responsible awareness" of a ruling class. The schools won't work for the workers until there is a workers' state. Conventional schooling suggests nonetheless, as Gramsci's own experience suggests, what needs to be done.

Gramsci's educational arguments are stern, with a personal as well as an ideological sternness. His letters have the same tone. I can only speculate about its sources in his own life, but the speculation seems worthwhile; the dilemma of the Gramscian intellectual, after all, is ultimately a personal dilemma. I want to make a simple claim: that what Gramsci demanded of the workers is what he thought he had achieved himself. They must break as radically with the "Sardinia" of common sense as he had done with the actual Sardinia where he was born and raised. They must come to hate their "spiritual slavery" as he hated Sardinian backwardness. In Sardinia, he once wrote, he had known only "the most brutal aspect of life." The truth is that he had known something more: the first stirrings of revolt, sympathy with the oppressed, even solidarity—in the form of Sardinian patriotism, an emotion long repressed by the time he wrote the *Notebooks*.[38] But all that was inchoate feeling, closely tied to the local version of common sense, and it had to be, as Gramsci's English editors say, "transcended." So too with the common sense of the workers, even if it sometimes makes for a "rudimentary" solidarity.

At the same time, Gramsci worried about intellectual transcendence. Here is that worry expressed in theoretical terms:

> The popular element "feels" but does not know or understand; the intellectual element "knows" but does not always understand and in particular does not always feel. . . . The intellectual's error consists in believing that one can . . . be an intellectual (and not a pure pedant) if distinct and separate from the people-nation, that is, without feeling the elementary passions of the people, understanding them . . . and connecting them dialectically to the laws of history and to a superior conception of the world, scientifically and coherently elaborated—i.e. knowledge.[39]

And here is a similar worry expressed in personal terms: in a letter to his wife, Gramsci recalled a life (before he met her) without love and confessed that he had often wondered whether "it was possible to tie myself to the mass of men when I [had] never loved anyone, not even my own family, [whether] it was possible to love a collectivity if I had never been loved deeply myself by individual human beings?"[40] The unloved and self-pitying intellectual is a common enough figure, I suppose, and I don't want to focus on that but rather on the first of Gramsci's questions, which expresses his rejection of home and homeland. At great personal cost, he had broken loose. Could he now form comradely ties with men and women who had not broken loose, who embodied the backwardness he had transcended? With no feeling for his own past, how could he find fellow-feeling with men and women who still lived in that past?

It is at least an honest question, recalling again Rousseau's contempt for philosophers who loved humanity and despised their nearest neighbors. Did Gramsci ever "love" the workers? It is a question I would hesitate to ask, at least in these terms, if Gramsci had not asked it himself. It's not a question addressed at all, so far as I know, in the vast Gramsci literature, whose authors are concerned almost exclusively with cultural life and Marxist theory. But the *Notebooks* do suggest an answer: he loved the workers only as a stern teacher might love a backward, recalcitrant, but somehow promising student. It's not the love of a brother or a friend. Gramsci must have expressed himself differently in face-to-face encounters, especially in the factories in 1919 and 1920. His style in the prison writings, however, is distant and demanding. Of course, he wants to feel the elementary passions of the workers, but he knows that he knows a superior doctrine.

What Gramsci demands is that the promising student give up his own "culture and society." This is the demand that the party makes upon the working class as a whole (though always with the caveat that the practical activity of the workers already represents a new culture and society, of which only the party intellectuals and a few "advanced" workers are fully aware). Can one ask this of adult men and women and still call oneself their comrade? Gramsci's educational program amounts to treating the workers as if they were immigrants to a foreign country, "greenhorns," as he himself had been when he first arrived in Turin. They have made the crucial move—into the modern factory—and now they must adapt themselves to, or let themselves be reeducated for, the new world they have entered. But a program like Gramsci's works best with children, that is, "after the creation of a new state" (and then it works, very much like "Americanization" in the early twentieth-century United States, largely through the public schools). It is more coercive and less attractive as a program for adults. Since Gramsci isn't a native of the new world, one might expect him to see the difficulty. In fact, having made the move and the adaptation, having repressed his own past, he seems all the more ready to lead others (to force others?) through the same process.

Gramsci's Doctrine

The completion of this process is the crucial requirement of the war of position. But I can best complete my own account of Gramsci's politics by looking at two descriptions (from the *Notebooks*) of wars of maneuver, that is, of actual revolutionary struggles. The first of these deals with the Bolsheviks, who maneuvered brilliantly and seized state power without ever having won a positional victory:

> An elite consisting of some of the most active, energetic, enterprising and disciplined members of the society emigrates abroad and assimilates the cultural and historical experiences of the most advanced countries of the West, without however losing the most essential characteristics of its own nationality, that is to say without breaking its sentimental and historical ties with its own people. Having thus performed its intellectual apprenticeship it returns to its own country and compels the people to an enforced awakening, skipping historical stages in the process.[41]

The reference to "sentimental ties" is necessary, I suppose, to explain why these enterprising intellectuals, having assimilated Western culture, don't just remain in the West. They see the sun but nevertheless go back to the cave. Except for two brief visits, Gramsci himself never went back to Sardinia, but perhaps his reiterated insistence that the Italian communists address themselves to the problem of the peasantry ("the Southern question") is a gesture toward a return. If so, it is a gesture that studiously avoids sentimentality. Nor did the Bolsheviks ever allow their sentimental ties to old Russia to interfere with the task they had set themselves: "to compel the people to an enforced awakening." The verb makes the adjective redundant, but the two together make the meaning of the sentence especially clear.

The second description deals with the French Revolution and the Jacobins, the revolutionary elite that Gramsci most admired, who led a class that had already won the war of position. The Jacobins, Gramsci writes, "made the demands of the popular mass their own" and then pursued those demands with "extreme energy, decisiveness and resolution." It wasn't only their energy, however, that made them an elite. Somehow, they represented future as well as present and actual demands: they "forced the hand" of the popular mass, though always "in the direction of real historical development" (much as a stern but devoted teacher forces a favorite student in the direction of his promise). Gramsci compresses the story he wants to tell into a single image when he describes the Jacobins as "a group of . . . determined men driving the bourgeoisie forward with kicks in the backside."[42]

But this is a strange story, surely, for in the case of France enlightenment had preceded revolution; the bastions of civil society had been conquered, and there should have been no need to kick the triumphant middle classes along the path to their own hegemony. The chief reason for Gramsci's appeal to latter-day Marxists is his revaluation of civil society—which seems to open the way to a politics free from dictatorship and terror. Whatever the case in Russia, in the West the state won't be seized until a popular base has been established: a shared culture will soften and legitimate the exercise of power. That is indeed what Gramsci hoped for but never saw his way clear to having. Even a class led by organic intellectuals, a powerful and self-enlightened class like the French bourgeoisie, scarcely dared to challenge the debilitated forces of aristocracy and absolutism. What then can one expect from the Italian workers, who are so "poor in organizing elements" and who cannot dispense with the leadership of expatriates like Gramsci? Would Gramsci have kicked the backsides of the workers? All we can say is that he never had the chance.

Gramsci's theoretical argument is deeply contradictory. He believes that in countries like Italy the cultural war of position will come before the political war of maneuver and will be "decisive definitively." And this positional victory ought to make coercion, at least coercion of the "popular mass," unnecessary. But he also believes that the war of position won't finally be won until after the seizure of power. Who then will maneuver to seize and hold the state? "A group of determined men," whose personal lives must be as contradictory as their theory: for they love and don't really love the people they coerce.

It is the gulf between elementary feeling and common sense, on the one hand, and Gramsci's own absolute knowledge, on the other, that generates these contradictions. They rise out of the void between the people and the intellectuals, a vast space that even the dialectic can't bridge. Gramsci wants to be a "democratic philosopher," and his account of hegemony, had he fully worked it out, might well provide the ground on which democratic philosophers could stand. Certainly no communist theorist comes closer than Gramsci in his prison cell to a revolutionary strategy that fits, or might be fitted to, the norms of a functioning democracy. For he suggests that the servants of hegemony necessarily create, by incorporation and concession, a common culture, assimilating to their own "ideological complex" the interests and values of subordinate groups. Subordinated men and women need not be described, then, as wholly unaware of the meaning of their own practical activity, ideologically shaped by borrowed ideas: they have, after all, extracted the concessions. Criticism can come from within, and they themselves can be subjects as well as objects of critical activity.

Criticism of this sort "makes possible," writes Gramsci, "a process of differentiation and change in the relative weight that the elements of the old ideologies used to possess. What was previously secondary and subordinate . . . is now taken to be primary and becomes the nucleus of a new ideological and theoretical complex."[43] This is abstractly stated and without illustration in the text; it lacks the concreteness and intensity that Gramsci brings to the themes of backwardness and hegemony. But the point is important. Moral and intellectual reform begins with inner-hegemonic struggle, and the new culture is never wholly new; it is in large part a rearrangement of ideas already present in the old. Think, for example, of the place of equality in bourgeois and oppositional thought. Equality is a real but distinctly limited value in the hegemonic culture, but it also has larger, "utopian" meanings at least occasionally invoked by ruling intellectuals, if only as a concession to subordinate groups. So it is more generally available, a contested or contestable value—and the war of position is the name of the contest. Why shouldn't Marxist intellectuals participate in this war as real comrades, democratic philosophers, identifying simultaneously with ideas that are "secondary and subordinate" in the cultural system and with men and women who are "secondary and subordinate" in the social structure? But Gramsci never quite manages this broad and generous identification; he is the proud defender of "advanced" ideas, and he identifies only with the "advanced" members of subordinate classes. Like Randolph Bourne in the United States, he is, he can only be, "fiercely and concentratedly intellectual." But he is also, in contrast to Bourne, an intellectual firmly possessed of a doctrine, a new and certain science, superior to every other form of knowledge.

Gramsci is a victim, we might say, of Marxist teleology. Advancement is the form of his detachment, and it is a bar to a comradely politics. The more advanced his theory, the more detached he is in practice from working-class backwardness. His political activity is an irregular movement toward and then away from the people he hopes to lead. He knows that he can't lead them without their consent, but he also knows, and this time with a "scientifically and coherently elaborated" knowledge, that they ought to consent, and in the course of "real historical development" will consent, to his leadership. This is the knowledge he won when he left Sardinia behind, and it makes him a self-confident and, in his own eyes, an objective critic of common sense. But objectivity has a price, which Gramsci also acknowledges: "The intellectual element 'knows' but does not always understand." And without understanding, criticism and leadership are alike corrupted.

Imprisonment saved Gramsci from the practical consequences of this corruption—or from the practical need to save himself. In prison, with admirable courage and extraordinary physical and mental discipline, he wrestled with the dilemmas of intellectual militancy. He did not resolve those dilemmas, not for himself, not for us. He never gave up his commitment to the party and to the true doctrine that it embodied. He never ceased to hope that the war of position, led by the party, could nevertheless be a democratic war. It's not, I suppose, an impossible dream: the vanguard connected to the rearguard, not with the coerciveness of steel but with the persuasiveness of words. An intellectual's dream—endangered, though, by an intellectual's confidence that when he marched, he always marched at the head of the line.

6

Ignazio Silone: "The Natural"

Common Sense and Communism

Ignazio Silone, Arthur Koestler once wrote, was a "natural communist . . . the only one among us."[1] Koestler meant that no one had converted Silone to communism; no radical guru, no spiritual or political guide had led him into the party; he had followed what he himself called (describing his later break with communism) the "obscure dictates" of his heart. Koestler applied the laws of Newtonian physics to party life: there is no movement without some initiating force. Intellectuals, beset by inertia, must be pushed or pulled into the orbit of communist discipline. But Silone was an anomaly—self-propelled, naturally in motion.

In fact, Silone has provided several accounts of his decision to join the party (and several more circumstantial accounts of his decision to leave), and it is clear that nature had little to do with it. It is second nature that guides such decisions: character, commitment, and what we might think of as the habits of moral life. Koestler's real claim is that Silone did not have to break his habits, alter his commitments, reshape his character. He was not born again into the Italian Communist party; he became a new member (he was actually present at the founding in 1921) without becoming a new man. All this Silone confirms in his collection of autobiographical essays, *Emergency Exit*, and his two partially autobiographical novels, *Bread and Wine* and *The Seed Beneath the Snow*. But there is nothing in these writings to suggest that he was, or that he thought himself, anomalous. Silone is unusual because of the courage and integrity with which he followed his chosen course. But the course itself is not unusual, and so I shall take him as a representative of all those men and women who become critics of their own society and even revolutionaries, who pay the common price in inner turmoil, quarrels with their families, and personal danger, but who have no experience at all of conversion, rebirth, or moral transformation. Their radicalism is somehow continuous with their previous life, the acting out of principles they first learned at home. Whereas Gramsci repressed whatever there was of Sardinia in him, Silone preserved and cherished the "traces" left by his native Abruzzi.

He is a writer with a powerful sense of place—not only a physical sense, though one comes away from his novels feeling as if one has lived for a time in the peasant villages and small towns of the Abruzzi. The Abruzzi is also a moral world, and Silone evokes it in order to answer the question of origins: "By what decree of fate, or through what inner strength or neurosis, does one decide at a certain age to be a 'rebel'?" What is the source of the rebel's "spontaneous intolerance of submission" and his "incapacity to let injustice go by—even if it only affects others"?[2] No doubt there are a large number of sources, just as there are many different kinds of rebellion, but Silone is not speaking only for himself, he speaks for many other radicals too, when he writes that:

> The facts which justified my indignation and the moral reasons which made that indignation necessary were given me by the place where I grew up. The step from submission to subversion was very short; all I had to do was apply to society the principles that were considered valid for private life. And that is how I explain the fact that everything that I have written up to now, and probably everything I will write in the future, even though I have travelled and lived abroad for many years, refers only to that part of the country which can be seen from the house where I was born.[3]

Principles "given" by a place—so that there was no adventure in finding them, only in following them. Silone is describing the principles considered valid and taught to their children by the people of the Abruzzi. The principles aren't in any way extraordinary; he might have learned them, or something very like them, in exile in Switzerland or in France or in Belgium (though probably not at the Comintern meetings that he attended in Moscow). In fact, however, he learned them at home; morality for him was less an acquisition than an inheritance, and it was delivered in a local dialect—which Silone then "spoke" for the rest of his life. Nor was this a morality valid only for private life. Visible and effective only within the family or among intimate friends, excluded from public life by oppression and fear, it pointed nonetheless toward a pattern of economic and political relationships. Silone's application of principles to society was implicit in the principles themselves. What was implicit, however, was also repressed, so that ideas like justice and freedom took on either an ideological or a utopian appearance. Toward the ideology the peasants of the Abruzzi were resigned and cynical. The utopia was a resource, though one without immediate usefulness: heretical, subversive, and secret. "Under the ashes of skepticism," Silone wrote, "the ancient hope for the Kingdom, the ancient expectation that love will take the place of law, the ancient dreams of Gioacchino da Fiore, the Spirituals and the Celestines have never died out among those who suffer most."[4] So the principles were applied long before Silone's application—but only in dreams. Still, these were real dreams, somebody's dreams; they weren't the personal or idiosyncratic inventions of a novelist. They were a significant part of Silone's inheritance.

Even the local ideologies were a part of his inheritance. There is a lovely moment in Silone's first novel, *Fontamara*, when the peasants decide to publish a newspaper, the first paper that would be entirely their own. What should they call it? The village cobbler suggested the name *Justice*. Someone else protested that justice was always against the peasants; justice was represented by the *carabinieri*. " 'But it's real justice I mean,' said the old cobbler, losing his patience. 'Equal justice for everybody.' "[5] *Real justice*: the idea survives the crimes committed in its name, and this will be true as long as the name remains the necessary cover for the crimes. The peasants may doubt the possibility of real justice in the economic and political life of the countryside, and they may be right or wrong about that, but they know what the word means; they know what justice really is.

In fact, everyone knows, even the town orators and politicians, masters of forensic eloquence, whom Silone treats rather more cruelly than Plato did the sophists. The orators are doubly opportunistic—eager for applause, eager for money. They pose as tribunes and speak to the people for the sake of applause; they practice law and serve the landlords for the sake of money. Bloated with words, they still have some dim sense of the power of the ideas they simultaneously express and exploit. Thus Zabaglione, in *Bread and Wine*, once the local leader of the Maximalist Socialists, who, at great personal cost, has given up his socialist convictions: "That is the root of the trouble. . . . Taking things literally. No regime ought ever to be taken literally, otherwise what would the world come to?"[6] Pietro Spina, the central figure of the novel, communist and Christian saint, makes the same argument. We begin, he says,

> by taking seriously the principles taught us by our own educators and teachers. These principles are proclaimed to be the foundations of present-day society, but if one takes them seriously and uses them as a standard to test society as it is organized and as it functions today, it becomes evident that there is a radical contradiction between the two. Our society in practice ignores these principles altogether. . . . But for us . . . they are a serious and sacred thing . . . the foundation of our inner life. The way society butchers them, using them as a mask and a tool to cheat and fool the people, fills us with anger and indignation. That is how one becomes a revolutionary.[7]

It may be true, as Marx argued, that another "radical contradiction," between new forces of production and old relations of production, somehow produces men and women ready to "test society" and join in the revolution. But it is hard to believe that anyone would become a communist militant, a professional revolutionary, as Silone did, choose a life of agitation and danger, because of this second contradiction alone. Marx's contradiction is not a matter—how could it be?—of immediate experience. Nor does anyone choose revolution by opting for a new set of moral principles, hitherto unknown, designed for a new set of productive relations. Revolution is born in anger, and what makes for anger is the experience of principles already known and yet ignored, affirmed and then "butchered." One must learn what is right—this is never a single-handed discovery or contrivance, as if the revolutionary were some mad inventor working away in his basement—and then see what is wrong. The true madness of the revolutionary is "seriousness" or literal-mindedness.

At least, that is the madness of the rebel, as Silone acted out the part and Camus later described it. Professional revolutionaries, by contrast, may need some new theoretical disclosure, some account of human nature or history, before they can settle into their role. Professions require doctrines. But the original impulse, without which no one would enter the profession, doesn't come from the doctrine. It comes instead from what Silone calls "the ordinary sense of the relations between [oneself] and others, the ordinary sense of rights and duties, the ordinary standards of moral judgement."[8] No human society is possible without an ordinary morality, and in every known society ordinary morality is a critical standard. The task of the town orators is to sound the moral notes in such a way that one doesn't hear the words—or in such a way that the words make for comfort or amusement and not for incitement. But a man or a woman who listens for the words and takes them to heart is on the way to rebellion.

Not that the way is smooth: though it begins with what is ordinary, it doesn't end there. Silone was led into the Communist party by a Christian faith that was at once commonplace and heretical, a product of what Gramsci called the "common sense" of the oppressed. But once in the party, he could not remain a Christian; the party had its own creed, which had no room for either the time or the place from which Silone came—the mountain villages of the Abruzzi or "the 'Middle Ages' rooted in my soul." However natural his choice of communism was, it required a great deal of uprooting; he broke with his family, left his home, lost his faith. "Who can describe the private dismay of an underfed provincial youth living in a squalid bedroom in the city, when he has given up forever his belief in the . . . immortality of the soul?"[9]

But it is possible to lose one's immortal soul and hold on to one's practical principles, to leave the Church but cling to the teaching of holy books and faithful priests. The world of commitment and belief is never so coherent that we can only take it or leave it. Full-blown integration, integration in detail, is a sociological fantasy. What we experience instead is complexity and instability, anomaly and contradiction. We change the world—at least we change it for ourselves—simply by choosing one among the possibilities it offers, by "taking seriously," say, its official ideology and breaking with its officials. Or, another version of the same thing, by siding with those men and women whom the officials pretend to serve and actually oppress:

> One fine Sunday some of us stopped going to Mass, not because Catholic dogma seemed to us, all of a sudden, false, but because the people who went began to bore us and we were drawn to the company of those who stayed away. . . . What

> characterized our revolt was the choice of comrades. Outside our village church stood the landless peasants. It was not their psychology we were drawn to: it was their plight.[10]

Silone chose the landless peasants, whose daily oppression and grinding poverty revealed the "radical contradiction" between principles and practice. But there was no way to make that a politically effective choice except by leaving the world of the village. The peasants were frightened, ignorant, resigned; their resistance was passive and evasive; they were incapable of organizing themselves and infinitely suspicious of outside organizers. The corrosive irony that is so central to Silone's novels is a peasant irony, the product of a long schooling in the falseness of political appearances. The hypocrisy of landlords and lawyers, the ironic resignation of the peasants, his own seriousness—together these forced upon Silone an "emergency exit" from the countryside he loved.

He came to the city, where his choice of the peasants led him "naturally" into the party of the proletariat: first the Socialist Youth and then the new Communist party. Anomalous moves—he had broken with the established Church only to find himself in a new establishment with its own "language, symbols, administrative norms, discipline, tactics, program and doctrine."[11] At no point did Silone stand free, the way the critic is commonly supposed to stand, look around, choose the best moral principles, design the ideal society, compare party programs, decide on the strategically appropriate course of action. The story that he tells is moving and powerful because it is a story of infinite entanglement and subtle constraint. "We proclaim ourselves revolutionaries . . . for motives, often ill-defined, that are deep within us, and before choosing we are, unknown to ourselves, chosen. As for the new ideology, we learn that, usually, at the [party] schools."[12] In Silone's case the learning was hard; staying in the party required a kind of conversion that joining had not required, and it wasn't easy, he writes, "to reconcile my state of mental rebellion against an old and unacceptable social order with the 'scientific' requirements of a minutely codified political doctrine."[13] Obviously, the reconciliation was never complete; unlike Gramsci, Silone never became a scientific socialist. But he remained in the party and lived by its discipline for almost ten years, a "Marxist of the heart."[14]

Ignazio Silone: "The Natural"

The Underground

After the fascist coup, the party went underground, and by the late twenties, Silone was the leader of the underground organization (while his friend Palmiro Togliatti, in exile, presided over the Central Committee). Those were difficult years; Silone went into hiding, changed his name ("Silone" is a pseudonym), shunned friends and relatives—anyone, outside the party, who might know who he was. "I . . . adapted myself to living like a foreigner in my own country."[15] Later on, he thought the adaptation had come too easily: this was a way of life "in no way incompatible with Communist mentality." For someone whose radicalism derived from his Christian faith, the party line must often have seemed an alien creed and living according to the line not very different from "living like a foreigner." *Bread and Wine* and *Seed Beneath the Snow* are simultaneously novels about leaving the party and coming home—to the villages and people of the Abruzzi and to the hero's (and Silone's own) "paleo-Christian heritage." "He . . . returned and found himself."[16] But how had he lost himself? In what way was communism compatible with, even suited to, an alien and underground life?

The underground is by no means a negative concept in Silone's writing. When he withdrew from party work, Silone left Italy and lived in exile from 1929 to 1945, a foreigner in someone else's country. Nor could he live openly, even in neutral Switzerland, for he was soon involved in politics again, this time in the noncommunist resistance to fascism. At a meeting of writers in Basel in 1947, Silone described himself as a representative of the resistance, "that invisible, underground country without frontiers which we created . . . during the long years of persecution, that country of which we wish to remain free and loyal citizens."[17] Here the underground is assimilated to the invisible church, though Pietro Spina, in *Seed Beneath the Snow*, insists upon a this-worldly end to invisibility: "I don't mean that ours is the kingdom of heaven; we're only too happy to leave that to priests and sparrows;* no, our kingdom is, for the moment, underground, and there it will remain until we have cleared the surface of the earth of the

* The reference is to Heinrich Heine's "Germany—A Winter's Tale": "We gladly leave to the angels and birds / The dainties of the gods" (translation by Aaron Kramer, in Heinrich Heine, *Poetry and Prose*, ed. Jost Hermand and Robert Holub [New York: Continuum, 1982], p. 232). Written in 1844, at the height of Heine's involvement in radical politics, this was a favorite poem on the European left. Silone might have read it in the party schools.

tiresome presence of you [the police] and your masters."[18] But this underground, though it may require one to live in hiding, does not require one to live like a foreigner; it is entirely compatible with the firm sense of being at home. Spina indeed is sitting in his grandmother's house, describing to her an imaginary conversation with a policeman; Silone in 1947 had only recently returned to Italy and joined, openly now, the Socialist party. Silone's underground is simply the solidarity of the stalwart, the band of men and women who take seriously the moral principles that everyone else merely accepts and routinely ignores. Silone had originally joined the Communist party thinking that it was a band of this sort—and sometimes it was; sometimes, among communists who were "simple left-wing socialists," he found "those traits of generosity, frankness, solidarity and lack of prejudice which were the genuine and traditional resource of socialism in its struggle against bourgeois decadence and corruption."[19] These simple socialists, in the face of fascism, also lived underground or participated sometimes in underground activities, but they didn't live like foreigners in their own country.

Living like a foreigner meant living at a distance from the people one hoped to mobilize and lead—a critical distance, perhaps; more importantly, a distance mediated by an ideology and an organization. It meant not knowing what the critic and revolutionary most needed to know (and had begun by knowing), that is, the social conditions and the moral reasons that made the established order intolerable. Instead, the party member was taught a substitute Truth, which had more to do with what was inevitable than with what was intolerable. Pietro Spina returns to Italy carrying with him an unfinished essay on the agrarian question, aimed at expounding this Truth. Like Silone himself, Spina had become a communist because of the agrarian question: he first recognized injustice in the oppression of the peasants. In the party, however, the peasant was an unknown figure, the member, as Gramsci wrote, of a "surpassed" social class. Spina's fictional essay is probably meant to recall Gramsci's actual essay on the Southern question, unfinished at the time of his arrest in 1926. A major theoretical turning point, so Gramsci scholars tell us, "The Southern Question" is nonetheless a peculiarly lifeless document. And so Spina's essay seems to him after he has lived for a while in the countryside:

> He took his notebook from his bag and [read] the notes he had started in exile. He read them through and was astonished and dismayed at their abstract character. All those quotations from masters and disciples on the agrarian question, all

> those plans and schemes were the paper scenery in which he had hitherto lived. The country . . . was a paper country, with paper mountains, paper hills, fields, gardens, and meadows. The great events recorded in them were mostly paper events, paper battles, and paper victories. The peasants were paper peasants. The heresies and deviations against which he fought had been paper heresies and paper deviations.[20]

Spina "was seized with a great fear of abstractions." Not an entirely plausible fear, I suppose, since abstraction is an ordinary and also an indispensible intellectual activity. But Silone means to associate it here with an inauthentic distancing of the self from ordinary life, a posture of theoretical understanding, indeed, absolute understanding, that merely conceals practical ignorance. And he associates this in turn with the party and its "minutely codified doctrine." Like the Church, the party cultivates its own Truth and has lost touch with the concrete truths of "social reality." It exists for its own sake, not for the sake of the cause it was originally intended to serve. Real peasants exist for the sake of paper peasants; their function is to act out the "paper battles" described in party ideology—and woe to them if they act incorrectly! Party members lose the sense of their own instrumental role: that is the moral meaning of living like a foreigner. If the Communists are for the moment driven underground, it is all too easy to imagine them ruling the country (and still living like foreigners). They have already adopted the fascist doctrine that Silone caricatures in *Seed Beneath the Snow*: "A handkerchief does not exist for the nose, but the nose for the handkerchief."[21]

The corruption of the Communist party had, of course, another and more direct cause. Its members were foreigners in a second sense: they were imaginary citizens of the "first workers' state," which was not an invisible but an actual state with borders and bureaucrats and policemen. Communist politics in Italy in the 1920s and 1930s was little more than a distorted echo of communist politics in Russia. The "paper events, paper battles, and paper victories" to which Italian realities were ruthlessly subordinated were not even written out on Italian paper. This subordination was justified in theoretical terms (world-historical terms: the *first* workers' state), and the effect of the theory was to relativize every local struggle. Once again, the party looked very much like the Church that Silone had left, which had its own historical mission and its own practical and expedient reasons for neglecting the principles it was supposedly founded to serve. Thus Spina in *Bread and Wine*:

> He had broken with a decadent Church, rejected opportunism, and declined to compromise with society. But had he not succumbed to another kind of opportunism . . . dictated by the interests of a political party? He had broken with the old world and all its comforts, cut himself off from his family . . . set himself to live for justice and truth alone, and entered a party in which he was told that justice and truth were petty-bourgeois prejudices.[22]

And so Spina drifted away from the party, and Silone himself withdrew: they were both of them natural ex-communists.*

The Naturalistic Phase of the Revolution

The first thing that Silone did after giving up party work was to write *Fontamara*. Instead of a pamphlet on the agrarian question, he wrote a novel about a peasant village. Critics of the novel have suggested that the peasants in it are still paper peasants, but that seems to me a misconceived critique. *Fontamara* is a political fable as much as it is a realistic novel; its characters are representative, therefore fabulous, men and women, but they don't merely walk an ideological line. Silone finds in them an integrity that the bureaucrats of the party (and the Church) had long ago surrendered. But he also finds ignorance, degradation, fear, and selfishness. "I haven't the illusion that the poor possess the truth; I know that their spiritual poverty . . . is often as great as their material misery."[23] A French critic wrote of Tolstoy in his later years that "he always has his *muzhik* in his pocket."[24] Against every social evil, Tolstoy summoned up the primitive but sublime goodness of the Russian peasant. Occasionally, Silone seems engaged in a similar operation, but he doesn't in fact have Tolstoyan illusions. He only insists that radical politics must exist in some close relation to the needs and values of the oppressed. Silone's socialism, writes his friend Nicola Chiaromonte, "lies wholly in the memory of the . . . warp and weft of peasant life and the fact that the need for justice is an integral and daily part of that life, just as an integral and daily part of it is the hope that the reign of *force*

* Silone left the party, according to his old friend and comrade, Togliatti, because of his *anima bella*, his beautiful soul. The phrase is meant to be a sneer, and the sneer is a commonplace in the tough-minded, realistic, and (in one sense or another) official criticism of social critics. Togliatti acknowledges the principles on which Silone acts but holds them to be merely personal and aesthetic principles, not morally or politically serious. See Giorgio Bocca, *Palmiro Togliatti* (Rome: Editori Laterza, 1973), p. 416. (I owe this reference to Franco Ferraresi.)

majeure will one day end. Silone is bound up with this need and this hope, and by comparison nothing else matters to him."[25]

Fontamara represented a return to the sources of Silone's radicalism. Living in exile, he could return only in imagination (and on paper). But the return henceforth controls his politics, as Marxist theory and Russian battles could no longer do, and so we need to understand exactly what it involves. Is critical force lost by this mental homecoming, this willful surrender of distance? The loss is predicted by the common understanding of social criticism, and that prediction, naturally enough, was fiercely endorsed by Silone's former comrades. The common understanding is nicely stated by Thorstein Veblen in his essay on the Jews. One becomes a "disturber of the intellectual peace," Veblen wrote, "only at the cost of becoming an intellectual wayfaring man." The critical intellectual, with his "free-swung skeptical initiative," has necessarily given up "his secure place in the scheme of conventions into which he has been born" and, equally necessary, has found no new security elsewhere.[26] But this perfect homelessness, this endless detachment, is a barely tolerable human condition. Something like it may be the fate of radically innovative artists and scientists who find, even in the world of bohemia or among professional colleagues, few people willing to share their isolation and insecurity. But among politically engaged intellectuals, Silone's career is more likely: they move from one creed or discipline to another. Even a detached social critic must stand somewhere, and he will probably manage to convince himself that his is a secure standpoint (even a likely rallying point). Benda is an example of someone who, for all his Jewish "wayfaring," took his stand on the sure ground of eternity and defended, without much skepticism, the abstract and universal ideals of the enlightenment. Silone, after his emergency exit, chose the security of the Communist party. Certainly, his membership in the party made the criticism of Italian society easy; it supplied him, indeed, with an ideologically correct critique. It didn't, however, make it easy to criticize the ideology. Silone became a critic of the party only when he returned to the moral conventions and the heretical Christianity he had learned as a child. The adjective "free-swinging" never quite describes him.

One could, of course, become a critic of communism simply by taking communist principles seriously. So far as criticism goes, intellectual wayfaring is never necessary. But physical wayfaring and all the hardships of exile often are necessary, because someone who takes conventional principles seriously is likely to find it difficult to earn a living or to measure up to the ideological versions of propriety and respectability or to avoid the attentions of the police. Silone left the Abruzzi and never lived there again, though he did go back for a visit and, unlike Gramsci, wrote about it: one of the finest essays in *Emergency Exit* is the story of a failed return. And his fictional heroes regularly go home to live: home, for them, is an urgent moral need. "I came back here," says Spina, "to be able to breathe."[27] One might think that it's the air of exile that makes a man free. But the party knows better. Thus the functionary Oscar to the communist rebel Rocco in *A Handful of Blackberries*, one of Silone's later (postwar) novels: "Your case goes to show what dangers we all incur if the party sends us back home for any length of time. . . . In our home surroundings we tend to relapse into the primary, infantile, romantic phase of the revolution—its naturalistic phase."[28] Nature again, and again it is second nature, moral conventions, that Oscar is attacking. Freed from these conventions, men and women are indeed available for party discipline; but they are not free (or, better, they are not free for long).

Oscar's argument has been given a more specific, and a more benign, formulation by Michael Harrington: "The appearance of peasant figures in the political fiction of the Left," Harrington wrote in the 1960s, "is a sign of despair. [The despair is evident] in Silone's turning back from the Communist party to the traditional wisdom of his native province, from proletarian revolution to *jacquerie*."[29] Here it is less a matter of coming home than of coming home to a peasant village. Harrington worries that Silone will succumb to the parochialism, moral narrowness, sporadic anger, and deep resignation of the Italian countryside—one more weary radical wrapping himself in the shroud of organic connection, returning to his birthplace to die with his ancestors. But what Silone shares with the peasants of the Abruzzi is not their everyday life but their discontent with their everyday life. A rebel when he left, he returns to renew the sources of his rebellion, to explore again the heresies and utopias of peasant consciousness.

I don't know if he got the peasant village right; in any case, he never made it into an ideological small-holding. If Pietro Spina and Rocca had returned to the factories of Turin, say, the political meaning of the act would have been the same. Silone was searching for a certain purity of need and rebelliousness, and he could have found this in Turin, too, had he been born and raised there. The return is not a sign of despair, it seems to me, but rather the acknowledgment of a particular failure and defeat, the failure of vanguard politics, the defeat of communism. It's not that the party will never come to power—in A *Handful of Blackberries* it has come to power, at least in a small piece of the Italian countryside—but that it isn't capable of achieving, it no longer seriously stands for, a just society. Surely it is better to recognize this than not to recognize it: the recognition is even a small victory for truth and perhaps for justice too. And if Spina finds in "traditional wisdom" some basis for resistance to oppressors new and old, left and right, that is another small victory.

Small victories still, to set against a great defeat, a world-historical defeat, the death of the dream inspired by the Russian Revolution. Henceforth, radical critics must be doubly critical, first of the established social order and second of the historically chosen, now corrupted, instrument of transformation. The double critique makes for a political impasse, and *Bread and Wine* and *Seed Beneath the Snow* are above all novels of impasse. Torturous, grim, often painful to read, they are nevertheless not novels of surrender—certainly not critical surrender. *Seed Beneath the Snow* is in fact the most dense and fully developed of Silone's novels, and its portrait of the provincial elites of fascist Italy is unremittingly savage. Brilliantly caught in a moment of baseness and opportunism, frozen by fear, these elites are set against Spina's few comrades, seeds beneath the snow, whose friendship and good humor represent not (for the moment) a political but a moral alternative. *Only* a moral alternative, and Spina has "not forgotten that the social question . . . is not resolved by purely moral means."[30] Nor can it be resolved, however, by men and women who have lost touch with the moral reasons that once drove them to seek its resolution.

Comrades

What are those moral reasons? Again and again, in his novels and his essays, Silone expresses them in terms of "the choice of comrades." His own moral history begins with a lesson taught by his father. Once, as a child, he made a joking remark about a "small, barefoot, ragged little man" who was being led away to prison, "handcuffed between two policemen." His father was very angry:

> "Never make fun of a man who's been arrested! Never!"
> "Why not?"

> "Because he can't defend himself. And because he may be innocent. In any case because he's unhappy."[31]

When Silone left the Church, he was choosing as his comrades those members of Italian society who were in any case unhappy. And when he left the party he was acting from similar motives (though now with an international perspective): "Do we side with the inmates of the slave labor camps or with their jailers?"[32]* The political history of the twentieth century suggests that the answer to this question is less obvious than it might appear. Perhaps it is just a peasant prejudice, a sentimental identification (the "naturalistic phase" of the revolution) to prefer inmates to jailers. What if the jailers represent true doctrine, the workers' state, historical progress? If he is to justify his choice, Silone requires a doctrine of his own.

"In essence this consists of the permanent validity of certain moral values"—embodied at least sometimes in kinship and friendship. Most men and women are unlikely to experience these values anywhere else; or, everywhere else, in school and church and marketplace, they are loudly proclaimed and yet ring false. Socialism is the promise that they won't ring false, hence, for Silone, an "extension of the ethical requirements of the restricted individual and family sphere to the entire realm of human activity."[33] This is a recurrent theme—I began with it—but Silone is nowhere concerned to defend a particular list of ethical requirements. Generosity, frankness, and solidarity probably capture his meaning, which is in no sense esoteric. These are and will always be the values that inspire the demand for justice. "Under the domination of Marxism," party members have come to treat them as relative values, but they are in fact permanent, and because of them socialism is a "permanent aspiration of the human spirit."[34]

This is Silone's doctrine. As he grew older, he expressed it more and more in Christian and messianic terms, but the Christianity is always that of the Gospels, not of Paul or the Church Fathers: it has the form of a moral tale, not a theological argument. Silone's doctrine is simple, ordinary, unadorned; it requires interpretation nonetheless. The relativism of the

* Compare George Orwell's comment, in *Homage to Catalonia* (Boston: Beacon Press, 1955), on the repression of anarchist and Trotskyite workers in Barcelona: "When I see an actual flesh-and-blood worker in conflict with his natural enemy, the policeman, I do not have to ask myself which side I am on" (p. 124). The theory of class struggle may have something to do with these statements, but not much. Silone and Orwell would probably attribute them to common decency. I am not sure that the same attribution is right for Sartre's line: "Every time the state police fire on a young militant, I am on the young militant's side." "Militant" doesn't have the same moral resonance as "worker" and "camp inmate." (Sartre is quoted in Simone de Beauvoir, *Adieux*, trans. Patrick O'Brian [New York: Pantheon, 1984], pp. 106–7.)

party is a strategic relativism; behind it stands an absolute Truth that is supposed to guarantee the ultimate moral outcome of each successive strategy. What happened to Silone was that he ceased to believe in this absolute Truth or, better, he came to see it as a paper Truth, which could not possibly justify those acts of meanness, deceit, and betrayal that party officials found expedient. But it wasn't Silone's intention to oppose the absolute Truth of the party with an absolutism of his own. His doctrine is not a total ideology or a general theory or a full-scale religious creed. "In a situation where the premises of metaphysics and even of history are uncertain and open to question," he writes in "The Choice of Comrades," "the moral sense is forced to extend its scope, taking on the additional function of guide to knowledge." This can be a misleading guide; social critics readily fall prey in such a situation to "an abstract and superficial moralism"—which is fully as bad as the arrogance of the ideologically correct. But now it is enough to recall whose moral sense the critic is relying on: "a creature of flesh and blood, a man of a certain region, a certain class, and a certain time."[35] In Silone's work, Christian humility serves the cause of moral particularism.

The principles of morality are permanent but they are also local. They reflect the needs and hopes of particular people with faces and proper names, occupations and places of residence, customs and beliefs. One reaches mankind only through serious engagement with such people—though it seems to me that Silone is in no great hurry to reach mankind. He is seized by a fear of abstractions; he is in retreat from world history; he is content to begin and end his narratives with the peasants of the Abruzzi. Peasant endurance is the practical proof of moral permanence. "The truth of the *cafoni*," writes Chiaromonte, "is rustic and inarticulate, but it lasts, being forged from necessity."[36] This is the truth that Silone sets against the Truth of the party. The opposition between what is permanent and what is relative doesn't capture the difference between the two. Silone's truth is commonplace, practical, and enduring; the Truth of the party is esoteric, theoretical, and historically mutable. Silone, we might say, is committed to his dialect, the party to its dialectics.

I don't want to suggest that Silone is himself a rustic or a would-be rustic who wants to return to the soil (or who wants the rest of us to return to the soil). It is indeed a high compliment when someone says of Pietro Spina, in *Seed Beneath the Snow*, that "he is not a mere theorist, a slave to reasoning, a hair-splitter."[37] Yet Spina is nothing if not an intellectual; the two novels in which he appears are accounts of his reflections far more than of his activities. And Silone, after his "emergency exit," first from the Abruzzi and then from the party, is an urban and urbane social critic—even if he never writes about any place else than the countryside. He describes himself as one of "the legion of refugees from the International." But unlike many of the other refugees, he never gives up the principles that led him to his initial choice of comrades; he gives up only the ideology learned afterward in the party schools. And then he sets himself to construct, if not a new ideology, at least a new understanding of the political world. No doubt this new understanding doesn't have the analytic power (or the buoyant optimism) of Marxist theory, but it has the considerable advantage of moral relevance: it confronts the realities of the twentieth century, not only capitalism but also bureaucratic dictatorship. "Two evils," says Don Severino in *Seed Beneath the Snow*, "Money and the State . . . as old as fleas and coughing, hateful in themselves but bearable as long as they are kept within certain limits."[38] Like Camus some years later, Silone comes to recognize the moral importance of limits—a doctrine at once simple and sophisticated.

This is the wisdom of the ideological refugee but not, I think, of the intellectual wayfarer. As a critic and a novelist, Silone is steady, patient, stubborn, faithful—in contrast to Koestler, say, to whom none of these adjectives could possibly be applied. "What do . . . refugees do from morning to night? They spend most of their time telling one another the story of their lives."[39] Silone's story, transmuted into fiction and fable, is something more than this. It represents a critique of injustice and oppression sustained with remarkable power through all the vicissitudes of a bad time. But is this a critique capable of inspiring other people, who aren't members of the legion of refugees? Silone's emergency exits may well leave him isolated and without influence. Certainly his stories have not produced a succession of "Silonians" in the way that Marx's theoretical arguments produced a succession of Marxists (Gramsci only one in an impressive and continuing series). There are, however, other forms of continuity: Silone's stories have helped to create, not a succession, but a critical tradition, a certain way of talking into which people enter in part because they admire him, in part because they feel it to be, of the available alternatives, the better way. George Orwell and Albert Camus, I think, belong to this tradition, sharing in Silone's enterprise and taking their bearings, as he did, from common sense and commonplace morality.

7

George Orwell's England

Radicalism and Rootedness

Like "Ignazio Silone," "George Orwell" is a pseudonym; unlike "Silone," it is not a political pseudonym, an underground name chosen out of necessity, on the run. "Orwell" was Orwell's free choice and not a choice that is easy to understand. Why did he need a pseudonym at all? Perhaps we don't have to answer this question in order to come to grips with the man and his work—indeed, I incline to this philistine and distinctly Orwellian opinion. But there is a sharply critical view of Orwell that makes much of his pseudonym, almost as if names were ontologies. He chose his new name in the early 1930s, on this view, when he became a new man and a radical critic of English society. But the name corresponded to no stable moral reality, and he could not sustain the critical stance to which it committed him. Imitating the heroes of his own novels, so Raymond Williams has argued in the most powerful version of this critique, Orwell breaks with the "orthodox routines" of his class and culture, fails to realize the hopes that motivate the break, and then, disillusioned, returns. He begins as Eric Blair and, without acknowledging what has happened, ends as Blair again; begins as an imperial policeman and ends as a cold war ideologist. In effect, Williams reinstates the communist condemnation of Silone's "return," but he does so from an independent leftist position and with far greater attentiveness and literary grace.[1]

It comes as no surprise, of course, that Orwell's last books, *Animal Farm* and *1984*, made many people on the left uneasy; but so did *The Road to Wigan Pier* and *Homage to Catalonia* much earlier. There seems to have been a roughly determinate group of people, leftists of a particular sort, who winced every time Orwell took up his pen (this gave him great pleasure), and such people must see his last books prefigured in his earliest political writings. Raymond Williams isn't quite a leftist of that sort; he tells a more sophisticated story. *Homage to Catalonia* is for him an unqualified success, the grand moment of Orwell's political career—the first pages, the celebration of Barcelona as "a town where the working class was in the saddle," the grandest moment. In fact, Orwell's celebration is characteristically restrained: "There was much in [the life of the city] that I did not understand, in some ways I did not even like it, but I recognized it immediately as a state of affairs worth fighting for."[2] It is Orwell's roughly similar judgment of England in 1940, based on much greater understanding, that Williams takes as the sign of his disillusion and return. The crucial text is *The Lion and the Unicorn*, published in February 1941, in which Orwell succumbs to a disease called "social patriotism," rejoins the family of "sensible, moderate, and decent" Englishmen, and ceases to be a radical critic.

Williams isn't entirely unsympathetic—or wasn't unsympathetic when he wrote his study of Orwell in 1970; seven years later in an interview with the editors of *New Left Review*, bullied a bit by the editors, he took a harder line. Class identity is his central theme, and given his view of class, social patriotism looks very much like an inherited disease.[3] Orwell's political difficulties and his final defeat, as Williams describes them, are the (predetermined?) outcome of his heroic effort to make himself over as "Orwell"—cool, dispassionate, relentlessly honest, freed above all from the conventional respectability of his class. So he left the police, went down and out in Paris and London, descended again into the mines of the North Country, fought and was wounded in Spain. But he never became, could not become, an organic intellectual of the working class. He tore up his roots and then found himself rootless, without a clear social identity. This is the ideal position for the radical critic—so goes the standard argument, elegantly expounded by Julien Benda, about the prerequisites of criticism itself. But Williams's argument is different, more overtly sociological, perhaps, or more committed to his own (Welsh working-class) roots. Rootlessness for him is a condition of loss, from which even an Orwell, who chose his condition much as he chose his name, must eventually seek an escape. Hence Orwell's return to England and English patriotism, "an act not so much of membership as of conscious affiliation." Standing nowhere, he can't keep up the struggle that criticism requires. He is trying in his "patriotic" pieces to prove that he really belongs to the extended English family: "The emotions are understandable, and honorable," says Williams, "but . . . they are too easy, too settling, too sweet."[4]

Ironically, this criticism of Orwell coincides in part with Orwell's criticism of the left intellectuals of the popular front—though Orwell is rather more savage. Middle-class intellectuals, alienated at home, become communists or fellow travelers through an act of the will, he argues, and then their willfulness knows no bounds; it is matched only by their ignorance of the world they have entered. They become willful proletarians, party stalwarts, apologists for the Soviet Union. The popular front, Orwell says in a phrase that Williams might have applied to Orwell's own politics, is the "patriotism of the deracinated."[5] Orwell has an intense dislike for deracination, and his mockery of the men and women who display its symptoms like badges of honor is often very cruel. There isn't much excuse for his reiterated lists of the cranks and eccentrics, the marginal, graceless people who are drawn to socialism and then to communism because of some dim hope for kinship and discipline: "all that dreary tribe of high-minded women and sandal-wearers and bearded fruit-juice drinkers" and so on. Clearly, Orwell did not want to be associated with *them*, though it is too quick a piece of psychologizing to suggest that he feared he might himself be one of the tribe. Sometimes, in any case, his mockery is more perceptive, as in his brief comment on W. H. Auden's line (which Orwell immortalized) about "the necessary murder." The time will come, Auden writes, for poetry readings, walks by the lake, and "perfect communion." But today something else is required:

> Today the deliberate increase in the
> chances of death,

> The conscious acceptance of guilt in
> the necessary murder;
> Today the expending of powers
> On the flat ephemeral pamphlet and
> the boring meeting.[6]

These lines sketch, says Orwell, a day in the life of a "good party man." "In the morning a couple of political murders, a ten-minutes' interlude to stifle 'bourgeois' remorse, and then a hurried luncheon and a busy afternoon and evening chalking walls and distributing leaflets."[7] Auden is striking a political pose, and the pose is wholly inauthentic, therefore available for caricature. The "conscious acceptance of guilt" is all too easy when one has no experience of crime. This sort of thing is considerably worse than wearing sandals or drinking fruit juice, and Orwell's critique is serious, a crucial indication of his political commitment. It suggests that he had a view of his own radicalism very different from the one that Williams provides. Despite his new name, he did not think of himself as a deracinated intellectual, a socialist-by-virtue-of-will-alone. What was he, then, this man who "became" George Orwell?

At bottom, he was always Eric Blair, the "lower upper-middle class" Englishman who went to school at Eton and who joined, and left, the Burmese police. One can easily enough describe Orwell's life as if it were a parade of selves, himself a one-man cast of characters—though the description requires more than Williams's trio of Blair, Orwell, and Orwell betrayed. It is at least as important, however, to notice a broad continuity not only of moral character but also of social identity. He gave up the authority of his class and its claims to wealth and prestige (his own family had never known either); he changed his mind—more than once—and his political positions too. But there were no radical conversions and no "emergency exits." He avoided the Communist party, never worshipped the god that failed, was only distantly a Trotskyite, had no experience with what Silone called "the situation of the 'Ex.'" He was not easily a comrade, never a proletarian. One can find in *Wigan Pier* and *Homage to Catalonia* idealized portraits of individual workers, but the authorial voice in the two books is consistently that of a middle-class (lower, upper) reporter. Interviewed in 1940 on the subject of "The Proletarian Writer," he said what he would have said at any point in the previous decade: "I believe that [the proletariat's] literature is and must be bourgeois literature with a slightly different slant."[8] *Wigan Pier*, written in 1936, ends with a political argument that points directly to his World War II politics. If you bully me about my "bourgeois ideology," he told the members of the Left Book Club,

> if you give me to understand that in some subtle way I am an inferior person because I have never worked with my hands, you will only succeed in antagonizing me. For you are telling me either that I am inherently useless or that I ought to alter myself in some way that is beyond my power. I cannot proletarianize my accent or certain of my tastes and beliefs, and I would not if I could. Why should I?[9]

Orwell was faithful to what he was, as if following the moral injunction that Albert Camus later made the maxim of his own politics during the Algerian war. He did resign from the Burmese police, and he did become a socialist, but he did both these things without renouncing his "tastes and beliefs." He moved left and remained whole. One can see something of the inner process earlier on in the controversial second part of *Wigan Pier* when he describes the dawning sense of British imperialism as an "oppressive system." He resigned from its service, he says, "with an immense weight of guilt," with the memory vivid in his mind "of subordinates I had bullied and aged peasants I had snubbed, of servants and coolies I had hit with my fists in moments of rage." Out of this experience he constructed "the simple theory that the oppressed are always right and the oppressors are always wrong: a mistaken theory, but the natural result of being one of the oppressors yourself."[10] The comment is important, "a mistaken theory," and it is equally important that Orwell sensed the mistake almost from the beginning; the simple theory is hardly in evidence, for example, in his first published novel, *Burmese Days*, which turns a critical eye on English and Burmese alike.

Guilt is a bad guide to politics, and cant about guilt a worse guide; the two together probably account for much of the self-abnegating willfulness of middle-class intellectuals in the 1930s, dressed up for the occasion as workers and revolutionaries. When he went down and out, Orwell dressed up too: "I wanted to submerge myself, to get right down among the oppressed, to be one of them and on their side against their tyrants."[11] But he learned that he could not be one of them, and he always came back and changed back into his own clothes. It was possible to be "on their side" without pretending to an unfamiliar identity. Williams seems bound to deny this last point, even if he also denies that the pretense can ever be the basis of a lasting socialist commitment. But Orwell managed to connect his old self and his new politics. Bourgeois ideology, after all, had fueled the commitment of many generations of English radicals.

Coming back is one of Orwell's central themes, though the return is always more wary than Williams suggests. The last paragraph of *Homage to Catalonia* is a nice example. Orwell describes his homeward voyage from Spain to England, the seasickness of his Channel crossing, and the dawning sense of his country's deep and dangerous sleep, "from which I sometimes fear we shall never wake till we are jerked out of it by the roar of bombs."[12] That return, at least, isn't "too easy, too settling, too sweet." Orwell doesn't end his books in places like Wigan or Barcelona or even Lower Binfield but typically brings himself or his hero home, to a place he knows, though always uneasily, as his own. He doesn't return like a prodigal son, however, and after the publication of *Animal Farm*, when conservative cold warriors gave him a prodigal son's welcome, he did not like it. To what, then, was he faithful? The standard answer is, to some construction of "ordinary decency." That's not wrong, but it isn't specific enough; it doesn't help to explain his resistance to crucial, and by no means indecent, aspects of leftist ideology (collectivism and Marxist internationalism, for example); nor does it suggest the critical force of his writings about England. The resistance and the criticism are closely connected, but I will take them up separately, beginning with Orwell's anti-ideological socialism. For Williams, that last phrase must be an oxymoron, and perhaps that is why he describes Orwell, after the war, as an ex-socialist. But Orwell comes back to "England, Your England" without giving up his opposition to the men and women who tyrannized over the working class. His success has something to do with his ability, on all his journeys, physical and intellectual, to take himself along. He travels light, says Williams.[13] I don't think so.

English Socialism

One of the most persistent themes of left-wing thought in the twentieth century is the critique of "consumerism." Marx had described the "fetishism of commodities" as a feature of capitalist production: the things the worker makes take on an existence independent of his own productive work, out of his control. But fetishism is present also in capitalist consumption, so post-Marxist critics like Herbert Marcuse have argued, where the commodity is the be-all and end-all of everyday life. The desire for goods, for possessions and conveniences, turns into a social force distinct from the men and women whose desire it is; and the more that desire is met, the more inexorable it becomes. Modern belongings are things to which people belong, a form of domination, like work itself. The endless stream of shoddy and replaceable goods is a sign simultaneously of capitalist success and popular corruption. All this is fairly standard among leftist writers and it has a right-wing counterpart, a generalized dislike of commerce, industry, urban life, the mass market, and the mass media. One can find traces of this sort of thing in Orwell; indeed, one can find both its left- and right-wing varieties. He was never at ease in the world of modern conveniences, and he was capable of a remarkably sustained and almost lyrical nostalgia, as in his last thirties novel, *Coming Up for Air*. But he never expressed an ideological aversion for things themselves, the physical objects that men and women long to possess; his critique of English capitalism does not extend to the "fetishism of commodities." On the contrary, he seems to sense, in *1984* especially, that everyday fetishism has a kind of saving grace.

It is never a good idea for the left to set itself in stark opposition to the values of ordinary people. The attack on consumer goods is the work of social critics at the farthest reach of their willfulness. For men and women deprived of things are not liberated for radical politics any more than starving artists are liberated for art. Deprivation is deprivation; one can't escape from the world of getting and spending by not getting and not spending. Ordinary life makes its own demands, not only for what is absolutely necessary but also for what is merely desirable. Orwell was from the beginning sensitive to these demands. Or, better, almost from the beginning: there was a time, he says in *Wigan Pier*, when "failure seemed to me the only virtue."[14] A mistake, again, and Orwell's *Keep the Aspidistra Flying* is a novelistic working out of the mistake. When he wrote the book, Orwell was not yet politically engaged; its terms are set by the traditions of bohemia, not those of radical militancy. Its hero, Gordon Comstock, the author of a slim but "promising" volume of poetry, has dropped out of bourgeois life and declared war on the "money world." The war is intensely private, fought mostly by self-imposed suffering and internal diatribe. Gordon's denunciations of the power of money, though they have no political resonance, could have come out of the pages of the young Marx. But his is a losing war, partly because of his own absolutism, his rejection of any compromise with bourgeois respectability. He brings himself too low, can't write, can't find friends, can't live with Rosemary whom he loves, can't find any degree of contentment or joy. Orwell's novel is about the failure of "failure." It ends with Gordon's return: back from bohemia to the lower middle class. The last pages celebrate the apartment that Gordon and Rosemary have found and furnished. "It seemed to them a tremendous advantage to have this place of their own. Neither of them had ever owned furniture before. . . . And it was all their own, every bit was their own—at least, so long as they didn't get behind with the installments!"[15]

Strange sentences from a writer who was only a few months away from declaring himself a socialist. Lionel Trilling finds in them "a dim, elegaic echo of Defoe and of the early days of middle-class ascendency as Orwell's sad young man learns to cherish the small personal gear of life, his own bed and chairs and saucepans—his own aspidistra, the ugly, stubborn, organic emblem of survival."[16] Not quite "his own," in fact, his and Rosemary's, and the point is worth making for Rosemary is almost the only sympathetic and strong woman in all of Orwell's writing.* Gordon is not alone at the end of the novel. But the novel is, at the end, a celebration of private life and private ownership, and so it does recall the earlier triumphs of the middle class. But it also points to Orwell's later conviction that socialism cannot, should not, any more than art or literature, require the reversal of those triumphs.

This is a conviction often evident in Orwell's work, but it finds its most remarkable expression in *1984* where, also remarkably, it has gone largely unnoticed. It's not only sexual love that symbolizes opposition to the regimented life of party members on Airstrip One but also the love of things: the notebook in which Winston Smith writes his diary, "a peculiarly beautiful book [with] smooth creamy paper"; the coral paperweight, smashed later on by the thought-police, "a beautiful thing"; the bed in the furnished room where he and Julia make love, "a beautiful mahogany bed." For Winston and Julia, the room is as much an adventure as the apartment is for Gordon

* She is a petty-bourgeois Julia, but unlike Julia (in *1984*) triumphant in the end. Orwell's treatment of these two, and of all the other women in his novels, has been severely and intelligently criticized by Daphne Patai in *The Orwell Mystique: A Study in Male Ideology* (Amherst: University of Massachusetts Press, 1984). Certainly Rosemary is molded to a gender stereotype: she is no more interested in Gordon's poetry, for example, than Julia is interested in Winston's politics. Orwell was no critic—but probably a supporter—of gender stereotyping. He did, however, find strength in the stereotypes—or better, he found strength in these two women, Rosemary and Julia, embodiments of human connection, defenders of the concrete and immediate against (male) abstraction. Still, it is not a good idea, morally or politically, if only women play this role.

and Rosemary—and its joys are not only those of sex but also those of privacy and possession. It inspires fantasies of ordinary life: "He wished that he were walking through the streets with her . . . openly and without fear, talking of trivialities and buying odds and ends for the household."[17]

Is this the wish of an oppositional figure, a social critic? Only, it might be said, in the world of *1984*, while in Orwell's own world, it represents a reconciliation with bourgeois society, a surrender of critical weapons. That seems to me exactly wrong. The recognition that things have their place and value, that "the very stupidity of things," as Trilling says, "has something human about it, something meliorative, something even liberating," sharpens the critique of inequality and oppression.[18] It repudiates, indeed, an ascetic or puritanical socialism but not a socialism that aims to make "the small personal gear of life" equally available to everyone—and if available, why not beautiful? Orwell's socialism is conditioned and concrete; hence his interest in material possessions. He is an advocate of collective control of the means of production but not of collectivism as an abstract ideal. His is a socialism suited to himself and defended with a firm sense that this self, at least as it aspired to beds, chairs, and saucepans, and even as it aspired to beautiful books and paperweights, was sufficiently ordinary. With "small-scale ownership," he wrote in *The Lion and the Unicorn*, describing his political program, the state should not interfere.[19]

Socialism with a bourgeois face? Orwell might better have said that it was socialism with an English face. As he was attached to things, so he was attached to place and culture; and once again he thought the attachment ordinary. "Above all," he told what he must have assumed were skeptical readers, "it is *your* civilization, it is *you*. However much you hate it or laugh at it, you will never be happy away from it for any length of time. The suet puddings and the red pillar-boxes have entered into your soul."[20] Any knowledgeable leftist would indeed be skeptical. From the time of *The Communist Manifesto* onward, he would have been taught that the workers had no country; they were a class radically dispossessed, first of things, then of places, and the love of these two was an inauthentic love, concealing social reality. Preached by the ruling class, consumerism and patriotism were ideological mystifications; the task of the social critic was to demystify commodities and countries alike. I suppose that Raymond Williams marks out *The Lion and the Unicorn* as Orwell's turning point, the beginning of his backsliding, because it is in this text that he most explicitly adopts a patriotic stance: "I believe in England." Orwell does try, however, to appropriate patriotism for the left. That's why he isn't merely a patriot, but a "social patriot."

Patriotism, Orwell writes,

> has nothing to do with Conservatism. It is actually the opposite of Conservatism, since it is a devotion to something that is always changing and yet is felt to be mystically the same. It is the bridge between the future and the past. No real revolutionary has ever been an internationalist.[21]

That last sentence is probably wrong, unless the word "real" conceals some further qualification. But it is not difficult to see what Orwell means. Revolutionary politics requires the mobilization of the people; the people can be mobilized only by appealing to their sentiments and values as well as to their interests; and those sentiments and values are historically formed, culturally specific. The workers he knew or knew about, Orwell thought, "have a great deal to lose besides their chains." In 1941, one of the things they had to lose was their country. For it was theirs, even though they were not in control of its social arrangements or governmental policies. Put them in control and England would become more English: "By revolution we become more ourselves, not less."[22] That sentence, I think, is not wrong. Every genuinely popular revolution (perhaps that is the meaning of Orwell's "real") has intensified the particularity, the political or religious specificity, of the society in which it takes place. Old and established elites, aristocracies especially, are always more cosmopolitan than the men and women they rule. So, indeed, are Marxist vanguards; internationalism is a vanguard ideology. Orwell himself, of course, was acting on internationalist principles when he fought in Spain (he tried several times to join the International Brigade). But he did not believe that these principles could ever be a source of authority in Spanish or in English politics. They determined the allegiance of individuals, not the substantive creed of revolutionary movements. Local struggles were sustained by local values.

At the same time, Orwell despised nationalism, to which he gave a very broad meaning: it included every sort of collective self-aggrandizement, every claim to group advantage or superiority. English nationalists wanted to rule India; English patriots wanted only to defend England against the Nazis.[23] It is a morally neat distinction, but it avoids the hard question: why do patriotic feelings so often take on nationalist political forms? Orwell seems to believe that the success of right-wing nationalism has a lot to do with the unwillingness of left-wing intellectuals to value and work with patriotism. That may well be part of the story, but it can hardly be the whole of it. Here, and elsewhere too, Orwell exaggerates the importance of left-wing intellectuals. He may still have been right, however, to criticize the intellectuals for "their severance from the common culture of the country." (One can be both disconnected and ineffective.) The disconnection did not make it any less likely that many intellectuals would become nationalists in Orwell's extended sense of the term; they merely defended the aggrandizement of foreign collectivities, Stalin's Russia above all. Orwell's internationalism, by contrast, required the critique of every form of aggrandizing politics, the defense of local and particular arrangements; one might think of it as the reiteration of patriotism.

The Critique of Hierarchy

"A family with the wrong members in control—that, perhaps, is as near as one can come to describing England in a phrase." Thus wrote Orwell in 1941.[24] Williams concedes that many people on the left felt that way during the war: the blitz made England whole, even if it didn't reconcile leftists to the rule of the Tory upper class. But Orwell, writing at this critical moment, gave the myth of wholeness lasting life, and for this Williams cannot forgive him:

> If I had to say which [of Orwell's] writings have done the most damage, it would be . . . the dreadful stuff from the beginning of the war about England as a family with the wrong members in charge, the shuffling old aunts and uncles whom we could fairly painlessly get rid of. Many of the political arguments of the kind of laborism . . . usually associated with the tradition of Durbin or Gaitskell can be traced to those essays.[25]

Not quite fair, for Orwell in *The Lion and the Unicorn* warns of a "bitter political struggle" and thinks that "at some point or other it may be necessary to use violence": "The bankers and the larger businessmen, the landowners and dividend-drawers, the officials with their prehensile bottoms, will obstruct for all they are worth. . . . It is no use imagining that one can make fundamental changes without causing a split in the nation."[26] What he doubted was not the ability of the ruling class to defend itself but its ability to defend the country, to mobilize the people and win the war. He thought that revolution, "a fundamental shift of power," was the prerequisite of victory. Here Orwell turned out to be wrong. England won the war without dislodging the "prehensile bottoms" of the old elite. There was indeed a shift of power; the war initiated, and the first postwar election confirmed, the triumph of English social democracy. But this was not the fundamental shift that Orwell anticipated. It did not make London (or Manchester or Liverpool or Glasgow) into a second Barcelona, with the workers "in the saddle." It did not create that matey egalitarianism that Orwell had relished so much in Spain and that had made socialism come alive for him.

But it would only repeat Orwell's exaggeration of the importance of intellectuals to blame *The Lion and the Unicorn* for the emergence and remarkable stability of "laborist" politics. The family image as Orwell develops it does indeed suggest the absence of revolutionary fervor. Images, however, do not cause absences; they only evoke and record them. Orwell points, honestly enough, toward a popular culture that isn't wholly estranged from the hegemonic culture of English capitalism. Williams's charge is that he missed, or perhaps that he deliberately repressed, the systematic character of capitalist hegemony and so misled his readers about the necessary harshness and inevitable difficulties of the coming struggle. In fact, Orwell seems to have recognized that even politics-in-the-family can get pretty rough. What he did not recognize was the possibility, even the likelihood, of compromises along the way and stopping points short of victory. Nor did he acknowledge that patriotic feelings like his own made compromise more likely, not less. For reasons available in his text, but not fully articulated there, England achieved only a welfarist socialism. Was this a defeat? Perhaps; but one might also say that this was (at least the beginning of) the socialism "native to England" that Orwell had always called for. It's that thought that Williams rejects, clinging to the hope of a socialism at once native and far more radical. And then he is driven to argue that the divisions in English society go much deeper than Orwell admits. It is not a family at all, or it is more like Freud's primordial family, with the sons plotting to overthrow and kill the father.

Thus far, however, the plot has not been successful; it has, in fact, hardly engaged the energies of the people whom Williams would call its subjects. Nor has it produced a critique of English society more powerful than Orwell's—though it has certainly produced critiques harsher, more violent, nastier in tone. Orwell's power derives from his intimate grasp of the society he is criticizing and his admiration for many of its cultural and material artifacts: English gentleness, respect for the law, tolerance of eccentricity; English pubs, music hall songs, even English cooking; cricket, comic postcards, country gardens, flowers, Stilton cheese, suet pudding, warm beer, and "a nice cup of tea."[27] Orwell appropriates all this for an egalitarian socialism, much as he appropriates "the small personal gear of life" in the same cause. It's not surprising that revolutionary ferocity is lost along the way. Of course, the appropriation is meant to be provocative. Though Orwell was the most European of twentieth-century English writers (a point I will come back to later on), he disliked intensely what might be called the continentalizing tendencies of well-placed or upwardly mobile Englishmen. He loved to offend high-minded intellectuals and the culturally ambitious middle class. But this was more a hobby than a serious politics, and it would be wrong to see in Orwell's critical work only an easy, if occasionally perverse, sentimentality about the life of the common people. His opposition is directed against the class system itself. Hatred of hierarchy is the animating passion of his social criticism.[28] Domination and arrogance on the one hand, subordination, deference, and fear on the other—these are the features of English life that he sets himself against. The real purpose of cricket, flowers, and the nice cup of tea is to establish his own connection to the life he is criticizing. I think of it as a kind of home remedy for intellectual pride and vanguard presumption.

But this very connectedness, Richard Wollheim has argued, presses Orwell toward a view of society that is deeply conformist in character. Socialism for him meant the realization of a "determinate way of life." Men and women would be free, of course, to lead whatever individual lives they chose, but Orwell anticipated a particular set of choices, defined by English decency and working-class self-respect. "It would be no great parody of Orwell to say that for him a free society was [nothing more than] a society in which no man touched his cap to another." He rejected servility, but then he also rejected crankiness, affectation, and perversity—whatever might seem (in England) indecent. He would not have suppressed such things, writes Wollheim, but he also would not have thought it any great breach of liberty to crowd them out. "And there I am sure he was wrong."[29] Wollheim captures something of Orwell's tone here, but he misses the extent of his commitment to democracy—not the sovereign people only but also the political process: the rough and tumble of debate and the mutual tolerance that keeps the rough and tumble from getting too rough. Orwell railed unfairly against crankiness on the left, but he admired the larger society that tolerated leftist cranks.

Orwell is less a radical egalitarian than he is a simple democrat. His goal was the transfer of power to ordinary men and women and the creation of a lively, open, frank, and plain-spoken politics. This would require only an "approximate" equality of income: the highest income should not exceed the lowest, he argued in *The Lion and the Unicorn*, by more than ten to one. It would also require, and this was at least equally important, a democratic reform of the schools—a demand frequently repeated on the labor left after the war. In his autobiographical essay, "Such, Such Were the Joys," Orwell took the prep school he attended as a child as a prime example of an unjust society and explored the connections between class snobbery and political tyranny. It is an oblique but savage piece of social criticism; no ferocity is lost here. Where other "laborist" radicals held back, he straightforwardly advocated a state takeover of public (i.e., private) schools like his own Eton. Finally, and most important, the transfer of power, he argued, required a more direct and continuous control by the people over their government. What institutional arrangements might make this possible, Orwell didn't say; he would no more have abolished Parliament than he would have shut down the local pub. He meant only to bring the two into some closer contact.

His democratic commitments are best revealed by his literary and cultural interests. Consider, for example, his enthusiasm for the pamphlet (he was a collector and anthologist as well as an occasional author), which Alex Zwerdling nicely contrasts with Auden's reluctant readiness to "expend his powers" (but did he ever actually make the expenditure?) on "the flat ephemeral pamphlet."[30] This is the more common attitude among literary intellectuals whose true ambition, I suppose, is never to write anything ephemeral. But the ephemeral pamphlet, Orwell believed, is the concession one makes to a lively politics and a mass audience. A pamphleteering intelligentsia, writing in a plain English and aiming to reach that audience, would be connected to the people in a way that Orwell thought exemplary. Here is another "dim, elegaic echo of Defoe and the early years of middle-class ascendency." Such connections had once existed in England; a successful socialism would restore and enlarge them.

But Orwell was always alert to the dangers of an unsuccessful socialism—more alert, his leftist critics might say, than to the dangers of an established capitalism. He has, in fact, little to say about capitalism. Though he recognized its political strength, he assumed its failure as a productive system, and his program for an economic succession was the standard left program of his time: "nationalization of land, mines, railways, banks, and major industries" (this is from *The Lion and the Unicorn*).[31] He was more concerned, however, to argue that nationalization would only bring new forms of oligarchy and privilege unless it was accompanied by "a fundamental shift in power." Not a shift from capitalists to state bureaucrats: that would not be fundamental, since the same people or the same sort of people, educated in the same schools, would fill both categories. For Orwell, a fundamental shift required a democratic revolution. Much of his critical writing was aimed at the two groups that he thought might obstruct or usurp such a revolution once the capitalists had been defeated—the political and technical intelligentsias, the masters of ideological truth and scientific knowledge. He is a student of James Burnham in this regard, but his argument is very much his own.[32] His social criticism follows his literary criticism; in both he aims at breaking through the barriers of elite culture. Hence his interest in the appeal of good writers like Charles Dickens and of "good bad" writers like Rudyard Kipling across the lines of class and schooling. "The fact that good bad poetry can exist," he says in his essay on Kipling, "is a sign of the emotional overlap between the intellectual and the ordinary man."[33] There is a mental overlap too, and so vanguard ideologies not only should be, but can be, opposed. It's because opposition is possible that the degradation of the proles in *1984* represents such a terrible defeat.

Orwell's hatred of hierarchy, shared in principle by other leftists, also expressed itself as a fear, hardly shared at all, that one set of inegalitarian arrangements would merely be replaced by another—and this in the name of socialism. And so he was a critic of oppositional as well as of established elites, more savage, perhaps, in his criticism of the first than of the second, not only because the opposition was nearer to hand but also because he thought it was going to win. What separates him from other "laborist" radicals is his intense uneasiness about that victory and his constant irritation with advanced ideas that served only, he thought, to feed the pride of the few. He was, says Zwerdling, "an internal critic of socialism."[34] Writers like Williams deny the internality and see in the criticism only Orwell's obsession with totalitarian politics—as if this wasn't an obvious and necessary socialist obsession in the age of Stalin. Anyway, that is only part of the story, not the whole of it. Orwell's internal critique begins before his obsession;

it begins at the beginning, in his first socialist book, *The Road to Wigan Pier*. He worried even then that socialism might reproduce the old hierarchy in a new form, that it might mean nothing more than "a set of reforms which 'we,' the clever ones, are going to impose upon 'them,' the Lower Orders."[35] The clever ones are the products of the old regime, not of Ingsoc but of bourgeois society. Orwell knew them well, and when he attacked them, he evoked their own putative commitment to the central values of the bourgeois revolution: freedom and equality.

These were also the values of the English working class. They had penetrated, he wrote in his essay on Dickens, "to all ranks of society."[36] That's why Orwell could be a patriot and still, in his own fashion, a revolutionary. And that's why his criticism of the hegemonic culture is never so wholesale as to satisfy Raymond Williams—and why, again, his criticism of popular culture and working-class "common sense" entirely lacks Gramsci's ideological edge. Orwell was, nonetheless, the very model of a "national-popular" intellectual; perhaps for that reason he sensed that a democratic politics was more readily available, more immanent in English life, than any Marxist analysis could allow. At the same time, he worried that the defeat of democratic politics might open the way for a hegemony far worse than anything the bourgeoisie had ever achieved.

Nightmares

Orwell's essays on Dickens and Kipling, on patriotism and radical politics, on pubs, postcards, and popular culture, belong to his daylight hours. They are sometimes clouded but never dark. Totalitarianism is his nightmare. By day, Orwell is an Englishman; at night, he is a European, fully responsive to a range of experience from which England had been shielded. In an essay on Arthur Koestler, written in 1944, he argued that the twentieth-century English were virtually incapable of serious political writing; they had produced no equivalent of Ignazio Silone, André Malraux, Gaetano Salvemini, Franz Borkenau, Victor Serge, or even Arthur Koestler (to whom they gave refuge but did not really understand). They suffered from their own good fortune: "There is almost no English writer to whom it has happened to see totalitarianism from the inside . . . England is lacking, therefore, in what one might call concentration camp literature. The special world created by secret police forces, censorship of opinion, torture, and frame-up trials is, of course, known about and to some extent disapproved of, but it has made very little emotional impact."[37] Almost no English writer: Orwell himself is the exception, partly because of his months in Spain, partly because of a remarkable imaginative effort sustained over a number of years, which turned out to be his last years. He made himself into a European writer and produced the first, virtually the only, English examples of the political *roman noir*.

Raymond Williams's judgment of these dark novels, as if by perverse design, bears out Orwell's claim about the failure of English political writing. "As for *1984*," Williams told the editors of *New Left Review*, "its projections of ugliness and hatred . . . onto the difficulties of revolution or political change, seem to introduce a period of really decadent bourgeois writing in which the whole status of human beings is reduced."[38] "The difficulties of revolution" invites comparison to Auden's "the necessary murder"—a line that could never have been written, Orwell rightly said, by anyone who had ever seen a man murdered. So Williams's line could never have been written by anyone who had actually experienced those "difficulties." It represents a refusal to respond, intellectually or emotionally, to the central events of the twentieth century.

What is the political meaning of Orwell's response? Not, surely, to close off all hope of democratic or socialist success: nightmares threaten to do that but don't finally do it; one wakes up sweating and goes on with daytime life. But Orwell did want to make English socialists sweat. The description of totalitarian politics has often had a conservative intention; its purpose is to turn the minds of one's fellow citizens toward horrors far away, so that local faults look like mere blemishes and efforts to deal with them seem overly zealous. The horrific description is curiously comforting. It is hard, indeed, not to produce effects like that whatever one's purpose, but that was not what Orwell had in mind. He thought that Western socialism could not succeed unless its defenders recognized *and learned to worry about* what was happening in the East. *Animal Farm* and *1984* were part of his "internal critique."

It is an interesting question whether one can be a social critic of someone else's society. By now, Orwell has become an honorary East European, and his books have been incorporated into the literature of resistance. But he himself aimed only at local effects: "Even if I had the power, I would not wish to interfere in Soviet domestic affairs. . . . But on the other hand it was of the utmost importance to me that people in western Europe should see the Soviet regime for what it really was . . . for the past ten years I have been convinced that the destruction of the Soviet myth was essential if we wanted a revival of the socialist movement." This is from the preface to the Ukrainian edition of *Animal Farm*.[39] Among Orwell's Ukrainian readers the destruction of the Soviet myth had been accomplished long before; they would put the book to other uses, and Orwell has nothing to say about what those uses might be. As he wrote on an earlier occasion: "What I am concerned with is the attitude of the British intelligentsia. . . ."[40]

I don't think that Orwell feared—not in his daylight hours anyway—the internal transformation of English socialism into Ingsoc. Bureaucratic aggrandizement and elite presumption might generate new inequalities, but nothing quite so drastic as the inequality of proles and party members. English culture as he himself described it had strong built-in defenses against that sort of thing. The overt argument of *1984*, nonetheless, is that *it can happen here*: immunity is an illusion. Totalitarian politics had an international logic; it invited, perhaps even compelled, imitation. And so the experience of total war and then of ideological cold war could, over time, produce repression at home, against the grain of English decency. That's why Orwell was so radically unwilling to leave socialism in the hands of men and women who talked too quickly about "necessary" murders. Nor would he have been willing to leave it in the hands of men and women who thought of Stalinist crimes as "difficulties" encountered in the course of the revolutionary process. He insisted that English intellectuals face those crimes, name them, imaginatively experience them. The "neo-gothic torture scenes in Room 101," sometimes taken as a sign of Orwell's final illness, a loss of literary control, have instead a firm political intention.[41] They enlist the fears and fantasies of the reader in an act of recognition: this is what politics in the twentieth century can come to, has come to in countries that are not, after all, so far away.

One senses in *1984* a barely contained fury at the complacency of English leftists, still sleeping England's deep sleep. Even the bombs had not awakened them, for those were Nazi bombs, right-wing bombs, as it were, and required no confrontation with the crimes of the left. It was still possible, in England, "to be anti-fascist without being anti-totalitarian"—the "sin" of leftist intellectuals since the early thirties.[42] Given the sin, *1984* is the punishment. To make sure the punishment hurt, Orwell named the totalitarian regime of Airstrip One "Ingsoc," though he must have known to what uses the name would be put. It is not so much that he wanted English socialists to have minds free of sin (their hands were free enough: they had not actually committed any "necessary" murders). He wanted them to have comprehending minds; he wanted them to understand, even if the politics he described defied complete understanding. "I can understand HOW," says Winston Smith, "I do not understand WHY."[43]

But the novel seems to reject the idea that understanding might open the way to an alternative politics. That, according to Williams, is Orwell's final betrayal. The vision is too grim, denying any hope of resistance; there are no positive heroes. Indeed, there aren't; both *Animal Farm* and *1984* are fables, not tracts or programs. What they describe is the nightmare of the boot pressing down on the human face . . . forever. Nightmares would not be what they are if they marched toward some upbeat ending. They inspire fear, not hope. *1984* particularly is a novel of absolute bleakness, not so much a reduction of humankind as a refusal of political comfort, an unremitting portrait of totalitarianism in its own terms. And yet, Orwell's purpose in writing the book was surely to inspire opposition: disgust with the apologists, hatred for the dictators. He tells the story of Winston Smith, "the last man in Europe," to other men and women in whose power it is to deny that finality. The positive hero of the book is its author—and, possibly, its reader.

"The book appalls us," writes Irving Howe, "because its terror, far from being inherent in the 'human condition,' is particular to our century; what haunts us is the sickening awareness that in *1984* Orwell has seized upon those elements of our public life that, given courage and intelligence, were avoidable."[44] Are avoidable: since "England, Your England" is not yet Airstrip One. Orwell's England has only a dim presence in *1984*, symbolized by the old jingle, which Winston Smith can't quite remember, about the bells of St. Clement's. But we remember, we know intimately, the life and values that Ingsoc obliterates and to which Orwell consistently appeals. Writing *1984* was not an act of closure. Orwell undoubtedly felt the pressure of his illness, and that may have added to the urgency with which he wrote. But he was not dead yet; nor had he withdrawn from the world in order to pronounce a final judgment upon it. He meant to write again. The story of the last man was not intended to be his last word on politics. Nor need it be ours, so long as we speak with the terrifying awareness that was his gift.

8

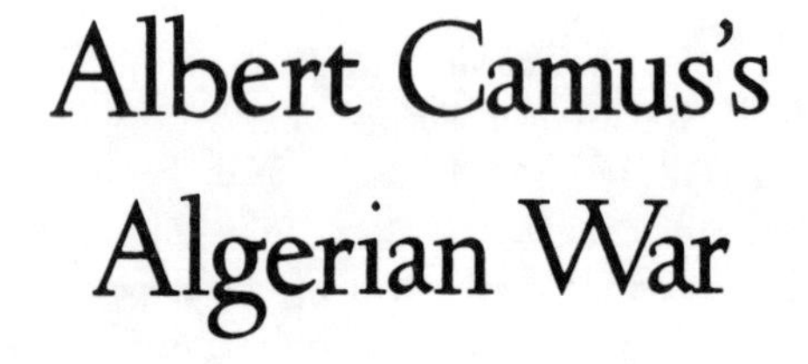

Albert Camus's Algerian War

A Just Man?

For men and women of the liberal and democratic left, Albert Camus is an exemplary figure. His writing and his life, both of them enhanced, perhaps, by his early and senseless death, have taken on mythic proportions, so that we can plausibly feel that we know him well even without knowing much about him. We know what he stood for: he was a man of principle, a "just man." (We also know, because of Herbert Lottman's recent biography,[1] what he did every Monday, Tuesday, and Wednesday; oddly, that doesn't dispel the myth, any more than it reveals the inner man.) But there is one moment in his life when Camus is commonly said to have betrayed his principles—an all-important and long-drawn-out moment, dominating the last years of his life: the moment of the Algerian war. Here he became "that just man without justice," described by Simone de Beauvoir in her memoirs; austere urgency collapsing, says Conor Cruise O'Brien, into hollow rhetoric.[2] From 1954 on, he provides an example only of the inability of the "moderate bourgeoisie" of France (O'Brien's phrase) to come to grips with the brutality of colonialism. Even this failure serves, in a way, to sustain the myth: it makes Camus into a disfigured hero, human, all-too-human. But how exactly did he fail?

I want to reconsider Camus's Algerian moment, to defend him against his critics and at the same time to free him from the bonds of myth. I don't think that Camus was a hero in the 1950s—he may have been a hero in the 1940s—and I don't much like the phrase "just man," which suggests a moral absolutism that he explicitly repudiated. More accurate to say that he was a good man; in a bad time he did better than most of his fellows. He was also a working intellectual, a radical critic, who faced the hardest choices and who flinched sometimes but didn't walk away. And that is why we can learn from his experience something about the obligations and limits of the critical enterprise.

Against Maps

Man of letters and *moraliste*, Camus represents an old French tradition. An honorable tradition but not without its temptations, the greatest of which is the god-like pronouncement, the voice from offstage. Like many others, Camus sometimes succumbed, but he was programmatically committed to resist. If we stand sufficiently apart, he admits, we can indeed see the moral world much as God must see the physical world. "There is no more nature," Camus wrote in his notebook after a plane flight from Paris to Algiers; "the deep gorge, true relief, the impassable mountain stream, everything disappears. There remains *a diagram*—a map. Man, in short, looks through the eyes of God. And he perceives then that God can have but an abstract view. This is not a good thing."[3] It is no better in ethical life than in geography. As true relief requires contact and closeness, so true morality requires involvement and love. And yet love fits uneasily into a general moral theory, for it always favors the near and the few. "Love is injustice," Camus wrote, "but justice is not enough."[4] This tension is one of the reiterated themes of the *Notebooks* during the years of Camus's "second cycle," when he was writing *The Plague*, *The Just Assassins*, and *The Rebel*. He attempted different formulations, always maintaining an antinomy that he might better have avoided by saying simply that a justice without room for love would be itself unjust. I think that is what he believed; it is what his critics commonly deny.

Camus's response to the Algerian war has been criticized in two different ways. He has been blamed, first, for a failure of concreteness, for the very abstraction he hated, a rigid universalism. High-mindedly, he applies the same standards to oppressors and oppressed alike, without regard to their actual circumstances. And he has been blamed, second, for a failure of distance, for sentimentality and an unrestrained particularism. Low-mindedly, he defends his friends and relatives. But the two charges are really one. The fundamental criticism is that Camus's universalist pronouncements are only a cover for his particularism; talk about justice masks a merely local love. "The humanist in him," de Beauvoir wrote in her autobiography, "had given way to the *pied noir*."[5] Hence, the hollowness of his rhetoric—the stylistic sign of bad faith.

Rereading *Actuelles III*, Camus's Algerian chronicle, it is hard to see the bad faith. Moral anxiety lies right on the surface of the reprinted articles and speeches; universalism and particularism, justice and love are equally in evidence; nothing is concealed. These are essays in negotiation, the work of a social critic continually aware of the on-the-ground obstacles that the map of right and wrong only inadequately represents. His opponents are critics of a different sort, who maneuver by the moral (perhaps better, the ideological) map. The two are distinguished not merely by their conclusions but by the way they set about their work, by the way they locate themselves among their fellows. Before taking a stand one must find a standpoint. Where? Too close, say Camus's opponents, and one becomes an apologist; too far, Camus responds, and one becomes a terrorist. We see once again the centrality of distance, which is at issue every time an intellectual is accused of betrayal.

An excerpt from Camus's *Notebooks*, 1942: "Calypso offers Ulysses a choice between immortality and the land of his birth. He rejects immortality. Therein lies perhaps the whole meaning of the *Odyssey*."[6] The common view of Camus is similar. He had to choose between eternal justice and French Algeria, and he rejected eternal justice. Maybe so; it is certainly true that he never rejected French Algeria. He was indeed a *pied noir*, born and raised in Algeria; he learned to write in Algeria, and he never wrote more lyrically than when he wrote about the sun and sea of his native land. "For Algeria . . . I have unbridled passion, and I surrender to the pleasure of loving."[7] The only authentic example of Camusian nonsense is provided by his many pages (most of them written early on) about Mediterranean culture—an imaginary world of classical "measure" that neither Camus's own people nor the Arabs of Algeria ever gave any sign of inhabiting.

It can hardly be said, then, that Camus is an objective critic of French colonialism. One might well prefer someone from Japan or Iceland or, even better, someone from Mars, an impartial spectator or ideal observer for whom critical distance is not, so we might suppose, a problem. But such people are unlikely to take an interest in French colonialism. God is the ideal "ideal observer," and it is a commonplace of the philosophical tradition that He is chiefly interested in observing Himself. In any case, His omniscience is in the service of abstraction, and He is likely to miss the deep gorges and impassable mountain streams. What we really want is a social critic who emerges out of his own society. Someone who is inside, connected, emotionally close, must learn to draw a line, take a stand, say *no*. How to do that?

The Detachment of Sartre and de Beauvoir

Writing in 1965, very much in the shadow of the Algerian war, Sartre argued that the only way to learn to say no to one's fellow citizens was through "perpetual self-criticism."[8] The life of a social critic must begin with the rejection of his own socialization, the refusal of society-in-himself. He can't just deny that he is a petty-bourgeois intellectual or a *pied noir* or whatever, leap into universality, and take his stand on Benda's heights; he must acknowledge his conditioned self and then subject it to an unrelenting analysis and critique. It isn't entirely clear who the analyst is here and who the analysand. In theory, the same petty-bourgeois intellectual, the same *pied noir*, functions in both roles: a strenuous business, though not impossible. In practice, however, the analysis and criticism are more likely to be aimed at one's fellow intellectuals or *pieds noirs*—not at oneself but at the ones who look like oneself. The purpose of the exercise is differentiation.

This can sometimes take slightly comic forms, as in de Beauvoir's announcement, after the overwhelming popular vote endorsing Charles de Gaulle's return to power in 1958, that she was no longer a member of the French people: "The result of the referendum had severed the last threads linking me to my country."[9] Nothing in her life seems to have changed in the years afterward. Of course, the severing of threads had begun much earlier, and I suppose one can say that it began with self-criticism, though self-criticism of a very special sort: "I could no longer bear my fellow citizens. . . . I couldn't sit down near them anymore. . . . I felt as dispossessed as I had when the Occupation began. It was even worse, because, whether I wanted to be or not, I was an accomplice of these people." Or again: "All those people in the streets . . . they were all murderers. Myself as well. 'I'm French.' The words scalded my throat like an admission of hideous deformity."[10] But it isn't *her own* deformity that de Beauvoir is describing in these passages.

I don't mean to mock Simone de Beauvoir; her autobiography is wonderfully lively and open-hearted. Though she is a very sophisticated writer, as we will see, her politics is always artless—which Camus's never was. The shame she expresses over Algeria and the pathology of shame that she also expresses both find their echo on the American left during the Vietnam years. I only want to suggest that such feelings are not the precondition, they are the result, of social criticism. It's not that one cuts the threads in order to become a critic, but that the force of one's criticism leads one to think about cutting the threads. Criticism will falter and fail, however, if the threads are really cut, for the social critic must have standing among his fellow citizens. He exploits his connections, as it were, not his disconnections. If he hates his fellows and breaks his ties, why should they pay attention to what he says?

That last is not only a prudential but also a moral point, and I want to develop it briefly before asking again how social criticism properly begins. The bourgeois social critic, Sartre says, must escape his own conditioning. But he doesn't then enter into a world of universal principles. He must first "universalize" himself; criticizing his past, he must join in a political struggle that projects universal principles into the future: so he transforms himself even as he transforms the world. More simply, he must consult the moral map and cross the border that separates oppressors like himself from the mass of the oppressed. He must undertake, says Sartre, "a concrete and unconditioned alignment with . . . the underprivileged classes."[11] This doesn't require going to live and work among the underprivileged. Like the schoolmaster Daru in Camus's fine short story "The Guest," one can do that without making anything like an "unconditioned" commitment. What Sartre has in mind is a shift in political position, not in social location. Still, it is something close to a new life that the critic must create for himself, and the creation is hard.

How is he to live? Who are his comrades? He can never be assimilated on the other side of the border; however fierce his self-criticism, he cannot be born again as an organic intellectual of the working class. And so he is tempted to "pass," making up in zeal what he lacks in familiarity and ease. Sartre hopes that the committed intellectual will "never renounce his critical faculties," but this is a matter of some difficulty, touch and go, for his critical faculties are the product of his social conditioning. Radically desocialized, he is a candidate for ideological discipline: hence (as Silone and Orwell argued) the appeal of the Communist party. Sartre himself, de Beauvoir too, avoided party discipline, though it can't be said that they gave their critical faculties free rein. It is to their credit that party hacks, whose alignment was really unconditioned, always thought them to be petty-bourgeois intellectuals. In the case of the Algerian war, however, they made the more radical move recommended by the Sartrean program: guiltily, they separated themselves from the French people, and they supported the Algerian National Liberation Front (FLN), so far as I can see, without a word of criticism.

Of course, they did not go to Algiers and plant bombs in cafes and dance halls. They supported such actions from a distance. Despite the "severance" of their links with France, they remained at home, where they were resolute and sometimes courageous critics of their own government. So far as France is concerned, they fit the standard model of the social critic; they detached themselves (intellectually, morally) and denounced the local barbarians—and condemned Camus for refusing to join their denunciations. But though much that they said was true, there was much that they failed to say, and their failures were closely connected to the radical character of their "self-criticism." Detachment had its cost. A small cost, perhaps, if one conceives of human life in existentialist terms: the petty-bourgeois intellectual, aspiring to be the author of himself, invents himself as a social critic. It is a heroic project, and the result is the familiar heroic figure, standing apart from his fellows, bound to his critical principles. But then, like God, he can only take an abstract view.

Wrenched loose from bourgeois France, unable to become Algerians,

Sartre and de Beauvoir see an ideologically flattened world. The FLN represents liberation, the French are fascists. Political choices are extraordinarily easy, a direct function of critical distance. "The lives of Moslems were of no less importance in my eyes," writes de Beauvoir, "than those of my fellow countrymen."[12] In fact, there is little evidence that she attached much importance to any particular lives. Terrorist attacks on French civilians left her unconcerned; and she was outraged by Algerian deaths only when they were caused by the French (there were, no doubt, enough of those to provoke anyone's outrage). She knew about the brutality of the FLN's internal wars but chose not to write about it; she seems never to have given a thought to the likely fate of the *pied noir* community after an FLN victory. So her hard-won impartiality slides into a cold indifference. For all her passion, she writes without the complexity of love. Reading her account of her Algerian years, one feels the force of E. M. Forster's injunction: "Only connect!"

The Difficulties of Connection

Though he is said to have been cool and aloof in personal relations, Camus was a connected social critic. Moreover, he was connected in a way that tests the theory of critical distance—to a group that benefited, or that thought it benefited, from the oppression of others. In the Marxist scheme, a *pied noir* intellectual was exactly like a bourgeois intellectual: Camus belonged, wrote Albert Memmi in 1957, "to a minority which is historically in the wrong."[13] Memmi, a Tunisian Jew whose people had also benefited from French colonialism, was not entirely unsympathetic. But the standard left argument is simple and straightforward: that kind of "belonging" must be repudiated. It turns out that the repudiation is easier in the case of class membership than in the case of nationality, for the nation is commonly the deeper tie. Camus, born among the poor, had no difficulty criticizing the wealthy elite of the *pied noir* community. It was much harder for him to take Memmi's view and describe the entire community as somehow "in the wrong." No more could he accept Frantz Fanon's description, which underlies and rationalizes the terrorism of the FLN: "The Frenchman in Algeria cannot be neutral or innocent. Every Frenchman . . . oppresses, despises, dominates."[14] On this view, social criticism from within is literally impossible; the *pied noir* intellectual must make himself over—first into a detached observer and then into a supporter of Algerian liberation. But the historicism and collectivism of these arguments are further examples of abstract morality. They miss the texture of moral life.

In 1939, the young Camus visited the Kabyle Mountains and wrote (for a socialist newspaper in Algiers) a series of articles on the suffering of the Berbers and the indifference of the colonial regime. The articles, the most important of which are reprinted in *Actuelles III*, constitute a powerful piece of social criticism, and they led, a year later, to Camus's "exile" from Algeria. His "cry of indignation," Jules Roy later wrote, made him "suspect in the eyes of the authorities."[15] But though the articles required a physical journey that few *pied noir* journalists undertook, they did not require that Camus stop being a *pied noir* journalist. Independence was necessary, perhaps courage, but not the repudiation of national identity: he simply applied the standards of the French left—the putative standards, indeed, of the colonial regime—to the case of Kabylia. This is the simplest and most direct form of social criticism; the critic lifts the veil, exposes the actual experience of oppression; the remaining critical work is done, so to speak, by the mores. Camus went on to call for a redistribution of land, technical assistance on a large scale, local self-government, equal rights for all the inhabitants of Algeria.[16] He did not call for an end to French rule, but his program was very close to that of the Algerian nationalists of the thirties, who were themselves francophile—their faces turned toward Paris, their politics revolutionary only in the sense of 1789. These Algerians were aliens-at-home, living in a colonial limbo, and they would become effective nationalists only when they reinvented their politics in an Algerian (Islamic, Arab) context. But Camus was not an alien, even though he would soon leave his homeland.

The social critic works from principles naturalized in his own society. He applies those principles with a stringency that makes his fellow citizens uncomfortable: hence he often finds himself alone and may well come to admire himself for being alone. "*Le vrai intellectuel est un solitaire.*"[17] But he doesn't begin by cutting himself off; nor need he embrace and cultivate his solitude. He has his own obligations and loyalties. Camus's description of the intellectual makes better sense than Benda's: *solitaire et solidaire*, apart and united. "After all," he wrote mockingly of the ancient argument about rootedness and nomadism, "we need a native soil and we need travel."[18] Even "true intellectuals" have parents, friends, familiar places, warm memories. Perfect solitude, like existential heroism, is a romantic idea, and it is closely connected to another romantic idea: the absolute opposition between art, philosophy, and moral value, on the one hand, and ordinary life, mundane concern, "bourgeois society," on the other. As if the critic plucks his principles from the sky! In bad times, it is precisely the principles of ordinary life that need to be asserted. "The values I ought to defend and illustrate today," Camus wrote in his notebook in October 1946, "are average values. This requires a talent so spare and unadorned that I doubt I have it."[19]

Camus's prose is sometimes too elevated, too "noble," to capture average values. Here he resembled Martin Buber, despite the radical difference in their self-presentation: *résistant* with a cigarette, bearded prophet. Both men were capable of sentences more full of portent than their occasions warranted, though the occasions were serious enough. But the two had another problem, more pressing for Camus than for Buber. The values Camus wanted to defend were shared only formally—in practice they were rejected—by the overwhelming majority of his own people. The rejection was visible already in 1945, at the time of the Sétif rising and the savage French repression, and it was a permanent presence in Camus's life from 1954 on. After Sétif, he returned to Algeria and wrote for *Combat* a second series of articles, denouncing the repression and calling again for absolute equality: France must demonstrate its commitment "to export to Algeria the democratic regime that [its own citizens] enjoy." "Nothing French will be saved in North Africa . . . unless justice is saved."[20] But the export of democracy was pressed only half-heartedly from Paris and vehemently opposed by *pied noir* spokesmen. What then did justice require?

In the case of the other North African colonies, Morocco and Tunisia, the argument was easy. As soon as there were serious and organized demands for independence, independence had to be granted. That was the meaning, and the inevitable result, of exporting democracy—even if the export was effective only for that one moment when the people of the two colonies voted for freedom and simultaneously submitted themselves to new masters. But the case was different in Algeria where over a million Europeans had settled. In effect, there were two nations in Algeria, and it was not clear that they could both be free. From the beginning of its revolt, in 1954, the FLN demanded independence and full sovereignty. Camus, in all his writings, resisted this demand, for he understood that independence under FLN leadership meant the destruction of the *pied noir* community. Sometimes he expressed his resistance in terms of the simple antimony of justice and love that I have already cited from the *Notebooks*. His most famous statement on Algeria had exactly this form: "I believe in justice, but I will defend my mother before justice."[21] He said this to a group of students in Stockholm in 1957, when he received the Nobel Prize, and some of his friends have treated it as an offhand remark, a passionate but unreflective outburst. He repeated it later on, it is said, only because of the stir it created and the attacks from opponents on the left—who wrote as if they didn't have mothers or wouldn't think of defending them. But that remark, like all Camus's Algerian arguments, is prefigured in the *Notebooks*, and its repetition is of a piece with the preface to *Actuelles III*. One might well ask, however, whether a solution to the problems of Algeria that ignored Camus's mother or the interests of the *pied noir* community generally could possibly be just. Men and women don't lose their rights even if they are "historically in the wrong."

Certainly, when he canvassed the possible alternatives to independence, Camus was in search of justice, looking for an outcome that would respect the identity, the interests, the political aspirations of the two Algerian nations. "The 'French fact' cannot be eliminated in Algeria, and the dream of a sudden disappearance of France is childish. But there is no reason either why nine million Arabs should live on their land like forgotten men; the dream that the Arab masses can be cancelled out, silenced and subjugated, is just as mad."[22] After 1954, these two forms of madness were at war with one another, and it was Camus's proposals for equality and federation that looked increasingly dreamlike. Madness was practical, moral sanity utopian. The terrorist campaign against civilians signaled the FLN's commitment to eliminate the "French fact," and the extensive use of torture signaled the French commitment to "silence and subjugate" the Arabs. There was no choice, many French leftists argued, but to choose the least mad, the most just, of these alternatives. And it was when he refused to choose that Camus was charged with the crime he finally embraced—the crime of love, expressed now in terms of brothers rather than mothers: ". . . if anyone still thinks heroically that one's brother must die rather than one's principles, I shall go no further than to admire him from a distance. I am not of his stamp."[23]

He refused to cut himself loose from his *pied noir* relatives. Living in France, he still wrote about Algeria from close up. "He remained in fact a Frenchman of Algeria," writes O'Brien, and as time went on he came increasingly "to take the side of his own tribe against the abstract entities." He distanced himself not from his local setting and particular interests but from the universal values "that had hitherto dominated his language."[24] Camus's lines about his mother and his brother lend support to this view, but I think that it is, as I have suggested but not yet argued, fundamentally misconceived. From the beginning to the end, Camus displayed the same commitment to particularity; he was always drawn to the projections and gradations of "true relief." And his universalism was similarly consistent, though it took a shape that O'Brien did not recognize: it was constructed out of repeated particularities; it worked by what I have called reiteration, not by abstraction.

Camus would not have said, for example, that French and Arab lives were of equal importance in his eyes. French lives, even *pied noir* lives, on the wrong side of history, meant more to him—just as Arab lives meant more to the intellectuals of the FLN (though this latter point, it has to be said, was not always apparent: Camus was committed to particular people, the FLN intellectuals to a cause). Morality required the mutual acceptance, not the abolition or transcendence, of these different meanings. The Frenchman had his own loyalties, and so did the Arab; and each had a right to his own. Similarly, Camus's first commitment was to self-determination for the *pied noir* community, but he understood that the first commitment of the Arabs was to their own self-determination. The two commitments were equally legitimate, and the conflict between them could not be resolved by abstract reasoning (or by counting heads). Detach oneself, step back, step farther back; still the shape of a just settlement did not come into view. What justice required was that the French and the Arabs negotiate their differences. All Camus's schemes had this purpose: to find a formula sufficiently plausible to guide the negotiations. He never succeeded in doing this—"these reports," he wrote in the preface to *Actuelles III*, "are . . . the record of a failure"—but that is not to say that he was wrong to try.[25]

The attempt was especially urgent because what was at stake was the very existence of the *pied noir* community. This did not lead Camus, as long as he continued to write about Algeria, to temper his criticism of French policies, but it did make it impossible for him to line up, as Sartre and de Beauvoir did, with the enemies of the French. Nor was he willing to sign political manifestoes along with French supporters of the FLN. "It seemed to me both indecent and harmful to protest against tortures in the company of those who readily accepted . . . the mutilation of European children."[26] But there was also a more general point here. In his *Notebooks*, in late 1947 or early 1948, Camus had copied out the exclamation of a Russian émigré of the nineteenth century: "What a delight to hate one's native land and to long for its collapse." His comment: "the intelligentsia and the *totalitarian* interpretation of the world."[27] He returned to the same theme in his 1958 preface: "We could have used moralists less joyfully resigned to their country's misfortunes."[28] The joy derives from radical detachment and from the "totalitarian" understanding of ordinary people and everyday life that detachment facilitates: looked at from far enough away, we are all wretched sinners, historically in the wrong, ideologically corrupt, and the moralist can only rejoice at our discomfort. (But why at *our* discomfort and not *theirs*? Totalitarianism doesn't explain the reflexive turn of moral anger.)

Camus by contrast shaped his politics out of his primary loyalties:

> When one's own family is in immediate danger of death, one may want to instill in one's family a feeling of greater generosity and fairness . . . but (let there be no doubt about it!) one still feels a natural solidarity with the family in such mortal danger and hopes that it will survive at least and, by surviving, have a chance to show its fairness.[29]

And at this point he explicitly denied the antimony of love and justice, tribe and universe: "If that is not honor and *true justice*, then I know nothing that is of any use in this world." True justice must include one's own people, though not necessarily on their own terms. The terms have to be negotiated, and clearly the French would have had to accept a radical redistribution of land, wealth, and power; they would have had to give up the false universalism of "Frenchness"—"the perennial lie of constantly proposed but never realized assimilation"—and acknowledge Arab particularity.[30] Already in 1945, in his *Combat* articles, Camus had recognized that the great majority of Arabs did not want to become French citizens: there was an Arab nation ("*je voudrais rappeler aussi que le peuple arabe existe*").[31] There was also a French nation. The two would have to coexist, and the coexistence would require complicated arrangements of a sort incompatible with the currently favored principles of political life: state sovereignty and legal uniformity.

It is curious that Camus never considered the partition of Algeria, the only solution that was compatible with those principles and with the self-determination of the two communities—compatible also with Camus's assertion (in 1958) that "the way to human society passes through national society."[32] The pattern of French settlement probably made partition seem even more difficult than coexistence within a federated state. And I suspect that Camus had another reason for supporting federation: he saw it as a particular instance of the pluralism to which he was increasingly drawn. "Here as in every domain, I believe only in differences and not in uniformity."[33] Nor was this, in his view, merely the creed of a threatened minority; it was what justice (liberty too) required.

Silence and Defeat

After 1958, Camus wrote no more about Algeria. In the last two years of his life, years of rising opposition to the war among the French in France and increasing right-wing fanaticism among the French in Algeria, he was silent. He has been much blamed for his silence, and perhaps the blame is justified: what is the use, after all, of a silent intellectual? But it might be said that Camus's silence was eloquent in its hopelessness. Unlike Buber ten years earlier, he had reached a dead end. Every day it became more apparent that there was no chance of preserving, or of reforming and renewing, the Algeria of his youth. He could not join Sartre and de Beauvoir in supporting the FLN; nor could he support the *pied noir* ultras, committed now, to the point of no return, to policies he had opposed all his life. De Gaulle maneuvered between the two, but that was, however necessary, a politician's, not an intellectual's task. In effect, says O'Brien, Camus supported the government's policies, at least up to the point at which de Gaulle made his deal with the FLN; but by that time Camus was dead. He did not live to see the final spasm of Secret Army (OAS) violence, after which it was politically, if not morally, impossible for the *pieds noirs* to remain in Algeria. The FLN victory would have made it impossible anyway, as he foresaw. Should he have broken his silence and told his people that the struggle was over, that they had to leave? Maybe so, though there is also something to be said for Camus's claim "that too much is expected of a writer in such matters."[34]

In 1961, a year after Camus's death, his friend Jules Roy, another *pied noir* writer, published a powerful indictment of the French war. The last chapter, calling for immediate negotiations with the FLN, is a tense and passionate argument with Camus. Roy shares his friend's commitment to the reiteration of justice: for the Arabs, and for the French too. "I want to render justice on one side without stripping it from the other. But I respect an order of precedence: I move first to the injustice that cries out in pain, since the other for the moment constitutes only an hypothesis."[35] The war is a catastrophe in progress; the exile of the *pied noir* community is a catastrophe "that has not happened." It is clear from Roy's book that he doesn't believe it will happen; he lacked Camus's political realism. But his sense of precedence was almost certainly right—especially after the bloody (and as it turned out pointless) "pacification" campaigns of de Gaulle's first years in power. Camus's argument against the use of torture during the battle of Algiers applies also to the brutalities of pacification: "Even those who are fed up with morality ought to realize that it is better to suffer certain injustices than to commit them even to win wars . . . such fine deeds inevitably lead to the demoralization of France and the loss of Algeria."[36]

The fine deeds did lead to demoralization and loss, and perhaps Camus, had he lived, would have joined Jules Roy in calling for negotiations with the FLN and, in effect, acknowledging the loss of French Algeria. "As for your choice," says Roy to his dead friend, "I cannot doubt that it would have been like my own, at the cost of what anguish!"[37] At least, Camus would have known that something had been lost. He could not have written about the outcome of the war in O'Brien's easy tone: "Politically, Camus and his tribe . . . were casualties of the post-war period."[38] They were also victims of an absolutist politics with which we should not make our peace.

The Analogy with Intimacy

Camus's anti-absolutist politics depends not on critical distance but on critical connection. And so it invites us once again to doubt the standard view of the social critic as someone who breaks loose from his particular loyalties and views his own society from the outside—from an ideal point, as it were, equidistant from all societies. If the critic then sides with the oppressed, he does so because he sees their parties and movements as embodying universal principles. Particular men and women he does not see at all. He is like a judge, an activist judge, perhaps, whose judgments are resolutely impersonal. This is a role that Camus explicitly rejected, telling an interviewer in 1953 that his own choice, if he could choose, "would at least be never to sit on a judge's bench . . . like so many of our philosophers."* He would commit himself instead to "the common existence of history and of men, everyday life with the most possible light thrown upon it, the dogged struggle against one's own degradation and that of others."[39]

The order of that last phrase is important. First comes the struggle against one's own degradation and then, by extension, "that of others." Camus is as much a man of honor as a man of principle, and honor begins with personal loyalty, not with ideological commitment. Hence his Algerian politics, which can best be understood as a long, ultimately a failed, struggle against the degradation of the *pied noir* community. The threat came from within as much as from without: that is why he condemned French racism long before FLN terrorism. It's probably fair to say that he hated racism more for what it did to the French than for what it did to the Arabs, but he would have accepted the reversal of that priority in the writing of an Arab intellectual. What he could not accept was the claim that the *pieds noirs* were already degraded, condemned beyond hope of redemption, by their colonial history. That is indeed a view determined by distance, but it doesn't provide a ground for social criticism; it makes social criticism superfluous. On that view, as on Fanon's, there is nothing to do but abandon ship. But Camus conceived the critic as one of the crew, who can't leave before the passengers. "The task of men of culture and faith . . . is not to desert historical struggles. . . . It is rather to remain what they are . . . to favor freedom against the fatalities that close in upon it."[40]

So Camus remained what he was: a *pied noir* writer. Of course, he often found himself standing at some distance from his fellow *pieds noirs*. When he came to Algiers in 1956 to appeal for a "civilian truce," French thugs surrounded the hall in which he was speaking and shouted for his death—while Fanon, inside the hall, was bitterly critical of what he called Camus's

* Compare Bourne's rejection of the role of judge (see chapter 3) and also Breytenbach's (see chapter 12). But doesn't the critic in fact judge his fellows? Why this reluctance to acknowledge what seems an obvious fact? Certainly, Bourne, Camus, and Breytenbach make judgments, but these judgments are never verdicts. Nor are they "like" verdicts; they are argumentative in character and imply no claim to authority. The connected critic has no authority because he has no distance: he has instead, as Bourne writes, "a personal interest in the case."

"sweet sister" speech.* At that moment, and in the years after, Camus occupied a kind of no-man's land. But his homelessness was not self-made; he had set out from inhabited territory, and he longed to reach inhabited territory again. He was *solitaire et solidaire*.

The standard view of critical distance rests on a homely analogy: we are more ready to find fault with other people than with ourselves. If we are to be properly critical, then, we must turn our own people into "the others." We must look at them as if they were total strangers; or we must make ourselves into strangers to them. The trouble with the analogy is that such easy fault-finding is never very effective. It can be brutal enough, but it doesn't touch the conscience of the people to whom it is addressed. The task of the social critic is precisely to touch the conscience. Hence heretics, prophets, insurgent intellectuals, rebels—Camus's kind of rebels—are insiders all: they know the texts and the tender places of their own culture. Criticism is a more intimate activity than the standard view allows. And because it is intimate, it is sometimes reduced to silence, as impersonal judgment never is.

Intimate criticism is a common feature of our private lives; it has its own (implicit) rules. We don't criticize our children, for example, in front of other people, but only when we are alone with them. The social critic has the same impulse, especially when his own people are confronted by hostile forces. "Constantly present in Camus' mind," writes a relatively friendly critic, "was the thought that his mother, his brother, and his friends might be exposed to increased terrorism by words which he could utter without the slightest personal danger to himself."[41] But the social critic can never be alone with his people; there is no social space that is like familial space, and so the critic's intimacy can't take the form of private speech; it can only shape and control his public speech. A certain forbearance qualifies or alternates with his stringency. He must speak, however, and speak out loud, so long as there is any hope that he will be listened to among his own

* "Sweet sister" is like "beautiful soul," a denial of the seriousness of any critic who does not accept the necessary cruelties and deceptions of the political struggle. Curiously, when Fanon writes about his comrades in the FLN, he is himself all sweetness and light, as sure of their ideological advancement as he is of their personal courage. About the internal wars of the FLN he has nothing to say; his articles speak only of democracy and solidarity. But perhaps this is, in his eyes, a necessary deception, the suspension of criticism for the duration of the war. When the critic is hard pressed, should he stop writing or lie in print? See the comment of the Russian dissident Andrei Almaric, quoted by Breyten Breytenbach: "It is always better to be silent than to utter falsehoods" (Breytenbach, *End Papers* [New York: Farrar, Straus and Giroux, 1986], p. 249).

people. The detached and disinterested moralist drones on and on, and we don't care. But the silence of the connected social critic is a grim sign—a sign of defeat, a sign of endings. Though he may not be wrong to be silent, we long to hear his voice.

9

Simone de Beauvoir and the Assimilated Woman

Liberated by Her Subjects

Simone de Beauvoir's intellectual achievement has been obscured by her relationship with Sartre—more accurately, by her own account of that relationship. Writing about the philosophical opinions and political commitments that they shared, she almost always describes herself walking a step or two behind Sartre, sometimes dragging her feet, sometimes hurrying to catch up. She is, for a socialist and a feminist, rather excessively concerned to prove his primacy, as if she is worried that unless the matter is settled, their partnership won't endure. Contemporary feminists, recognizing the anxiety, have been critical of de Beauvoir for expressing it so naively (and critical of Sartre, sometimes, who must have done something to require the expression). A few feminist writers have argued for the originality of her philosophical work, but these arguments always seem to stretch the point; she was at best a Sartrean revisionist, working within his categories even when she resisted his conclusions.[1] And in politics, from the very beginning of their commitment, when he decided for the two of them that commitment was morally necessary, she was a follower: "A radical change had taken place in him," she wrote of Sartre on leave from the French army in 1940, "and in me too since I rallied to his point of view immediately."[2]

As a social critic, however, de Beauvoir undoubtedly comes first. There is nothing in Sartre's wide-ranging work that equals *The Second Sex* or even de Beauvoir's later, and much inferior, *Old Age*. All his life, Sartre was a savage critic of bourgeois society, but what he had to say about the bourgeoisie could have been said by a hundred others, and probably was. De Beauvoir's criticism is more original and at the same time more attentive to her own and other people's actual experience. Her anger is less ideological than Sartre's and more firmly and interestingly focused. And for all his influence, the first of her critical books, *The Second Sex*, has touched more lives and started more arguments than anything he ever wrote.

De Beauvoir's importance has a lot to do with the groups for which she chose to speak: groups not yet mobilized, not represented by organized parties or movements, without militants of their own, without a political "line." When, by contrast, she writes about the French working class or about Algerian nationalists (or about Cubans or Vietnamese or Chinese communists), she seems content to follow Sartre and defer not exactly to the people she was writing about but to their militants and political leaders. She writes with conviction, even passion, but with little intellectual engagement, hence without subtlety. She sounds shrill, fitting herself too easily into a bad stereotype. Her books about women and the elderly, however, are quite different. They are entirely her own—in part because she is herself one of the people she is writing about (she was sixty-two in 1970 when *Old Age* appeared in France), even if she is distanced from the fate of the others; in part because she isn't led to acquiesce, guiltily, in their politics. They have no explicit politics; they are "inert." De Beauvoir was a feminist before there was a significant feminist movement in France, and she was one of the first to recognize elderly men and women as victims of a society fixated on youth, power, and efficiency. She doesn't make the unconditional commitment recommended by Sartre to either of these groups; she doesn't have to do that since she is already a member, and she can't do it since there are no organizations or militants to define the conditions for her. She is set free for creativity by another fact: gender and age are not Marxist categories. From some point in the 1940s or early 1950s, she and Sartre were in principle committed to Marxism as the only adequate framework for social criticism. In *Old Age*, she tries to adapt herself to Marxist doctrine, as Sartre does also in most of his major works after *Being and Nothingness*. But she finds herself compelled to write against the Marxist grain, liberated by her subjects, despite their subjection. Presumably, the oppression of women and the cruel neglect of the elderly will be brought to an end by the triumph of the proletariat: de Beauvoir sometimes repeats this dogma. If she really believed it, however, she would have written a book about the proletariat. Instead, she looked more freshly at the world around her and made a different choice.

Her choice of women as a subject derives, she tells us, from her choice of herself, that is, from her decision to write an autobiographical account of her childhood and youth.[3] But I suspect that the choice also has a philosophical source in her uneasiness with Sartre's conception of freedom. She meant to describe herself in her autobiography as a free human being, but she sensed that her freedom had been won in a different way than Sartre's. It was won, so to speak, against all the odds, despite her female body and the situation of women in her society. She did not share her freedom with other women but with men, and while she relished the sharing, she also understood its problems. So her book is a critique of the unfreedom of women, an unfreedom undreamt of in Sartre's philosophy.[4] But the freedom she defends is the freedom she achieved side by side with him. She assumes that other women should be free, and should want to be free, in just this way. The force of her analysis, but also its difficulties, derive from this crucial assumption, which is at once a sign of generosity and of arrogance. These two qualities made her critique possible at the time she wrote it, in the absence of a feminist movement. They also guaranteed that once there was a movement, the terms of that critique would be called into question. It is said now that she wrote from a male perspective and at too great a distance from the experience of women. That may well be true, but what she wrote reflected her own experience as a woman. Had it not done that, her book would never have had the impact it did on other women; nor would it serve today as the necessary theoretical counterpoint for a different feminism.

Critic of the Female Body

Existentialist ethics is rooted in a peculiarly essentialist claim: that man is by nature free, radically, absolutely, universally free. His life is his project; he makes himself, and he is fully responsible for how he turns out. Any effort to blame anyone else, any reference to external determinations, is an act of bad faith. Planning our future lives, we justify our present selves—and leave ourselves, now and forever, without excuses. "There is no justification for present existence," writes de Beauvoir, faithful here to Sartrean doctrine, "other than its expansion into an indefinitely open future."[5] But is woman's existence justified in the same way? Is the existentialist understanding of our essential humanity gender-neutral? With regard to these questions, *The Second Sex* constitutes, it seems to me, a sustained and brilliant equivocation. On the one hand, de Beauvoir believes that women, herself the prime example, are free exactly as men are, responsible for their own fate; and if most of them are in fact unfree, passive, subordinate, then they are responsible for *that*, complicitous in their own subordination. On the other hand, she believes that women, herself excluded, are doubly oppressed, by nature and by man, victims of their biological condition and their social situation. "I have escaped many of the things that enslave a woman," she told an interviewer in the 1970s, "such as motherhood and the duties of a housewife."[6] Her book, though, is an analysis of the enslavement, not the escape—a grim analysis that piles cause on cause until woman's fate seems overdetermined. But isn't the plea of overdetermination one more act of bad faith?

In her opening chapter, "Destiny: The Data of Biology," de Beauvoir comes very close to the claim that woman is not free, hence not complicitous, not capable of bad faith. She simply is what she is; she never consciously chooses what she will be. Understood as a physical body, a generic sexual being, woman represents the existentialist *en-soi*, being-in-itself, rather than the *pour-soi*, being-for-itself. These are dangerous terms; they suggest the problems of existentialist philosophy as a language of social criticism. For the existentialists seem constitutionally (I mean, because of their doctrine, not because of their bodies) incapable of recognizing the experience of oppression: the literal *pressing down* of a person who, despite the pressure, is still a being-for-herself. Applied socially, the idea of the *en-soi* serves only to replicate the conventional masculine view of gender difference. Or worse, it provides a metaphysical ratification of that view. But de Beauvoir is not concerned to deny the conventions; she wants to explain them and then to find some way to alter the conditions that give rise to them. The first of these conditions, however, is biological. A hard truth, according to de Beauvoir, but one that she will not avoid: the "enslavement" of women has biological foundations. She equivocates on the force of those foundations, not on their reality. Indeed, some of her most vivid prose is devoted to what can best be described as a denunciation of the female body.

Man's body always provides the exemplary contrast. He seems shaped for purposeful activity: "He is . . . larger than the female, stronger, swifter, more adventurous." He is "a being of transcendence and ambition." His body opens for him the opportunity "to take control of the instant and mold the future. It is male activity that in creating values has made of existence itself a value."[7] Woman's body, on the other hand, is shaped for immanence, not transcendence, for repetition rather than invention and adventure. She is designed in the interest of the species, not the individual. She doesn't construct a project; she serves a purpose. "From puberty to menopause woman is the theater of a play that unfolds within her and in which she is not personally concerned." De Beauvoir's portrayal of human reproduction is extraordinary in its savagery—for reproduction on her accounting is cost-free to the male, deadly for the female. "First violated, the female is then alienated . . . tenanted by another, who battens upon her substance."[8] While men contend against nature and one another, "seeking always to exercise . . . sovereignty in objective fashion," women merely reproduce the agents (and the victims) of this exercise: "Giving birth and suckling are not *activities*, they are natural functions; no project is involved, and that is why woman found in them no reason for a lofty affirmation of her existence—she submitted passively to her biologic fate . . . imprisoned in repetition and immanence."[9]

Having said all this, there doesn't seem much point in saying anything more. The detailed ethnography of women's lives, which takes up most of the second half of the book, can be read as a mere extension and elaboration of the biological argument—a passage, as it were, from physical to social anthropology, where the first explains all but the surface variations of the second. De Beauvoir's description of housework, for example, directly parallels her description of childbirth and suckling: "Few tasks are more like the torture of Sisyphus than housework, with its endless repetition; the clean becomes soiled, the soiled is made clean, over and over, day after day. The housewife . . . makes nothing, simply perpetuates the present. She never senses [the] conquest of a positive Good."[10] Of course, women are not biologically designed for housework in the same way as they are designed for childbirth. But pregnancy and lactation confine them to the house, which then becomes their social "domain" or, more realistically, their prison (and remains so however much they commit themselves to its interior decoration). The argument has a marked deterministic tone, but de Beauvoir is nevertheless set against determinism. Even in the chapter on biology, she insists that woman "has the power to choose between the assertion of her transcendence and her alienation as an object."[11] What transcendence requires is the rejection of woman's life in the service of the species; she must live for herself.

De Beauvoir believes that she can't criticize her society unless she repudiates her body. More exactly, she cannot criticize the social construction of gender unless she can find a way to escape the biological determinations that underlie it. It is men, mostly, who create and enforce gender roles, but this is not creation *ex nihilo*; it begins from the fact of woman's bodily immanence, from her reproductive biology. Listen again to de Beauvoir's voice describing female sexuality and the experience of pregnancy:

> Feminine sex desire is the soft throbbing of a mollusk. Whereas man is impetuous, woman is only impatient; her expectation can become ardent without ceasing to be passive; man dives upon his prey like the eagle and the hawk; woman lies in wait like the carnivorous plant, the bog, in which insects and children are swallowed up. She is absorption, suction, humus, pitch and glue, a passive influx, insinuating and viscous.[12]

> Ensnared by nature, the pregnant woman is plant and animal, a stockpile of colloids, an incubator, an egg; she scares children proud of their young, straight bodies and makes young people titter contemptuously because she is a human being, a conscious and free individual, who has become life's passive instrument.[13]

Passages like this have a familiar ring to my ears; they ring with self-dislike. De Beauvoir joins the ranks of the assimilated Jew, Albert Memmi's "colonized" man, the American black before the age of "black is beautiful," whose standards of physical attraction and cultural excellence are borrowed and derivative. She doesn't mean to pass, obviously, else she would never have written a book calling attention to herself as a militant of the second sex. Nor, however, does she want to live like a woman or even to be thought of (by the men with whom she spends most of her time) as a woman.* It is, she decides, her own rejection of conventional womanhood, of marriage and mothering, that points the way to female liberation. She chooses her lovers like a man, and she refuses to bear children. The result is a double achievement. She ceases to be a mollusk, a bog, a passive instrument, that is, she escapes biological determination; and then she ceases to be a "woman" as men conceive women—the natural, mysterious, frightening, and enticing Other—and becomes a human individual.

The second achievement is, so to speak, her official program, for herself, for other women, and for any future feminist movement: to replace the social construction of gender with the individual project. It is a quintessentially liberal program, though she would disdain the adjective. It is also a program that somehow misses the extent to which the individual project is itself a social construction. "To take control of the instant and mold the future" (the verbs are important, as much so as in "dives upon his prey") is not what human beings do by nature; it is what men do in the world de Beauvoir inhabits—or better, what men are supposed to do. It is also, according to de Beauvoir, what women want to do. "Woman also aspires to and recognizes the values that are concretely attained by the male. He it is who opens up the future to which she also reaches out."[14] The repetitive "also" captures her meaning. She is not a critic of the world that men have made for themselves but only of the exclusion of women from that world. She demands woman's admission; that is her public message. But there is another message, not exactly concealed but also not quite brought to the fore: that women must qualify for admission. And while man qualifies with his body—"his sexual life is not in opposition to his existence as a person"—woman can only qualify by leaving her body behind.[15]

This is an offensive and deeply dissatisfying message, and since it is offensive and dissatisfying, one has to honor de Beauvoir for delivering it. She does believe, of course, that women (or at least some women) can qualify—as she herself has done—and this must have been what made her book an inspiration to so many of its readers. Home and family, woman's

* At one point in her memoirs, though, she suggests that she enjoyed the advantages of both sexes: "After [the publication of] *She Came to Stay,* those around me treated me both as a writer, their peer in the masculine world, and as a woman; this was particularly noticeable in America: at the parties I went to, the wives got together and talked to each other while I talked to the men, who nevertheless behaved toward me with greater courtesy than they did toward the members of their own sex" (*Force of Circumstance*, trans. Richard Howard [Harmondsworth: Penguin Books, 1968], p. 189). See the comment on this passage in Mary Evans, *Simone de Beauvoir: A Feminist Mandarin* (London: Tavistock, 1985), p. 58.

domain and woman's prison, despite their biological foundations, are not escape-proof. And if escape is difficult ("I think there are some women who really don't stand much of a chance"—where "some women" seems to encompass most married women),[16] then it is at least possible to avoid the original lockup. Don't marry and don't have children; or have children only on your own terms, by yourself. Though she is not a technological determinist, de Beauvoir places a great deal of faith in contraception and artificial insemination. The achievements of a universal science will rescue women from their sexual and gendered particularity. Better, some women will rescue themselves, using the achievements of a universal science, and then they will enter the realm of universality.

The concrete expression of woman's freedom is work outside the home. "Protected from the slavery of reproduction, she is in a position to assume the economic role that is offered her and that will assure her of complete independence."[17] It is only outside, in the marketplace and the public forum, that she can avoid immanence and repetition; it is only outside that work becomes an activity and life a project. De Beauvoir doesn't seem to have looked very closely at what economic roles were actually being "offered" to women in the late 1940s. Her conception of work and life outside the home derives in large part from her own experience; it can hardly be emphasized too much that she was living the life she advocated.

She repeatedly describes that life in terms suggesting a metaphysical melodrama: it is the acting out of "the imperialism of the human consciousness, seeking always to exercise its sovereignty in objective fashion." "Each separate conscious being aspires to set himself up alone as sovereign subject."[18] In fact, that is a bit more than the ordinary aspiration of working women. De Beauvoir herself, in her autobiographical volumes, manages to take pride in achievements that fall well short of sovereignty. Her intention is to evoke (once again with the vocabulary of existentialism) a world of struggle: competitive rankings, harsh choices, continual risk, solitary victories. But this has been, and still is mostly, a man's world. One might think it unattractive, but it plainly has its attractions. The ambition of women, according to de Beauvoir, is to share the ambition, the risks, and the victories of men. That means, to earn money, write books, make scientific discoveries, rule nations, and win glory. The great majority of women have been excluded from these activities, and that is the chief injury that men have done to them. It seems entirely possible, however, that this injury can be overcome and nothing else be changed. When women are "completely independent," they will simply be what men are now. De Beauvoir sometimes suggests an alternative (socialist) vision, but her immediate goal is this imitative independence. "The future can only lead to a more and more profound assimilation [of women] into our once masculine society."[19]

Male Universality

De Beauvoir is an assimilated woman, and then a critic of exclusion; she is most powerfully critical when she writes about the obstacles that women like herself encounter on the road that leads from (female) immanence to (male) transcendence. How, then, should we describe the standpoint from which she writes? She herself claims a kind of objectivity—because she has reached the end of the road. One might think, she says, that only an angel, "neither man nor woman," could be objective, but an angel would "be ignorant of all the basic facts involved in the problem." What is necessary is someone who knows "what it means to a human being to be feminine," who has "roots" in the feminine world, but who is at the same time "fortunate in the restoration of all the privileges pertaining to the estate of human being." De Beauvoir is that someone, though she acknowledges that there are other contemporary women who share her good fortune. Having "won the game," they can "afford the luxury of impartiality."[20] It seems to me extraordinary that anyone writing in the 1940s (or before or since, for that matter, though the 1940s was a particularly hard decade) could possibly think that she had won the game and was in full possession of the privileges of humanity. De Beauvoir means to say simply that she is living like a man, sharing what she hardly recognizes as a badly depleted estate.

She writes about the second sex as if she were one of the first. There is nothing secretive or perverse about this identification; it is entirely open and innocent. She makes no special claim for herself; she simply assumes that all liberated women will be like existentialist men (much as she assumes that liberated Algerians will be like French leftists). There is, after all, only one universal life, and it is men—beings of "transcendence and ambition"—who have lived it. If these same men, encountered as individuals, commonly have to be opposed and resisted, their achievements can only be imitated. "The fact is that culture, civilization, and universal values have all been created by men, because men represent universality."[21] Brave words from a feminist writer—especially brave in that the sentence I have just quoted comes from a conversation tape recorded in 1972, when many French feminists were in the process of repudiating just this argument, which they rightly identified with *The Second Sex*: they took it as an acquiescence in secondness. For de Beauvoir this acknowledgment of male universality is the only way to overcome secondness. What modern women want (or should want) is "not that they be exalted in their femininity" but rather "that in themselves, as in humanity in general, transcendence may prevail over immanence."[22] Or, more concretely, the modern woman "accepts masculine values: she prides herself on thinking, taking action, working, creating, on the same terms as men; instead of seeking to disparage them, she declares herself their equal."[23]

The central purpose of de Beauvoir's book is to make this declaration of equality. Nevertheless, her ethnographic account of inequality and immanence is a more powerful and moving achievement. When she is not belaboring the bad faith, she has a keen sense for the pain of women whose hopes and ambitions are first deferred, then repressed, then turned into sentimental fantasy. She writes about these women with a mixture of sympathy and repugnance that very few male students of women's lives could possibly match. The volatility of the mix suggests the intensity of her feelings, though personal reference is severely repressed throughout the account. We can tell from her memoirs how much of her own experience and the experience of her female friends is reflected at least in the early chapters of part 2 of *The Second Sex*. But there is no clue to the reflection in the text itself—except for the obvious fact that this universal ethnography is concerned almost entirely with Western, middle-class women. Her tone throughout is firmly impersonal: these, she reports, are the attitudes and customs of the natives. De Beauvoir deliberately distances herself from her material. Perhaps she has to do that since she is writing about experiences of immanence that she has escaped or that, having escaped early, she has missed entirely. From her new vantage point, the story she has to tell is a story of defeat and of complicity in defeat. "It is said that woman . . . wallows in immanence; but she has first been shut up in it."[24] De Beauvoir describes the method of the shutting up, and then she describes, in great detail, the wallowing.

As with woman's body, so with her situation and her life, the standard of comparison is always that of the generalized male. "If we compare these situations . . . we see clearly that man's is far preferable; that is to say, he has many more opportunities to exercise his freedom in the world."[25] Once again, de Beauvoir reveals the essentially liberal, individualist, and universal politics that her existentialism requires. Equal opportunity for men and women to compete in the world that men have made—that is her feminist platform. But it is only fair to describe it in her own terms. She wants women's lives to "expand," like men's lives, "into an indefinitely open future." Since she expects nothing new from this expansion, however, no new activities, understandings, or evaluations, the openness hardly seems indefinite. In fact, she is not proposing a reiteration of male experience, which might in principle produce genuine novelty, but only, again, an imitation. With regard to the present, the two formulations, equal opportunity and indefinite expansion, make for an identical rejection of woman's condition; and with regard to the future, they make for an identical acceptance of man's.

Since de Beauvoir is philosophically committed to the proposition that "inner liberty is complete in both [men and women]," and at the same time to the proposition that immanence is slavery, any acceptance of the female situation as a situation of value or even potential value would be an act of bad faith—an "abdication" of transcendence. Give women the same "opportunities to exercise their freedom" that men have had, and they will behave exactly as men have done throughout history (de Beauvoir's ethnography is pretty much ahistorical). "When woman is engaged in an enterprise worthy of a human being, she is quite able to show herself as active, efficient, taciturn—and as ascetic—as a man."[26] How does one know what enterprises are worthy of a human being? Worthy enterprises are those in which men have been active, efficient, taciturn, and so on; de Beauvoir attempts no independent evaluation. It is more important to win equal opportunity than to worry about what this opportunity is for. So the indefinitely open future is programmatically empty, or better, it is wholly determined by the male past.

As soon as one recognizes alternatives to transcendence and universality as these have conventionally been understood, that is, understood by men, de Beauvoir's "objectivity" disappears. She writes from a particular perspective, from a time and a place-in-the-world. This is, as her critics commonly say, a male perspective. But one can't stop there: it is a rare man who could have written a book like *The Second Sex*; most men, reading it, are made acutely uncomfortable by its argument. For male comfort has historically required the belief that women are contented with their situation and that they are contented *with reason*, that the lives they lead are right—for them. De Beauvoir doesn't deny the contentment ("wallowing in immanence") of at least some women, but she denies the rightness, and the denial is hard for male readers to resist. Her portrait of female immanence hardly invites imitation: what man would want to live like that? And yet the argument toward which male readers are driven is, after all, not very difficult, at least in principle: let women (if they can) live like us! De Beauvoir holds out the possibility of a masculine feminism, male universality made truly universal.

She may well be right to suggest that this masculine feminism is better expressed by a woman like herself who has adopted male values and "won the game" than by a disabused and alienated man. "In order to change the face of the world," she says in *The Second Sex*, "it is first necessary to be firmly anchored in it."[27] The case is the same with the criticism that precedes change: a woman who has found her anchorage will be a better critic than a man who has lost his—and this even if the woman is trying only to win the game while the man is trying to act justly. For she can more readily recognize "the values . . . concretely attained by the male," which he may feel bound to disparage and renounce. Many contemporary feminists would prefer the disparagement and renunciation of male values, but whatever the justice of their argument, it is an argument that can only be made after de Beauvoir. To disparage values from which one has been excluded is the classic form of *ressentiment*: it is, or it will commonly be experienced as, the politics of sour grapes. Better first to criticize and overcome the exclusion and then to judge the fruits of victory. When we consider the situation of oppressed human beings, our first demand (and theirs too) is simply that they be admitted to the rights shared among their oppressors. These will be called, as in *The Second Sex*, universal or human rights. In fact, they are always a particular set of rights, and admission to their enjoyment, even if everyone in the world were admitted, would not mark the end of political argument and contention. It will turn out that the male representation of universality is false, or at least that it is radically incomplete. But this male universality won't even be tested so long as women are excluded from its attainments. Hence the priority of de Beauvoir's "assimilationist" politics.

A Different Feminism?

But de Beauvoir insists also upon the finality of her politics—for women, if not for humankind generally. Indeed, women could do worse than to imitate male achievements in mathematics, science, literature, and even philosophy (just as Algerians could do worse than to imitate the politics of French leftists). It would be a mistake, however, to insist that these imitative efforts, and only these, can count as liberation. "I do not think," de Beauvoir told an interviewer in the 1970s, "[that] women will create new values. If you believe the opposite, then what you are believing in is a feminine nature—which I have always opposed."[28] But that can't be right. Surely the bourgeoisie, for example, created new values, significantly different from those of the aristocracy, even though there is no such thing as a bourgeois or an aristocratic nature; there are just different social experiences. De Beauvoir argues that women won't create new values because of her beliefs about their experience, not their nature (though she is more ambivalent than she admits here about natural, that is, bodily determinism): first, that the experience of immanence is entirely uncreative; second, that the experience of transcendence is or will be exactly the same for men and women. It follows, then, that there is no feminist politics beyond assimilation.

But both these beliefs are wrong. Social critics "firmly anchored" in the world of women seem more likely to see the mistake than critics already assimilated into the world of men. At least, the criticisms of de Beauvoir that I now want to rehearse come from women working within a feminist movement. These women obviously don't accept as their own the social domain of home and family to which gender makes them heir; if they did, they would never have been moved to create feminism as a political project. But they keep up connections there; they are committed to "the self-understanding of female subjects," even if these subjects, most of them, are wives and mothers who "don't stand much of a chance," as de Beauvoir said, in the struggle for transcendence.[29] It is the conviction of de Beauvoir's critics that woman's life before transcendence is already in its own way transcendent, that women, as they are, are beings-for-themselves. But what does this mean? And why doesn't it constitute an acquiescence in subjection?

One can as easily ask the opposing question: isn't it subjection that has led women, following men, to devalue their own experience? When de

Beauvoir writes in *The Second Sex* that, despite "all the respect thrown around it by society, the function of gestation still inspires a spontaneous feeling of revulsion," is she expressing a liberated sensibility?[30] Her critics, by contrast, are likely to begin with a more affirmative view of mothering. Sometimes the affirmation has the form of a Beauvoirist revisionism. According to *The Second Sex*, writes Mary O'Brien, contemporary contraceptive techniques make only for sexual freedom. Their real importance, however, is to open up "the choice of parenthood, the voluntary acceptance of a real as opposed to a philosophical risking of life." Contraception, O'Brien suggests, makes pregnancy into an existentialist adventure. But she goes on to ask, more sensibly, "if passivity is an accurate description of any form of reproductive consciousness at any time, in any society?" It isn't, and that means that immanence has no social reality. Human reproduction is always different from that of plants and animals because it is always susceptible "to the interpretations of a rational consciousness."[31] A complete ethnography of women's lives would provide us with an account of these interpretations—an account that did not simply assume them to be ideological in character, concealing the grim truth of biological determinism and/or bad faith. Biology determines that only women will bear children, but what women make of the experience, given the many different things they have made of it, cannot be biologically determined.

The most interesting philosophical argument made by (some) contemporary feminists is the argument for pluralism in transcendence. De Beauvoir, as her assimilationist politics suggests, was always a monist. Women have never succeeded, she writes in *The Second Sex*, "in building up a solid counter-universe."[32] Since there is no creative potential in immanence, they never will succeed. And since the universe that men have "built up" is already universal in principle, and women have only to enter it to make it universal in fact, there is no need for success. But what if this counter-universe already exists—not wholly different from the world of men, overlapping with it, but giving social embodiment, or even a variety of different embodiments, to whatever is different in women's experience? De Beauvoir doesn't see the counter-universe because she is writing from too far away, with too great a burden of dislike. She "portrays woman only as victim—maimed, mutilated, dependent," writes Iris Marion Young, "confined to a life of immanence and forced to be an object. She rarely describes the strength that women have had and the earthly value of their work: the ways

[they] have formed networks and societies among themselves, the lasting beauty of the caring social values [they] often exhibit."[33]

I have called this critical view of de Beauvoir pluralistic because it suggests the existence of different, though equally "transcendent," moralities. But when contemporary feminists go on to claim that "masculine values exalt death, violence, competition, selfishness, a repression of . . . sexuality and affectivity," they don't seem very securely committed to pluralism.[34] Then it is necessary to insist that while some men may have values of that sort, others don't. Nor do all women display or even recognize the "lasting beauty" of nurturance and cooperation, "the caring social values." A pluralism of two, the first ranked negatively, the second positively, is no different from an antipluralism of one. It is possible, however, to acknowledge differences without ranking them, and differences there seem to be: expressed not so much in two distinct sets of values as in a range of ethical sensibilities and orientations, with men and women distributed unevenly across the range.* And then women's oppression "consists not in being prevented from participating in full humanity, but in the denial and devaluation of specifically feminine virtues and activities." On this view, the very idea of a universal humanity is itself oppressive insofar as it holds subordinate groups to standards they have had no hand in shaping. "Only an explicit affirmation of difference and social plurality . . . offers the hope of overcoming sexism."[35]

De Beauvoir cannot provide an affirmation of that sort. But she was brought to make concessions to the idea of difference in the 1970s; they take a characteristic form that is worth looking at closely. Certain "male failings," she told Alice Schwarzer in 1976, are absent in women:

> For example, that grotesque masculine way of taking themselves seriously, their vanity, their self-importance. . . . And then the habit of putting down all the competition—generally women don't do that. And patience—which can be a virtue up to a certain point, though after that it becomes a weakness—is also a female characteristic. And a sense of irony. And a straightforward manner, since

* It makes no sense to talk of categorical differences; better to say that the *distribution of differences* is different in the two sexes. Then one can sustain a genuine pluralism and evaluate the different differences . . . differently. Some of de Beauvoir's feminist critics are too quick, I think, to praise whatever she dispraises in women's lives—as if oppression had no ill effects on the oppressed. But "if women's labor has been as creative or more so than men's labor, if women's networks and relations with children have been the source of values more life-giving than the public activities of men, if female desire is more playful, less rigid, than male desire, then what warrants the claim that women need liberating?" (Iris Marion Young, "Humanism, Gynocentrism, and Feminist Politics," *Hypatia: A Journal of Feminist Philosophy*, no. 3 [1985]: 181).

> women have their feet on the ground because of the role they play in daily life. These "feminine" qualities are a product of our oppression, but they ought to be retained after our liberation. And men would have to learn to acquire them.[36]

It is interesting that de Beauvoir's list omits the "caring values." A number of feminist writers, rather in her spirit, have criticized her for falling into the conventional female role of caring for Sartre, especially in his last years. Kate Soper makes the right response to this criticism: "It is a *human* convention—or should be—to minister to a dying lifelong lover or companion. Any feminism that would sacrifice such a practice to its ideological purity would seem to hold out little promise of bliss to either sex."[37] But if the sacrifice is to be resisted, it is probably important to acknowledge, even to take pride in, the fact that this *human* convention has been sustained largely by women. For the rest, de Beauvoir's list is attractive enough. Her last sentence makes it clear, however, that she doesn't intend to affirm a pluralist position. It's as if she regards morality as a kind of United Fund to which liberated women will make a (somewhat marginal) contribution. And then men "would have to" accept the contribution—else the fund would cease to be united. This is still the assimilationist view, even if women are no longer seen as empty-handed petitioners. Given this view, de Beauvoir is right: after liberation, when men and women live identical lives, seize the same opportunities, expand into the same indefinite future, neither sex will be more patient, ironic, or straightforward than the other. All such qualities will be valued generally and distributed randomly.

But is it possible, after liberation, that men and women will live different lives? Is liberation compatible with difference, that is, with nonrandom distributions? There seems no necessary incompatibility so long as the distributions arise within more or less freely chosen or cooperatively shaped ways of life. Hence, again, the priority of de Beauvoir's argument for equal opportunity in politics, business, science, and literature—the career open to talents extended, finally, to women; the triumph at last of the French Revolution. Any defense of difference that obscures this priority is dangerous indeed: "a return to the enslavement of women," says de Beauvoir in a 1982 interview, "pure and simple!" She has no patience with "femininity," whether it is described in the old language of passive acquiescence or in the new language of active creation. And she despises any feminism that rejects the politics, business, science, and literature that men have made in the name of alternatives that have never yet been tested. This is to reject too much, since "this male world . . . is, quite simply, the world itself." Some women, she goes on, "won't do anything the man's way: whether it be organization, career, creative work or concrete action. I've always thought that one should simply borrow and make use of the systems men have at their disposal."[38] Borrowing is sensible enough, so long as one doesn't just stop there, as de Beauvoir seems content to do. She still draws her conclusions from the ethnography of immanence she wrote in 1948, when she was already what she hoped all women would become, a transcendent being—which is to say, manlike—studying the benighted natives. The natives cannot do anything more than imitate the culture and technology of more advanced people.

Is de Beauvoir really manlike? Is her politics merely borrowed? It is hard to imagine a male social critic taking as the central subjects of his criticism women and the elderly. There is in de Beauvoir's work a quality of nonideological compassion (entirely missing, for example, in Sartre's) which must have something to do with her gender. I don't mean with her female essence; I don't want to defend the claims that de Beauvoir so tellingly mocks: that "woman has a particular closeness with the earth, that she feels the rhythm of the moon, the ebb and flow of the tides . . . that she has more soul, or is less destructive by nature, etc."[39] Still, there is a story one can tell about the experience of women that explains de Beauvoir's intellectual choices better than the story she tells, focused on the imitation of men. Her imitation, indeed, provides her with critical standards. She attacks the male world from the inside, exploiting its "universal" values. But she is also a critic of women, from the outside. And here her criticism needs to be supplemented by critics differently positioned, who explicitly defend different values, who speak "in a different voice"—a voice that is just barely audible, though always repressed, in her own best work.

10

Herbert Marcuse's America

Transnational Marcuse

"It has a powerful, subtle, compelling impact," R. D. Laing wrote about the language of Herbert Marcuse's *One-Dimensional Man*, "and a beautiful dying cadence—the sad and bitter song of an aging scholar from old Germany in the New World."[1] In fact, Marcuse's prose is cumbersome, harsh, repetitive, abstract, only sometimes compelling, never beautiful. But his "song" is indeed sad and bitter, and it has most often been read as a European song about a despised America. But that is not quite right. *One-Dimensional Man* is an American song, or at least it is the song of an American. When he published the book, Marcuse had lived in the United States for thirty years. He left Germany in 1933, crossed the Atlantic a year later; and when, after the war, the greater number of his Frankfurt School colleagues went home, he chose to stay. How else does one become an American? In Randolph Bourne's transnational America, Marcuse was a typical citizen.

The antiheroes of his philosophy, the one-dimensional men, are also

Americans. I suspect that Marcuse did not know them all that well—not to talk to, anyway—but he thought himself surrounded by them, in the streets, the subways, the supermarkets. He wasn't much given to empirical research, but one-dimensionality imposed itself. To learn about it did not require any very adventurous program of study, only a minimal stoicism: "Perhaps the most telling evidence can be obtained," he wrote in the introduction to *One-Dimensional Man*, "by simply looking at television or listening to the AM radio for one consecutive hour for a couple of days, not shutting off the commercials, and now and then switching the station."[2] (It might be fatal for this particular piece of research if one turned by accident to an FM station playing classical music. Later on, Marcuse expanded his argument to take account of that possibility; and then research ceased to be necessary at all.) This is, no doubt, an American experience of the mass media; it is probably an American idea of "evidence" too—the quick fix as research method. But Marcuse could also sit in his study and read at his leisure about one-dimensional men. His book, as he admits, is radically dependent on the academic and popular social critics of the 1950s: C. Wright Mills, William H. Whyte, Vance Packard, Fred Cook, and (though they are unacknowledged in his introduction) David Riesman and John Kenneth Galbraith. All these were American writers describing an emerging social reality that they took to be quintessentially American. The air of theoretical closure that Marcuse added to their work might be called Germanic or, at least, transnational. But he thought the closure peculiarly American too, a sign of our advancement. Perhaps he chose to stay in the United States because he wanted to experience that advancement; he wanted a place, even a home, that needed his criticism.

Marcuse may also have relished the idea of living in what he took to be a post-Marxist society. All his life, in Germany and in the United States, he was at once a pre-Marxist philosopher, his attention focused on Hegel (on Marx only insofar as he was or could be read as a "left" Hegelian), and a post-Marxist social theorist, in the style, which he helped to create, of the Frankfurt School. He was far more concerned with the needs of a free consciousness than with the interests of this or that group of workers; and so he was entirely ready to adopt a characteristically American view of the (American) working class as a group radically lacking in "negativity," more or less accommodated within the existing society. Officially, so to speak, he mourned the disappearance of the proletariat, which had once provided the material basis of social criticism, the physical body for which critical philosophy could serve as head and brain. Now, he wrote, it was impossible to demonstrate that there were real social forces "which moved (or could be guided to move) toward more rational or freer institutions."[3] In practice, however, he was well attuned to this situation; it opened the way for his own social criticism. America's post-Marxist society was his subject: here was the place where human needs were most distorted and falsified—in part, paradoxically, because working-class interests were so nearly accommodated; here also was the place where those same needs were closest (potentially) to fulfillment.

The Happy Consciousness

Only thirty or forty years earlier, Gramsci had still been able to describe the subordinated consciousness of the Italian working class as a powerful, if latent and implicit, contradiction of bourgeois hegemony. The problem was to make it explicit, to reveal its categories, and then, of course, to arm its prophets. Like most social critics, Gramsci constructed a partial critique of his society—*partial*, because he found elements within it, social forces (actual men and women) that "moved, or could be guided to move" in directions he approved. By contrast, Marcuse's is a total critique. Not that American society is totally without contradiction, rather that its contradictions are no longer expressed in everyday experience; they are evident only at a very high level of philosophical abstraction. On the ground, as it were, "the integration of opposites," the reconciliation of opposing forces, is complete.[4] There is no class conflict, neither a war of maneuver nor a war of position. There is no forward march, no vanguard party, no serious politics. Hence Marcuse's critique does not have a partisan character or a class bias. In the last few paragraphs of *One-Dimensional Man*, he gestures toward a "substratum of outcasts and outsiders" that may still represent, as the proletariat once did, "the most advanced consciousness of humanity and its most exploited force."[5] But this is a gesture only, disconnected from the rest of the book, which has nothing to say about the everyday life or ideological grasp of this substratum. The book is about all the other strata, everyone else, the reconciled and integrated mass. It is addressed, at least formally, to all the one-dimensional men and women. The efficacy of the address is radically unclear, however, for it doesn't seem that there is anything these people can do (Marcuse has no suggestions). They hardly seem capable, even after reading his book, of feeling bad about their condition.

No society could be without practical contradictions unless it was also without everyday unhappiness. Marcuse vacillates a bit in his description of the mental state of one-dimensional men: "euphoria in unhappiness" is his first formula, suggesting that unhappiness is merely repressed or, perhaps, that it is misunderstood; "the happy consciousness" is the later and theoretically favored formula, suggesting a deeper transformation.[6] In any case, *One-Dimensional Man* is a critique of what would commonly be regarded as political and economic success. The critique is by no means without precedent. A host of social critics have condemned the contentment of their fellows—and not only because the contentment wasn't widely shared or because it was purchased at the expense of other people. The argument that contentment is the enemy of well-being is very old, and this in essence is Marcuse's argument. At the same time, it is a crucial feature of the happy consciousness that it *is* widely shared. And the happiness is, to some extent at least (Marcuse vacillates here too), real happiness. Americans are better off than men and women, ordinary men and women, have ever been before. And how can it be a bad thing to be better off?

American society "delivers the goods." Marcuse denies the ultimate goodness of these goods, but he doesn't deny, or at least he covers himself by seeming not to deny, their immediate goodness. He makes the argument against contemporary forms of consumption that Orwell refused to make—but always with a qualification at the end, the exact meaning of which is very difficult to judge. "The people recognize themselves," he writes, "in their commodities; they find their soul in their automobile, hi-fi set, split-level home, kitchen equipment." As these "beneficial" products become more and more widely available, their enjoyment becomes a way of life. "It is a good way of life—much better than before—and as a good way of life, it militates against qualitative change."[7] On the one hand, the human soul is not properly "found" in consumer culture; on the other hand, the relative goodness of the available goods makes any alternative "finding" increasingly difficult. If people are satisfied here and now, they have no motive to seek satisfaction elsewhere.

The same problem arises with regard to justice, and once again I had best let Marcuse describe it in his own terms. It is a question now of the substantive force and value of criticism itself. "Independence of thought, autonomy, and the right to political opposition are being deprived of their basic critical function," he argues, "in a society which seems increasingly capable of satisfying the needs of individuals. . . . Such a society may justly demand acceptance of its principles and institutions."[8] *Justly*, and yet the demand is not just, for this seeming satisfaction of needs masks a denial of the deepest human need—for freedom itself. The first sentence of the first chapter of *One-Dimensional Man* sums up Marcuse's indictment: "A comfortable, smooth, reasonable, democratic unfreedom prevails in advanced industrial civilization."[9] Once again, if we attend to the indictment, we must also attend to its (uncertain) qualifications, the noun "unfreedom" and its attached adjectives. Americans are indeed unfree, in Marcuse's view, but never before has unfreedom been so reasonable, its victims so comfortable, its establishment and maintenance so smooth, its institutions so democratic. What can this mean?

Our unfreedom, Marcuse writes, "is perpetuated and intensified in the form of many liberties and comforts."[10] Sometimes he is contemptuous of these (presumably petty) liberties and comforts—the mere indulgence of slaves. America's society has the form of a nonterroristic totalitarianism, which is entirely "compatible with a 'pluralism,' of parties, newspapers, 'countervailing powers,' etc."[11] Here the quotation marks and the "etc." are signs of disdain: the parties differ only over trivia, countervalence doesn't interfere with "economic-technical coordination," and everything else is just more of the same. But if all that were true, it is hard to see what we would have to be happy about. A political order so easily exposed would hardly require a Marcusean critique. The truth is that even the "subdued pluralism" of American democracy has real value. "Pluralistic administration is far better than total administration. One institution might protect [the individual] against the other; one organization might mitigate the impact of the other; possibilities of escape and redress can be calculated." Marcuse continues more strongly: "The rule of law, no matter how restricted, is still infinitely safer than rule above or without law." Infinitely safer, that is, than what most people through most of human history have endured. But "safer" is not the whole of "better": human beings have had higher ambitions than merely to be safe from the authorities. Once they are safe, will they still be ambitious? Marcuse's conviction that they won't be, *that they aren't*, leads to his (again, just barely qualified) conclusion: "Democracy would appear to be the most efficient system of domination."[12]

So we are happy with our commodities ("an ever-more-comfortable life for an ever-growing number of people") and we are happy in our political institutions ("infinitely safer" than the actually existing alternatives would allow). It is this rational happiness that requires the Marcusean critique; Marcuse is, among social critics, the great defender of the unhappy consciousness. He makes John Stuart Mill's maxim, "Better Socrates dissatisfied than a pig satisfied," into a critical principle. And his defense of the principle is like Mill's: if the pig knew what Socrates knows, he too would choose dissatisfaction.[13] But for Mill the defense is speculative only, while Marcuse is prepared, as we will see, to consider an "educational dictatorship" organized by the agents of Socrates to free the pigs from their piggish contentment. He is a Marxist (or, perhaps better, a Leninist) at least in this sense: he believes that prophets must be armed; the vanguard must seize and use the power of the state. What distinguishes the Marcusean vanguard, however, is less its practical/theoretical knowledge than its philosophical discontent—and it isn't obvious that this discontent will be sufficient to sustain the serious business of seizing power. The superiority of the unhappy consciousness lies in its sensitivity to values, possibilities, aspirations that are not realized, and perhaps cannot be realized, in the existing social conditions of one-dimensionality. Unhappiness is negative, and negativity is the second dimension.

The unhappy consciousness preserves the image of a higher happiness. The image has, indeed, no material representation in advanced industrial (American) society. It is mental only; it survives, as it were, in a brain in a vat, kept alive by philosophical transfusions. Marcuse holds out little hope for its longevity. All the agencies of modern civilization conspire to make people happy by making them comfortable and safe and by suppressing their sense of the unrealized potential and higher possibilities of human life. And yet these possibilities have Truth on their side; they correspond to the real needs of men and women, that is, those needs which, were they ever fulfilled, would make us really (or perhaps it is really, really) happy.

Most social criticism starts from the real, I mean now the actual *un*happiness of oppressed or subjugated people—the grinding poverty of Silone's peasants, for example, or the deep frustration of de Beauvoir's "second sex." The critic articulates at the level of theory what is already articulated at the level of common complaint. Theory and complaint are likely to stand in some tension—as accounts of "false consciousness" suggest—but however they differ from one another in explaining oppression or in proposing suitable responses to it, they share a subject, oppression itself. The false consciousness of the workers consists, say, in believing that they are responsible for their own unhappiness or that only God or the king in his mercy can do anything to help them. But at least they know their own unhappiness. Marcuse, by contrast, lives or thinks that he lives in a society whose members, *for good reasons*, have no such knowledge: they have no experience of oppression; they have nothing to complain about; they get what they want; their needs are met. Hence his social criticism must look to a deeper reality. These happy men and women, he must argue, don't get what they ought to want. The needs that are met are false needs, first "implanted" in them, then fulfilled for them. They have lost the capacity for self-determination; the self that they recognize in their commodities is not (really) their own.

Now, it makes sense to insist that the story of the happy slave is the fictional creation of slave owners or of the intellectuals they patronize; it isn't a plausible account of slave consciousness. But there is another, more interesting, story, according to which we are the slaves of our passions—alienated from our true selves but not owned by anyone else and, insofar as our passions are gratified, happy in our alienation.[14] This is a critical, not an apologetic story, and it is Marcuse's story, though he would regard it as mere moralizing were he not able to attribute the enslavement to malign social forces. Malign but, as it turns out, unnamed social forces: the attribution is made entirely with verbs, never with nouns; the verbs have an object but no subject. The slaves still have no apparent masters. Their passions are "implanted," their happiness "administered," they themselves are "indoctrinated and manipulated (down to their very instincts)."[15] Some unknown agency—the market? the state? the modern corporation?—working through the mass media, generates a host of "artificial" needs, and ordinary men and women (you and I) rush to satisfy these needs and do satisfy them and are happy. But this is not the happiness of a free people. Or, if there is a kind of freedom that consists in deciding which of these implanted needs to satisfy, in what order, with what particular commodities, that only proves that "under the rule of a repressive whole, liberty [itself] can be made into a powerful instrument of domination."[16]

In Marcuse's story we are enslaved because we are driven by passions that are not properly our own, and this slavery is governed by a "repressive whole," a system different from all previous systems. For in this system there is no distinction of rulers and ruled; we are all one-dimensional; we are all, simultaneously, victims and beneficiaries.* Only the philosophical critic sees or thinks that he sees the falsehood of the whole thing. But his insight is not demonstrably true until he can convince the rest of us. Only we can tell the truth about our own needs. Marcuse gestures, at least, toward a democratic epistemology: "In the last analysis, the question of what are true and false needs must be answered by the individuals themselves, but only in the last analysis." So long as we are enslaved, incapable of autonomy, indoctrinated and manipulated (down to our very instincts), our "answer to this question cannot be taken as [our] own."[17] Set free from the system, we would value our freedom, even if it made us unhappy. Unfree, our judgments about value are not to be taken seriously. But those judgments are serious enough insofar as they prevent us from setting ourselves free. It is the special feature of this modern system that the more we are enslaved the happier we are, and the happier we are the less we are capable of escape. "There is no reason to insist on self-determination if the administered life is the comfortable and even the 'good' life."[18] Hence the paradox of the Marcusean critique: *the better, the worse.*

Material Slavery

Happy slaves of the repressive whole: this was in the middle 1960s an exciting and, so many people thought, an enlightening view of the American and only a little later of the French, German, and English multitudes. But those who found it enlightening were rarely ready to acknowledge that it shed any light on their own lives. Marcuse was describing all the others, whose contentment and inertia made philosophical education so difficult. *One-Dimensional Man* is a grim book, and yet it warms the heart of anyone who thinks himself properly unhappy—hence two-dimensional. But is the argument about the others "really" enlightening? There is first of all the dark mystery of the repressive whole. How is modern domination organized? What are its hierarchical structures? What is the prevailing pattern of social

* Marcuse's argument here has some similarities with Michel Foucault's (see chapter 11), for both writers are in flight from Marxist class analysis and both have a strong sense of what might be called politics lost. But Foucault would obviously not accept Marcuse's claim that behind the false needs of "one-dimensional man," there is a recognizable set of true needs. The two men represent "modern" and "postmodern" articulations of a similar critical mood.

relationships? One-dimensionality is, after all, consequent to the advance of industrial society, the lateness of late capitalism, the totalitarian forms of economic-technical coordination. But Marcuse provides no substantive account of any of these, and so one-dimensionality looks like a consequence without a cause, much as it also looks, as I have already suggested, like a predicate without a subject.

Marcuse might have argued that one-dimensional men and women were their own causes, self-produced in the course of long, hard, bitter struggles against tyranny and oppression. Aren't comfort and safety, even in his disparaging descriptions, the achievements of bourgeois and working-class political movements? There is a story here of patient organization and conscious action, of risks taken and lives lost. Marcuse has no interest in any of this; he manages to suggest that comfort and safety are the gifts of manipulative (but unknown) donors whose only aim is social control. The recipients are rational but not active on their own behalf; indeed, their rationality doesn't come to much, since the long-term effect of the affluent society's flood of goods is, so Marcuse writes with bland assurance, "moronization."[19] It isn't easy to accept his parallel assurance that the culture of consumption is far better than what came before (*before* we were morons!). In fact, Marcuse doesn't display much curiosity about the day-to-day life of ordinary men and women either before or after the advent of one-dimensionality. Another failure of Marcusean enlightenment: it sheds no light on the life of the unenlightened. What is it like, how does it feel, to live under the aegis of the happy consciousness? Marcuse asks us to believe in the existence of people instantly and totally responsive to modern commercial advertising, instantly and totally content once they have purchased the advertised goods and services. But I don't know any people like that. One-dimensional man, it seems to me, is a creature of Marcuse's text, not of any actual society (not even of twentieth-century America). He is far too thin and pliable a creature to evoke recognition.

But *One-Dimensional Man* (the book now as well as its subject) invites a more general skepticism, which I would express in the form of a maxim: if a slave, then not happy; if happy, then not a slave. The maxim applies collectively; I allow for individual exceptions—masochists who are made happy by domination and abuse; philosophers like Epictetus whose inner life, so they say, their masters cannot touch. But a whole nation of such people is unimaginable. Human beings as we know them will resent and resist enslavement, and if there is neither resentment nor resistance, we had best assume that what is being experienced is something other than slavery. Even slavery to one's passions, if one's passions are mastered and manipulated by someone else, will produce resentment and resistance. We might make slaves happy, of course, by giving them drugs or controlling their brain waves; perhaps Marcuse believes that commodities like cars and washing machines are literal narcotics. But that's not a view that could be sustained if one were to talk to the men and women who drive the cars and do the wash—and commonly manage to hold other ends in view at the same time; the state of mind induced by driving or washing is not what they commonly aim at. Indeed, the relation of people to their things is an important subject for philosophical criticism. But critics are unlikely to move beyond the standard pieties unless they are themselves moved by some degree at least of ethnographic curiosity. Marcuse is unmoved and invincibly pious.

"Slavery" is a critical word, but it isn't the only critical word, and a refusal to use it to describe conditions remote from actual enslavement doesn't mean that we can't make any criticism at all. Similarly "totalitarian" is a critical word, but not every society that we want to criticize has to be called totalitarian. Perhaps Marcuse believes the lines he quotes (with seeming approval but without specific comment) from Ionesco: "The world of the concentration camps . . . was not an exceptionally monstrous society. What we saw there was the image, and in a sense the quintessence, of the infernal society into which we are plunged every day."[20] His own version of this sort of thing is only a little more cautious: "For 'totalitarian' is not only a terroristic political coordination of society, but also a non-terroristic economic-technical coordination which operates through the manipulation of needs."[21] Maybe; but the suggested usage would be legitimate only if terrorist politics and nonterrorist economics have the same "total" effect upon individual lives, and Marcuse does not even begin to make the case for such a similarity. Nor could he make the case, were he sufficiently interested in the everyday life, say, of Stalin's subjects and of American citizens.

But this is too easy a criticism of Marcuse. I need to ask why he feels himself driven to such linguistic lengths. It isn't as if no other vocabulary were available to him. Think, for example, of one of his own sourcebooks, C. Wright Mills's *The Power Elite*. Mills manages to describe the failures of American democracy without suggesting that Americans are slaves (though in his case we would at least have known whose slaves we were) or that the power elite exercises anything like total power. His was not an unambitious book; no reader can doubt his far-reaching critical intentions; but his argument and the language with which he made his argument were alike constrained by his sociological perception: he did not name what he could not see.[22] The radical closure of the Marcusean critique, expressed in words like slavery and totalitarianism, has more to do with theoretical commitment than sociological perception. And I have not reached the end of Marcuse's theoretical commitments by recounting his views of working-class accommodation and material affluence. Thus far he has merely finished with Marxist hopefulness. The real radicalism of his theory lies in the account it provides of contemporary culture, of one-dimensionality as it is expressed in the art, literature, and philosophy of post-Marxist society. *One-Dimensional Man* is a book about the slow dying of the human spirit, the eclipse of *Geist* in the modern world (exemplified, still, by America). Measured by what is at stake, the dislike I have expressed for the book's vocabulary must seem small-minded.

Spiritual Death

Negativity in Marcuse's universe takes two basic forms. The first is material deprivation, which shapes or once shaped the working class into a "living contradiction to the established society." The second is mental or spiritual richness, out of which comes "the oppositional, alien, and transcendent elements [of] the higher culture by virtue of which it constituted *another dimension* of society."[23] Until now, every ruling class has had to confront the challenge of the oppressed on the one hand and the enlightened on the other, the peasant and proletarian mass and the intellectual elite. No doubt the mass is often fearful, passive, divided; and the elite is often coopted. But the very existence of deprivation and Spirit guaranteed the two-dimensionality of the social order. Marcuse's deepest interest is in the second guarantee, which, he believes, has been effectively suspended—and first of all in America. Not that high culture has been abolished, but rather that it has been "incorporated" (very much like the working class) and rendered innocuous.

Years before the appearance of *One-Dimensional Man*, Randolph Bourne argued that the American writer needed "protection from the liberal audience that will accept him though he shock them . . . that subtly tame him even while they appreciate."[24] I suspect that the readiness of audiences to be entertained at the very moment when authors mean them to be upset predates liberalism by hundreds, if not thousands, of years. What makes liberalism new and different is that the readiness of the audience is not repressed; nor is the author's meaning censored. The end of repression and censorship is a great achievement, and Bourne has no desire to call it into question. But it does have this consequence: that literature becomes less dangerous. In an open society, the negative force of high culture is diminished by the sheer absence of barriers. Bourne believed nonetheless that writers of real power (like Theodore Dreiser) could still generate resistance among their readers and so force a genuine engagement. Marcuse, half a century later, seems to think that the effort is futile. "The absorbent power of society depletes the artistic dimension by assimilating its antagonistic contents. In the realm of culture, the new totalitarianism manifests itself precisely in a harmonizing pluralism where the most contradictory works and truths peacefully co-exist in indifference."[25] Marcuse suggests only one of the physical sites of this peaceful coexistence: the drugstore bookrack, where "Plato and Hegel, Shelley and Baudelaire, Marx and Freud" stand cheek by jowl with gothic romances and murder mysteries—all of them, he supposes, taken by their purchasers to be similarly entertaining.[26] (But if that's what they think, then high culture may still be able to surprise them.)

The force of Marcuse's argument is hardly suggested by this example—which, characteristically, he immediately qualifies: "As far as they go," he says, paperback books "are truly a blessing." I would add that they go pretty far; I have just reread *One-Dimensional Man* in its twenty-fourth paperback printing. But Marcuse's uneasiness with Plato-in-the-drugstore does suggest a certain theoretical intention that is entirely missing in Bourne's work. Marcuse means to call into question the value of cultural equality. Not, at this point in his exposition, the value of liberalism, which, he would probably say, is a blessing as far as it goes. Equality is not a blessing and won't be until it goes much farther; effectively, it won't be a blessing until after the revolution. The assimilation of high and low culture and the democratic availability of "transcendent" art are, right now, "historically premature." Their effect is to "establish cultural equality while preserving domination." And these two, equality and domination, turn out to be mutually reinforcing. It was *inequality*, cultural privilege, which once "provided a protected realm in which the tabooed truths [of art and literature] could survive in abstract integrity—remote from the society that repressed them." When social remoteness disappears, so does cultural transgression. The tabooed truths become part of the common cultural stock, marked out, perhaps, as "classics" but "deprived of their antagonistic force."[27]

Is this right? It is hard to see how the antagonistic force of art and literature could ever be realized, could ever become a social force, unless the actual works of art and the poems, plays, novels, philosophical dialogues, and so on, are somehow appropriated by ordinary men and women. "Survival in abstract integrity" is certainly important, and remoteness may well serve survival. The text of the Bible, for example, was protected and preserved for many centuries by a tiny clerical elite. But it became a social force, it made for antagonism, only when it was translated into the vernacular and widely distributed and read among the vulgar. Admittedly, Plato-in-the-drugstore has not had a similar impact; perhaps *The Republic* is not a similarly transgressive text. Plato's work has never been conscripted into the service of a cause, but surely only a small number of religious and political texts are likely candidates for service of that sort. If *The Republic* provokes, it provokes individuals, one by one. Making it available in inexpensive paperback editions merely increases the number (expands the social range) of people who might be provoked. At the same time, this same availability inevitably increases the number of people who read Plato and are not provoked; it is as if they had never read him. That doesn't mean that he has been rendered unprovocative. He is what he was.

What would be the right treatment, today, when cultural equality is "historically premature," of books like Plato's *Republic*? Should they be read only by the members of an intellectual elite ("protected" by a social elite)? Or does Marcuse have in mind some alternative way of making them available to the rest of us? Is it wrong to treat *The Republic* as a marketable item, a cultural commodity, which one publisher might bring out for a few dollars less than another or with a more attractive cover? But how else might it be brought out? Perhaps we should seize the book in the course of revolutionary *praxis*? But what would we do with it once we had seized it? In any case, isn't the long struggle for democratic schools, for government scholarships, for academic freedom, for an end to censorship—isn't all this a form of seizure? And the result is what we see: reading Plato makes some of us a little wiser; it doesn't overturn the social order.

Marcuse has a moving faith in the power of great books; this is perhaps his most American quality. Consider his account of the effects of Freud-in-the-drugstore (and psychoanalysis in the marketplace):

> Invalidating the cherished images of transcendence by incorporating them into its omnipresent daily reality, this society testifies to the extent to which insoluble conflicts are becoming manageable—to which tragedy and romance, archetypal dreams and anxieties are being made susceptible to technical solution and dissolution. The psychiatrist takes care of the Don Juans, Romeos, Hamlets, Fausts, as he takes care of Oedipus—he cures them.[28]

Well, he doesn't really cure them, not even in Marcuse's presumably ironic sense—he doesn't teach them to adjust; he doesn't release them from the grip of alienation and sublimation. Psychiatry is not so frighteningly successful, neither as a form of medical practice nor as a form of cultural response. Freudianism has added a new way of reading *Hamlet*, say, without supplanting any of the old ways. What can it mean to claim that the play once provided, and now no longer provides, an "image of transcendence"? From his first appearance, the prince of Denmark has meant different things to different people; he is a hero to some, a figure of weakness and vacillation to others. He has often served the purposes of anti-intellectual (and, I suppose, antitranscendent) literary critics, who have made him a stereotype of highbrow impotence. But he never serves their purposes alone. No "technical solution" can deprive us of Shakespeare's enigma. What is the prince to us? He remains a splendid occasion for self-scrutiny and public debate. The *Hamlet* of the old elite culture was no more disturbing, no more transgressive or transcendent, than this *Hamlet* of ours.

It is true, however, that Freudianism itself would be a more negative force in our culture if Freud's books were banned from the drugstore bookracks and if the practice of psychoanalysis (and of psychoanalytic literary criticism) were repressed. Alternatively, the negative force of Freud's doctrines might be preserved for some future time were psychoanalysis excluded from the common culture and discussed only in the narrow circles of a privileged elite. Art and literature generally would be more transgressive and more transcendent in a less liberal, less "appreciative," less egalitarian society. Eastern Europe provides ample evidence for this proposition; South Africa, too. Relax the repression, reduce the transgression: here is another example of Marcuse's core argument *the better, the worse*. But the argument is more desperate now. What is at stake is the very idea (the artistic representation, the philosophical defense) of a radically new society—the essential contradiction without which one-dimensionality is irredeemable. But what can Marcuse propose? He cannot set himself up as the advocate of authoritarian repression and cultural inequality. Hence his constant (possibly insincere but in any case unavoidable) qualifications: as if remembering the Communist party in the Weimar Republic, he stops short of reversing the core argument and saying *the worse, the better*.

And, of course, he writes *One-Dimensional Man*, a book he presumably hopes won't be instantly assimilated, deprived of its antagonistic force, turned into one more entertainment for one-dimensional men. He must intend the book to serve as an example of critical philosophy. Certainly, he makes no concessions to the prematurely educated masses (those twenty-four paperback printings would probably have worried him). He writes for the *really* educated few, and he means to rouse them to a new effort to rescue whatever remains of transcendence in modern culture. He aims to be subversive, but he believes that one can only be subversive "from above," by reoccupying the heights that liberalism and democracy have abandoned.

Against Ordinary Language

There is no way around it: Marcuse is an antidemocratic critic. Almost alone among twentieth-century leftists, he is fully capable of sounding like Ortega y Gasset:

> The degree to which the population is allowed to break the peace wherever there still is peace and silence, to be ugly and to uglify things, to ooze familiarity, to offend against good form, is frightening. . . . In the overdeveloped countries, an ever-larger part of the population becomes one huge captive audience—captured not by a totalitarian regime but by the liberties of the citizens whose media of amusement and elevation compel the Other to partake of their sounds, sights, and smells.[29]

These are the democratic liberties that destroy Liberty itself, and at this point Marcuse is ready to contemplate a reversal: "To liberate the imagination . . . presupposes the repression of much that is now free."[30] *One-*

Dimensional Man aims to instruct and inspire the possible agents of this liberating repression (the antidote to what Marcuse later called the "repressive tolerance" of liberal society).[31] For how can more ordinary readers, who break the peace and uglify things and offend against good form and think themselves free and satisfied, "liberate themselves from themselves"? Their liberation can only come from above, at the hands of men and women who have some superior and philosophically correct understanding of peace, beauty, and good form.

For this reason, social criticism cannot speak in the language of the masses. At the center of *One-Dimensional Man*, Marcuse has placed a critique of ordinary language philosophy. I shall have nothing to say about that, but I am interested in the critique of ordinary language that lies just behind it, for which, indeed, the whole book serves as an example. Marcuse has no faith in the linguistic creativity of the common people. The triumph of the vernacular and then of popular dialects and argots within the vernacular, simply opens the way for political and commercial manipulation. Ordinary language is a "purged language, purged not only of its 'unorthodox' vocabulary, but also of the means for expressing any other contents than those furnished to the individuals by their society." Again: "The established universe of ordinary language tends to coagulate into a totally manipulated and indoctrinated universe." And again: "In speaking their own language, people also speak the language of their masters, benefactors, advertisers."[32] For Marcuse, the age of Newspeak had already arrived in 1964. But his version of Newspeak doesn't seem to require the highly specific apparatus of linguistic control that Orwell imagines; it is entirely compatible with pluralism (the existence of many different argots) and liberalism (the free expression of whatever ideas can still be expressed). I am half-inclined to say that all Newspeak requires, in Marcuse's view, is the death of Latin. When the intellectual elite no longer has a language of its own, then ordinary language "denies or absorbs the transcendent vocabulary."[33]

Marcuse really believes—though it seems unbelievable—that social criticism is impossible within the confines of ordinary language. The critical terms have been purged of their meanings, "totally" transformed, so that, like the biblical Balaam, one starts to criticize but can utter only words of praise. The words that we understand and know how to use allow only for collective self-congratulation. In a critical essay on Marcuse, Allen Graubard has made the best response to this:

> What can be said in "ordinary language" is that this society is lousy in many ways; that it is immoral to waste vast resources maintaining irrational and oppressive institutions while most of the world starves; that the lives of many people . . . are twisted and their potentialities distorted by the prevailing values and practices of this affluent society.[34]

Graubard makes his point by using an everyday vocabulary to express critical ideas, while Marcuse makes his point by cultivating an esoteric philosophical jargon—not a secret language but a deliberately difficult and abstract one. There is, he insists, "an irreducible difference . . . between the universe of everyday thinking and language on the one side, and that of philosophical thinking and language on the other."[35] The claim could hardly be stronger: if the difference is really irreducible, then translation must be impossible, and so philosophers can speak only to one another. Marcuse's many nonphilosophical readers, unless they all misunderstand him, would seem to belie the claim (though even Marcuse occasionally falls into what we might call the vernacular of indignation: in his case, high dudgeon).

Marcuse's commitment to a socially remote philosophical language helps to explain the highly distanced character of his criticism—perhaps also its total character, for he seems to think that nuance and modulation are concessions respectively to a nonphilosophical concreteness and an antiphilosophical positivity. The philosopher looks at society, as Camus in the airplane looked at the physical world, through the eyes of an absolutist God. Hence the view of American culture in *One-Dimensional Man*: not that it tolerates and "appreciates" criticism and so forces the critic to be more and more inventive (or outrageous), but that it makes criticism literally impossible; not that it invites passivity on the part of its newly enfranchised participants, but that it entirely rules out political participation; not that it shapes the lives of ordinary Americans in this way or that, but that it wholly controls them. These assertions are false, but what is more important than their falsehood is the great refusal they represent—a refusal to engage the popular culture or to talk with the people who talk in the ordinary language. Judging from some of his later books, Marcuse seems in fact to have valued certain forms of popular culture: jazz and rock music, for example.[36] But I can find no hint of this valuation, and no room for it, in the total world of *One-Dimensional Man*. As a social critic, he valued only high culture—and high culture only insofar as it was saved from the grasping hands of the semi-educated masses.

Marcuse believes, of course, that one day those grasping hands will seize the high culture and make it their own. But that day is far off, and it isn't brought nearer by any gradual process of education and cultural involvement. How it might arrive, he doesn't say. What he does say is that all efforts to interpret high culture for a mass audience in ordinary language must fail, for negativity and transcendence won't survive the interpretive effort. High culture won't be understood by the masses until after the "collapse and invalidation" of ordinary language and the culture of domination that it reflects.[37] But then ordinary men and women cannot be the agents of collapse and invalidation. The difficulty, remoteness, inaccessibility of cultural value seem to rule out the possibility of a politics that is at once democratic and transformative.

Negative and Positive

There is one important truth in *One-Dimensional Man*: the insistence on the negative character of high culture, both in its general form (the art and literature of the ages) and in its particularity (the art and literature of a given time and place). In the world of hegemony and ideology, Marcuse finds "oppositional, alien, and transcendent elements," and he values these elements in a way that goes considerably beyond Gramsci, with whose work he probably was not familiar: Marcuse is more enthusiastic and more systematic. Culture provides "images of conditions . . . irreconcilable with the established Reality Principle."[38] To be sure, this same culture is also, always, "accommodating" to the reality of privilege and domination, and ruling classes have rarely been discomforted by its contradictions. But the contradictions persist, if only "in abstract integrity." Art and literature are implicitly or latently critical, even in societies—if there are such societies—in which criticism itself is not a recognized or available genre.

The same argument holds with regard to the concepts and principles of the dominant philosophy or political theory. Marcuse takes the (standard) example of the Greek *polis*. Socrates is a social critic, his "discourse" is both political and subversive, because he explores the inner logic of the ruling ideas of Athens. "The search for the correct definition, for the 'concept' of virtue, justice, piety, and knowledge becomes a subversive undertaking, for the concept intends a new *polis*."[39] I am less sure than Marcuse that concepts have intentions or even "correct definitions," but they do have alternative meanings, apologetic and critical. And often, a critical interpretation of their meaning is the stronger, more plausible, even more "natural" interpretation. Socrates is a critical interpreter of the dominant concepts of Greek political and religious life, and, at least in what seem to be the authentically Socratic dialogues, he is the very model of an ordinary language philosopher. But this is not a model that Marcuse imitates. He makes no effort to identify the dominant concepts of American life; he is not committed to a dialogue with ordinary Americans. Despite his admiration for Socrates, he doesn't ask Socratic questions.

The form of his argument reflects the distance from which he writes. What he values in high culture is its articulation of universal reason, which is repressed and concealed (though not entirely obliterated) in everyday life. "The world of immediate experience . . . ," he writes, "must be comprehended, transformed, even subverted in order to become what it really is."[40] In fact, Marcuse displays little interest in "comprehending" immediate experience; he knows what "really is" without knowing what really is. The "essence of man" is freedom and creativity; these two in their ideal form are really real; and one has only to listen to the radio for an hour or so to understand that Reality is unrealized in modern society. Criticism of this sort is very easy, but it is also easy, it seems to me, to shrug off. It makes no demands on us of the sort that Socrates made on his fellow citizens: to live up to their own ideals. Marcuse too has fellow citizens, but he hardly attempts to understand or engage their inner life.

Marcuse's certainty about what is Real goes hand in hand with his naive acceptance of science (even social science!) and modern technology. Though science today serves the forces of darkness, the service is not determined. In principle, things might be different; science might be allied not with power but with philosophy, and then there would be no limit on our capacity to do good. "The historical achievement of science and technology has rendered possible the *transformation of values into technical tasks*."[41] Since the values are known—the essence of man, true human needs, and so on—and since they are beyond rational dispute, their realization is a matter for professionals and experts. It is hard to believe (again) that Marcuse believes this, but it is in fact the burden of the last part of his book, the utopian part. If the bulk of the book expresses a critical philosophy, a philosophy of negativity, the final chapters are an attempt at transcendence, Marcusean uplift. He sounds strangely like a modern practitioner of the "policy sciences" as he explains how the transformation of America might be taken in hand (after the revolution) by a technical elite:

> What is calculable is the minimum of labor with which, and the extent to which, the vital needs of all members of a society could be satisfied—provided the available resources were used for this end, without being restricted by other interests. . . . In other words, quantifiable is the available range of freedom from want . . . calculable is the degree to which, under the same conditions, care could be provided for the ill, the infirm, and the aged . . . quantifiable is the possible reduction of anxiety.[42]

Quantifiable also is the extent of our liberation not only from political domination but from politics itself: this liberation will be virtually complete. Once values have been quantified, realizing them is not a political matter: "Self-determination in the production and distribution of vital goods and services [that is, in the provision of what men and women "really" need] would be wasteful. The job is a technical one."[43] This is Marcuse's version of positivity. Freedom and the creative life lie beyond this sort of thing—presumably in the realm of culture, in the cultivation of Spirit. (But wouldn't Spirit now be deprived of its negative dimension?)

Marcuse doesn't believe, obviously, that this technical job will ever be undertaken; the political and cultural obstacles are overwhelming. His brief remarks at the very end of *One-Dimensional Man* about a revolution of outcasts and outsiders are more despairing than hopeful: pure domination requires pure negation, but the relative strength of the two is radically unequal. Marcuse's real interest lies elsewhere—in the "educational dictatorship" of the philosophical elite. The dictatorship, of course, is no more likely than the revolution, but it is more of a piece with all the rest of his argument: the analysis of true human needs, the critique of "premature" egalitarianism, the refusal of ordinary language, the technical translation of values, and so on. He knows the dangers of educational dictatorship; at least, he dutifully lists them. But only its advocates, he believes, have been willing to acknowledge the real meaning of one-dimensionality, "the conditions (material and intellectual) which serve to prevent genuine . . . self-determination." Because of these conditions, the risk that dictatorship involves "may not be more terrible than the risk which the great liberal as well as authoritarian societies are taking now."[44]

"To the degree to which the slaves [of modern industrial society] have been preconditioned to exist as slaves and be content in that role, their liberation necessarily appears to come from without and from above."[45] The word "appears" is another of those strange qualifiers that Marcuse regularly inserts in his sentences but doesn't ever elaborate. In essence, his critical theory is an explanation and defense of this claim about the fate of contented slaves, without the qualification. There is, however, an addendum: liberation necessarily comes from without and above *if it comes at all*; but it doesn't necessarily come. *One-Dimensional Man* is a deeply pessimistic book, despite the extraordinary confidence of its philosophical arguments. About what is above and without, about transcendence and the philosopher's grasp of transcendence, Marcuse is confident; about what is within, he is grim. The confidence and the grimness are not, I believe, unrelated. An absolute commitment to the Real makes Marcuse a savage (and a "total") critic of the actual, but it doesn't make him a perceptive or precise critic. He has no sensitivity to the immanent value or potential of everyday life. That is why he failed to understand the meaning (later on he failed to understand the limits) of the New Left political agitation that began while he was writing and into which his book was "absorbed"—without ever being deprived, as he should have expected it to be, of its antagonistic force. I doubt that it was much help, though, to those New Leftists who tried to use it as a guide to American society, a map of our iniquity.

A critical theory can only be worked out, Marcuse wrote, "from an independent position *within* a specific society."[46] *One-Dimensional Man* is evidence that this is a normative, not a descriptive, statement, as if Marcuse means us to do as he says, not as he does. It represents a wish more than a commitment, and a wish particularly poignant in that Marcuse freely chose the society he meant to criticize from within. But there was too much in American life that made him shudder. He chose to stay but always kept his distance, and his work suggests again that distance is the enemy of critical penetration. In the battles of the intellect, as in every other battle, one can win, finally, only on the ground.

11

The Lonely Politics of Michel Foucault

Author and Subject

One can hardly read Michel Foucault and doubt that he is a social critic, one of the more important critics of recent times, and yet his philosophical writings and his more powerful (and accessible) "genealogies" seem alike to deny the possibility of effective criticism. His tone is often one of anger, a fierce and insistent anger; his books can be read, and are read, as calls to resistance—but resistance in the name of what? for the sake of whom? to what end? None of these questions, it seems to me, can be satisfactorily answered. Foucault's criticism is a mystery, which I shall explore but probably not solve. At the heart of the mystery lies, once again, the problem of critical distance.

But before turning to that problem, it is necessary to look closely at

Foucault's politics, for his social criticism is in an important sense—and a sense not well understood—a critique of politics itself: a failed critique but no less significant for that. My concern here is not with the political positions that Foucault adopted in response to "events" like the student demonstrations of May 1968 or the French prison revolts of the early 1970s or the Iranian revolution of 1979. Though he insists that he doesn't have a political position and doesn't want to be situated on the chessboard of available positions (he doesn't play chess or any other game the rules of which the rest of us might know), he did indeed respond to events, and his topical statements and articles have a fairly consistent character, at least until his very last years. They are of the sort that I was taught to call, in the political world where I first learned to talk, "infantile leftism," that is, less an endorsement than an outrunning of the most radical argument in any political struggle. But Foucault's infantile leftism is not my main concern.

I want to deal instead with his political theory—though he also insists that he doesn't have a political theory. His purpose, he once said, is "not to formulate the global systematic theory which holds everything in place, but to analyze the specificity of mechanisms of power . . . to build little by little a strategic knowledge."[1] But strategic knowledge implies a coherent view of reality and a sense of purpose, and it is on these two things that I will focus: first, on Foucault's account of contemporary power relationships and their history or genealogy, and second on his attitude toward these relationships and his purpose (though that is part of the mystery) in writing about them.

Because Foucault is identified with a company of "postmodernist" intellectuals among whom the idea of the subject has been radically questioned, his work can be studied (as his own work) only by ignoring certain of his self-denials. It is probably best to be explicit about this: I take him to be an author in the conventional sense of the term, responsible for the books he wrote, the interviews he gave, the lectures published under his name. I believe that he makes arguments, even in some large sense, *an argument*. This belief situates Foucault inside the very structures of knowledge that he hoped to shatter. He was an antidisciplinarian (his own word), at war with the established intellectual disciplines. This may well have been a just war; at any rate, it was an exciting one. But each of Foucault's campaigns still took place, could only take place, within the overall discipline of language and the rules of plausibility (if not of Truth). His books are fictions, he says, but only because the power relations and the disciplinary establishments within which they could be validated don't yet exist.[2] At the same time, he has many readers who seem to inhabit such establishments, for they believe his genealogies to be accurate and even indisputable; and he has students and followers who pursue the research lines he laid out. His books are full of statements that lay claim to plausibility here and now. He wrote in declarative sentences, at least sometimes, though he had a fondness for conditional and interrogative forms, so that his arguments often have the character of insinuations. They are bolstered in any case by extensive footnotes and a rather erratic but (he has assured us) painstaking documentation. So I take him to be saying something that we are all invited to believe—and then to disbelieve its opposite, that is, "to detach the power of truth from the forms of hegemony . . . within which it operates at the present time."[3] I take him to be making an argument that is right or wrong or partly right and partly wrong.

Toward this argument, I shall adopt a "constructivist" position. Since Foucault never presented it in anything like a systematic fashion, I shall put it together out of the later (and more political) books and interviews, ignoring passages that I don't understand and refusing to live at the heights of his flamboyance. I will do what most of us do with any book we read: try to puzzle out what the author is saying. So great minds are subdued. . . . Reading Borges's Chinese encyclopedia, I would sit struggling to design a proper index.[4]

One last assumption, especially important since Parisian reputations are not hard currency in the United States today: I assume that my effort in this chapter is worthwhile, not only because Foucault has been influential but also because his account of our everyday politics, though often annoyingly presented and never wholly accurate or sufficiently nuanced, is right enough to be disturbing—and also because it is importantly wrong. Here Foucault resembles his great antagonist in the world of political theory, Thomas Hobbes. ("We must eschew the model of Leviathan," he says, "in the study of power.")[5] The comparison won't stand up with regard to insight or lucidity, only with regard to the general views of the two writers. Hobbes gives us an importantly wrong account of political sovereignty; rhetorically inflated and drained of moral distinctions, it nevertheless captures something of the reality of the modern state. Foucault gives us an importantly wrong account of local discipline; rhetorically inflated and drained of moral distinctions, it nevertheless captures something of the reality of contemporary society.

Pluralism

Foucault's political argument starts with the following two-part proposition, the second part largely unstated because it is (or was) so widely accepted on the French intellectual left: (1) in the *ancien régime*, the king was the actual ruler, the visible, effective, necessary agent, the concrete embodiment of political power; but (2) the people are not the rulers and not the embodiments of power in the modern democratic state; nor are their representatives. Elections, parties, mass movements, legislative assemblies, political debate—all these are absent in Foucault's "discourse of power," and the absence is eloquent. It requires only the briefest of explanations. "Power is not built up out of 'wills' (individual or collective)," Foucault writes, "nor is it derivable from interests."[6] There is no general will and no stable or effective coalition of interest groups; sovereignty works only when there is a physical sovereign. Popular sovereignty is a fraud, for the "people" don't exist except as an ideological abstraction, and abstractions cannot rule. No liberation followed from the defeat of the king, no process of collective self-government. In contemporary Western societies, power is dispersed, but not as democrats hoped to disperse it, not to citizens who argue and vote and determine the policies of the central government. Citizenship and government alike have been superseded by professional expertise and local discipline. And yet the whole point of modern political theory, first conceived in the absolutist states of the seventeenth and eighteenth centuries, has been to account for citizenship and government. Theorists still try to answer the Hobbesian questions, which Foucault puts this way: "What is the sovereign? How is he constituted as sovereign? What bond of obedience ties individuals to the sovereign?"[7] So they reveal the genealogical constraints of their enterprise, designed to legitimate a set of power relations that have now collapsed. This is another reason, perhaps, why Foucault does not want to call himself a political theorist. When the king's head was cut off, the theory of the state died too; it was replaced by sociology, psychology, criminology, and so on.

The king is headless; the political world has no practical center. Foucault nicely finesses the "legitimation crisis" described by the German philosopher Jürgen Habermas and hotly debated on the other side of the Rhine; the state has not been legitimate for a long time. The exercise of power and the acceptance or endurance of power now occur somewhere else. The argument of Hobbes and his theoretical heirs (liberal and democratic) was that subjects created and legitimized their own subjection by ceding some of their rights to the state; hence the state was rightful and a defender of rights. But this too is ideology; it merely "conceals" the "actual procedures of power," "the mechanisms of disciplinary coercion," which operate beyond the effective reach of the law. In fact, subjection has been continuous; it takes today a new form, claims a new legitimacy, creates new subjects—not the carriers of rights but of norms, the agents and also the products of moral, medical, sexual, psychological (rather than legal) regulation. Our interest shifts, because the action shifts, from the singular state to a pluralist society.

Many years ago, in a graduate seminar with Barrington Moore, I studied a group of American political scientists and sociologists, called "pluralists," who argued that power was radically dispersed in American society. There was no sovereign, no political elite, no ruling class, but a pluralism of groups and even of individuals. Everybody or almost everybody had a little power; nobody had so much as to be sure of getting his own way all the time. I was taught that this was a conservative doctrine.[8] By denying the existence of a directing center, it sought to rob radical politics of its object. And yet, of course, there was such a center, if not always visible or self-conscious or highly organized. Law and policy had a shape, corresponded to a set of interests; and the interests imposed the shape, dominating if they did not absolutely control the making of law and policy.

Foucault can be read, and not inaccurately, as a pluralist; he too denies the existence of a center. "Power comes from below . . . there is no binary and all-encompassing opposition between rulers and ruled at the root of power relations. . . . Power is not something that is acquired, seized, or shared . . . power is exercised from innumerable points."[9] Again: "At every moment, power is in play in small individual parts."[10] And again: "Power is employed and exercised through a net-like organization . . . individuals circulate between its threads; they are always in a position of simultaneously undergoing and exercising power. They are not only its inert or consenting targets; they are always also the elements of its articulation."[11]

This is not, of course, the same argument that the American pluralists made. Foucault is concerned not with the dispersion of power to the extremities of the political system, but with its exercise at the extremities. For the Americans, power was dispersed to individuals and groups and then recentralized, that is, brought to bear again at the focal point of sovereignty. For Foucault there is no focal point, but rather an endless network of power relations. Still, his account does appear to have conservative implications; at least (and this is not the same thing) it has anti-Leninist implications. There can't be a seizure of power if there is nothing at the center to seize. If power is exercised at innumerable points, then it has to be challenged point by point. "The overthrow of these micro-powers does not obey the law of all or nothing."[12] "There is a plurality of resistances, each of them a special case."[13]

This begins to sound like a reformist politics, and Foucault has indeed been accused of reformism. Challenged from the left, he sometimes stands firm, if uneasy: "It is necessary," he told the editorial collective of a radical magazine, "to make a distinction between [the] critique of reformism as a political practice and the critique of a political practice on the grounds that it might give rise to a reform. This latter . . . critique is frequent in left-wing groups and its employment is part of the mechanism of micro-terrorism by which they have often operated."[14] This is certainly right and conceivably, in a certain context, brave, but it avoids conceding the truth for which the collective was reaching: that Foucault is not a good revolutionary. He isn't a good revolutionary because he doesn't believe in the sovereign state or the ruling class, and therefore he doesn't believe in the takeover of the state or the replacement of the class. He doesn't believe in a democratic revolution, for the *demos* doesn't exist in his political world. And he certainly doesn't believe in a vanguard revolution: the vanguard is nothing more than the monarch *manqué*, one more pretender to royal power.

Disciplinary Society

The heroic moment when the king was overthrown can't be repeated (at least not by the French: Foucault thought for a time that the Iranians were repeating it and expressed an incomprehensible delight). But does Foucault believe in the possibility of a more modest heroism? His political theory, he once said, is a "tool kit" not for revolution but for local resistance. In order to understand what that might mean, and whether it is possible, we must consider more carefully the forms of social discipline that replace royal power. Every human society has its own discipline, and in every society above a certain size this discipline is exercised at micro as well as macro levels. On Foucault's understanding, as I understand it, the old regime required only a rather loose discipline at the micro level; or perhaps, and this is after all a traditional view of traditional societies, habitual routines and customary rules worked with little more than intermittent coercion. Political interventions were dramatic but occasional—like those horrifying punishments that Foucault describes in the opening section of *Discipline and Punish*, which made royal power visible and were entirely consistent with a generally ineffective system of law enforcement. But we live in a different age, where economy and society alike require a far more detailed control of individual behavior. This is a control that no single person or political elite or ruling party or class can establish and sustain from a single point: hence Foucault's "innumerable points" and his endless networks in which, he says, we are all enmeshed.

Many writers before Foucault suggested that we live in a more disciplined society than has ever existed before. This is not to say that individual behavior is more routinized or predictable, only that it is more intimately, more intrusively, subjected to rules, standards, schedules, and authoritative inspections. Some twenty years ago in an article on the welfare state, I argued that

> the most impressive feature of modern welfare administration is the sheer variety of its coercive and deterrent instruments. Every newly recognized need, every service received, creates a new dependency and a new social bond. Even [the] recognition of individuals—our hard-won visibility—becomes a source of intensified control. Never have ordinary citizens been so well-known to the public authorities as in the welfare state. We are all counted, numbered, classsified, catalogued, polled, interviewed, watched, and filed away.[15]

And so on: lots of people wrote that way, all of us probably overestimating the possibilities of surveillance and pacification. We worried that the revolt of the masses had somehow been deflected from its proper course or, worse, had found an unexpected fulfillment.

Foucault extends and dramatizes this view while at the same time shifting attention from the welfare state to the social agencies that operate on what he calls its "underside." His books are rather like the king's punishments: rhetorical statements of great power, though often ineffective in the scholarly version of law enforcement—the presentation of evidence, careful argument, the consideration of alternative views. They focus on three institutional networks of social discipline, all of them the work of eighteenth- and nineteenth-century reformers: asylums, hospitals, and prisons; with side glances at armies, schools, and factories. The focus is vivid; Foucault's sense for the telling detail is quite wonderful; no writer on the state can match it (the state being, after all, invisible and impalpable). Whatever disagreements one has, it is impossible to read his books without a sense of recognition.

I will come back to this sense, and so to the actual experience of living within the network of disciplines, in a moment. But first a word about the general character of the network—for it does have a general character, even if it isn't governed by a single will. Foucault is not the Kafka of the prison or the asylum; his account is frightening enough, but it is not surrealistic. The disciplinary society is a *society*, a social whole, and in his description of the parts of this whole, Foucault is a functionalist. No one designed the whole, and no one controls it; but as if by an invisible hand, all its parts are somehow fitted together. Sometimes Foucault marvels at the fit: "This is an extremely complex system of relations which leads one finally to wonder how, given that no one person can have conceived it in its entirety, it can be so subtle in its distribution, its mechanisms, reciprocal controls and adjustments."[16] Sometimes he is quite matter of fact: "If the prison-institution has survived for so long, with such immobility, if the principle of penal detention has never seriously been questioned, it is no doubt because this carceral system . . . carried out certain very precise functions."[17] The "complex system of relations" within which these functions are carried out is presumably modern industrial society, but Foucault sometimes prefers a more precise name. In his account of how sexuality was "constituted" in the nineteenth century, he writes: "This bio-power was without question an indispensible element in the development of capitalism; the latter would not have been possible without the controlled insertion of bodies into the machinery of production and the adjustment of the phenomenon of population to economic processes. But this was not all capitalism required; it also needed . . . etc."[18] Capitalism gets what it needs, though how the process works Foucault doesn't reveal, and his account of the local uses of power would appear to make the revelation less likely than it might be within a more conventional Marxist theory.

Some kind of functionalist (and determinist) Marxism, nonetheless, provides the distant underpinning of Foucault's account of power. In one of those dancelike interviews in which he both takes and doesn't take political positions, Foucault is led to say that the class struggle stands to the local power struggles as their "guarantee of intelligibility."[19] What this intelligibility might mean is a question never explicitly addressed in his work. But I do want to notice that the guarantee exists, like Bishop Berkeley's God, and that Foucault's stress on the particularist character of power relations is not an argument for disconnection or radical autonomy. He is, after all, in search of strategic, not merely tactical, knowledge. He argues from the bottom up, but that is a mode of analysis that suggests, at least by its direction, that the world is not all bottom. Even if he cannot find a state to seize, he might still locate, somehow, somewhere, in the complex system of modern society or of the capitalist economy, a comprehensible antagonist.

Foucault begins, however, with tactics, with local power relations, with men and women at the lowest levels of the social hierarchy or, as he would say, caught in the fine meshes of the power networks, with you and me. We can't understand contemporary society or our own lives, he argues, unless we look hard and closely at this kind of power and at these people: not state or class or corporate power, not the proletariat or the people or the toiling masses, but hospitals, asylums, prisons, armies, schools, factories; and patients, madmen, criminals, conscripts, children, factory hands. We must study the sites where power is physically administered and physically endured or resisted. In fact, this is not quite what Foucault does; he is more a theorist than a historian, and the materials out of which he constructs his books consist mostly of the written projects and proposals for these sites, the architectural plans, the handbooks of rules and regulations, rarely of actual accounts of practices and experiences. He never gets very close to the people he writes about. Still, it is exciting to see how the projects proliferate, how similar designs are repeated for different institutions, how the rules and regulations, though they often have the perfectionist character of an anti-utopia, as if in anticipation of *1984* or *Brave New World*, begin nevertheless to suggest the outlines of our everyday lives.

His institutional genealogies, *Madness and Civilization*, *The Birth of the Clinic*, and *Discipline and Punish*, are Foucault's strongest works, and they are strong even though, or perhaps because, they offer no "guarantee of intelligibility." They do point, though, to a certain sort of coherence. For it is Foucault's claim, and he is partly right, that the discipline of a prison, say, represents a continuation and intensification of what goes on in more ordinary places—and wouldn't be possible if it didn't. So we all live by the clock, get up to an alarm, work to a schedule, feel the eye of authority upon us, are periodically subject to examination and intimate inspection. No one is entirely free from the new forms of social control. It has to be added, however, that subjection to this control is not the same thing as being in prison: Foucault tends systematically to underestimate the difference, and this criticism goes to the heart of his politics.

All the microforms of discipline are functional to a larger system. Foucault sometimes calls this system capitalism, but he also gives it a number of more dramatic names: the disciplinary society, the carceral city, the panoptic regime, and most frightening (and misleading) of all, the carceral archipelago. The names are an indictment, but not an indictment that invites a political response. Should we overthrow the panoptic regime? That is not so easy to do, for this isn't a political regime in the usual sense of the term; it isn't a state or a constitution or a government. It isn't ruled by a Hobbist sovereign, shaped by a founder or a founding convention, controlled through a legislative or judicial process. Foucault's system is more like the physical embodiment of what he called in his earlier books an *episteme*; social structures take shape as the flesh and bones of dominant discourse.[20] Contemporary discipline, he argues, has escaped the world of law and right, which belongs to a dying discourse, and has begun to "colonize" that world, replacing legal principles with principles of physical, psychological, and moral normality. Thus, in his book on prisons: "Although the universal juridicism of modern society seems to fix limits on the exercise of power, its universally widespread panopticism enables it to operate, on the underside of the law, a machinery both immense and minute."[21] And the code by which this machinery operates is a scientific, not a legal code. Its function is to create useful subjects, men and women who conform to a standard, who are certifiedly sane or healthy or docile or competent, not free agents who invent their own standards, who, in the language of rights, "give the law to themselves."

The triumph of professional or scientific norms over legal rights and of local discipline over constitutional law is, again, a fairly common theme of contemporary social criticism. It has given rise to a series of campaigns in defense of the rights of the mentally ill, of prisoners, hospital patients, children (in schools and also in families). Foucault himself has been deeply involved in prison reform or—I had better be careful—in a political practice with regard to prisons that might give rise to reforms. And indeed there have been reforms: new laws about consent, confidentiality, access to records; judicial interventions in the administration of prisons and schools. Foucault has little to say about this sort of thing and is obviously skeptical about its effectiveness. Despite his emphasis on local discipline and struggle, he is largely uninterested in local victory.

But what other end can his criticism have? What other victories can he think possible, given his strategic knowledge? Consider: (1) that discipline-in-detail, the precise control of behavior, is necessary to the (unspecified) large-scale features of contemporary social and economic life; (2) that this kind of control requires the microsetting, the finely meshed network, the local power relation, represented in ideal-typical fashion by the cellular structure of the prison, the daily timetable of prison events, the extralegal penalties inflicted by prison authorities, the face-to-face encounters of guard and prisoner; (3) that the prison is only one small part of a highly articulated, mutually reinforcing carceral continuum extending across society, in which all of us are implicated, and not only as captives or victims; and finally (4) that the complex of disciplinary mechanisms and institutions constitute and are constituted by the contemporary human sciences—an argument that runs through all of Foucault's work, to which I will return later on. Physical disciplines and intellectual disciplines are radically entangled; the carceral continuum is validated by the knowledge of human subjects that it makes possible.

Given all that—and leaving aside for the moment whether it adds up to a satisfactory account of contemporary social life—how can Foucault expect anything more than a small reform here or there, an easing of disciplinary rigor, the introduction of more humane, if no less effective, methods? What else is possible now that political revolution is impossible? And yet sometimes, not in his books but in the interviews and especially in a series of interviews in the early 1970s, which still reflect the impact of May 1968, Foucault seems to see a grand alternative: the complete dismantling of the disciplinary system, the fall of the carceral city, not revolution but abolition. It is for this reason that Foucault's politics are commonly called anarchist, and anarchism certainly has its moments in his thought. Not that he imagines a social system different from our own, beyond discipline and sovereignty alike: "I think that to imagine another system is to extend our participation in the present system."[22] It is precisely the idea of society as a system, a set of institutions and practices, that must give way to something else—what else we can't imagine. Perhaps human freedom requires a nonfunctionalist society, whose arrangements, whatever they are, serve no larger purpose and have no redeeming value. The nearest thing to an account of such arrangements comes in an interview first published in November 1971. "It is possible," says Foucault, "that the rough outline of a future society is supplied by the recent experiences with drugs, sex, communes, other forms of consciousness, and other forms of individuality."[23] In that same interview, with some such vision in mind, he repudiates the likely reformist results of his own prison work: "The ultimate goal of [our] interventions was not to extend the visiting rights of prisoners to 30 minutes or to procure flush toilets for the cells, but to question the social and moral distinction between the innocent and the guilty."[24]

As this last passage suggests, when Foucault is an anarchist, he is a moral as well as a political anarchist. For him morality and politics go together. Guilt and innocence are created by the legal code, normality and abnormality by the scientific disciplines. To abolish power systems is to abolish legal and moral and also scientific categories: away with them all! But what will be left? Foucault does not believe, as earlier anarchists did, that the free human subject is a subject of a certain sort, naturally good and warmly sociable. Rather, there is no such thing as a free human subject, no natural man or woman. Men and women are always social creations, the products of codes and disciplines. And so Foucault's radical abolitionism, if it is serious, is not anarchist so much as nihilist.[25] For on his own argument, either there will be nothing left at all, nothing visibly human; or new codes and disciplines will be produced, and Foucault gives us no reason to expect that these will be any better than the ones we currently live with. Nor, for that matter, does he give us any way of knowing what "better" might mean. Among social systems as among *epistemes*, he is neutral; he attacks the panoptic regime only because that is the regime under which he happens to live. His only reason for climbing the mountain is that it is there.

Politics

Is he committed to his anarchism/nihilism? He has a way of turning on anyone who imitates it or tries to act it out politically, and I am inclined to think it is intended to have demonstrative, not practical, force. In a 1977 interview, he is savagely critical of some of his comrades in "the struggle around the penal system" who have fallen for "a whole naive, archaic ideology which makes the criminal . . . into an innocent victim and a pure rebel. . . . The result has been a deep split between this campaign with its monotonous, lyrical little chant, heard only among a few small groups, and the masses who have good reason not to accept it as valid political currency."[26] For Foucault, obviously, the prisoner cannot be an innocent victim, for he has denied the distinction between guilt and innocence. But his larger argument does seem to suggest the very claim that he here repudiates: that every act of resistance at every microsetting of the carceral continuum, whatever its motives, is a "pure rebellion" against the continuum as a whole—and one with which he is always ready to sympathize. What "good reasons" do ordinary men and women have for discriminating among these acts?

The same problem of discrimination arises when Foucault confronts young leftists who confuse the carceral archipelago with the Gulag archipelago, a confusion to which Foucault's terminology in this instance and, more generally, the language of his books, is a perpetual incitement. He himself resists the incitement and is severely critical of those who succumb. "I am indeed worried," he says, "by a certain use that is made of the Gulag-Internment parallel . . . which consists in saying, 'Everyone has their own Gulag, the Gulag is here at our door, in our cities, our hospitals, our prisons, it's here in our heads.' "* And he goes on, forcefully, to reject the "universalizing dissolution of the [Gulag] problem into the denunciation of every possible form of internment."[27] But he provides no principled distinction, so far as I can see, between the Gulag and the carceral archipelagos. I don't believe he can do that, not so long as he is also committed to rejecting the idea of "basic rights" and to blurring the line between guilt and innocence. Nor does he provide a genealogy of the Gulag and, what is probably more important, his account of the carceral archipelago contains no hint of how or why his own society stops short of the Gulag. For such an account would require what Foucault always resists: some positive evaluation of the liberal or social democratic state.

Here again a comparison with Hobbes is illuminating. Hobbes argues that political sovereignty is a literal necessity; without it life is nasty, brutish, and short. He supports every established sovereign; tyranny for him is nothing

* Obviously, it is not only *young* leftists who talk this way. Marcuse took a similar line and had his own epigones, who did not always attend to his ambiguous qualifications. He too argued for the hidden totalitarianism of liberal societies, though he was more interested in cultural consumption than in normative discipline.

more than "monarchy misliked." Since the only alternative to sovereignty is the war of all against all, social criticism is always dangerous and wrong. Foucault believes that discipline is a literal necessity; he abhors all its forms, every sort of confinement and control; liberalism for him is nothing more than discipline concealed. Since he cannot point to an alternative and better discipline, social criticism must always be a futile enterprise. For neither Hobbes nor Foucault does the constitution or the law or even the actual workings of the political system make any difference. In fact, I want to argue, these things make all the difference. One of Foucault's followers, the author of a very intelligent essay on *Discipline and Punish*, draws from that book and the related interviews the extraordinary conclusion that the Russian Revolution failed because it "left intact the social hierarchies and in no way inhibited the functioning of the disciplinary techniques."[28] Exactly wrong: the Bolsheviks created a new regime that overwhelmed the old hierarchies and enormously expanded and intensified the use of disciplinary techniques. And they did this from the heart of the social system, not from what Foucault likes to call the capillaries, from the center and not the extremities. Foucault desensitizes his readers to the importance of politics; but politics matters.

Power relations, he says, "are both intentional and nonsubjective."[29] I don't know what that sentence means, but I think that the contradictory words are intended (nonsubjectively?) to apply to different levels of power. Every disciplinary act is planned and calculated; power is intentional at the tactical level where guard confronts prisoner; doctor, patient; teacher, student. But the set of power relations, the strategic connections, the deep functionalism of power has no subject and is the product of no one's plan. Foucault seems to disbelieve in principle in the existence of a dictator or a party or a state that shapes the character of disciplinary institutions. He is focused instead on what he thinks of as the "micro-fascism" of everyday life and has little to say about authoritarian or totalitarian politics—that is, about the forms of discipline most specific to his own lifetime.

Critical Distance

But these are not the forms most specific to this own country, and Foucault does believe in sticking close to the local exercise of power. Nor does he often use terms like "micro-fascism." He is not a "general intellectual" of the old sort—so he tells us—who provides an account and critique of society as a whole.[30] The general intellectual belongs to the age of the state and the party, when it still seemed possible to seize power and reconstruct society. He is, in the world of political knowledge, what the king once was in the world of political power. Once we have cut off the king's head, power and knowledge alike take different forms. In his lectures and interviews of the middle and late 1970s, Foucault attempts to explain these forms, to work out what can be called a political epistomology. I want now to examine this epistomology, for it is the ultimate source of his anarchism/nihilism.

Sometimes Foucault seems to be committed to nothing more than an elaborate pun on the word "discipline"—which means, on the one hand, a branch of knowledge, and on the other, a system of correction and control. This is his argument: social life is discipline squared. *Discipline makes discipline possible* (the order of the two nouns can be reversed). Knowledge derives from and provides the grounds for social control; every particular form of social control rests on and makes possible a particular form of knowledge. It follows that power isn't merely repressive but also creative (even if all it creates is, say, the science of penology); and similarly, knowledge isn't merely ideological but also true. But this doesn't make either power or knowledge at all attractive. Penology is "constituted" by the prison system in the obvious sense that there could not be a study of prisoners or of the effects of imprisonment if there were no prisons. One form of discipline generates the data that makes the other possible. At the same time, penology provides both the rationale and the intellectual structure of the prison system. There could be no exercise of discipline, at least no sustained and organized exercise, without disciplinary knowledge.

It is a nice model, though perhaps a little too easy. In any case, Foucault proceeds to generalize it. "Truth is a thing of this world: it is produced only by virtue of multiple forms of constraint. And it induces regular effects of power." So for every society, for every historical age, there is a regime of truth, unplanned but functional, generated (for us) out of the multiple forms of constraint, and enforced along with them. There are certain types of discourse that the society accepts "and makes function as true" (the phrase is awkward in English, but it says exactly what he means).[31] There are social mechanisms that enable us to distinguish true and false statements—and sanctions, too, so we won't make mistakes. Foucault believes that truth is relative to its sanctions, and knowledge to the constraints that produce it.

There would appear to be no independent standpoint inside or outside the social system, no possibility for the development of critical principles. I don't mean that Foucault isn't detached; he is indeed so radically detached that he seems, as Charles Taylor has written, to stand nowhere at all—unconditioned by the reigning *episteme*, free of all disciplinary constraints, cut loose from the bonds of class or movement.[32] Of course, one can ask the obvious questions: what is the ground of his own work? To what set of power relations is the genealogical antidiscipline connected? Foucault is far too intelligent not to have worried about these questions. They are standard for any relativism. He responds in two ways: first by saying, as I have already noted, that his genealogies are fictions waiting for the "political realities" that will make them true. Each present invents its own past, but Foucault has invented a past for some future present. At other times, Foucault says more simply that his work is made possible by the events of May 1968 and by subsequent local revolts here and there along the disciplinary continuum. As the conventional disciplines are generated and validated by the conventional uses of power, so Foucault's antidiscipline is generated by the resistance to those uses. But I don't see, on Foucault's terms, how resistance can validate knowledge until the resistance is itself successful (as contemporary discipline is successful)—and it's not clear what success local resistance can have.

But this conventional demand that Foucault show us the ground on which he stands, display his philosophical warrants, is really beside the point. For he makes no demands on us to adopt this or that critical principle or replace these disciplinary norms with some other set of norms. He is not an advocate; he is not a *purposeful* social critic. We are to withdraw our belief in, say, the truths of penology and then support . . . what? Not every prison revolt, for there may be some that we have "good reason" not to support. Which ones then? At this point Foucault's position is simply incoherent. The powerful evocation of the disciplinary system gives way to an antidisciplinarian politics that is mostly rhetoric and posturing.

And yet Foucault was deeply involved in prison reform, and he sometimes seems to urge upon readers his own version of social criticism. His alternative to the general intellectual is the "specific" intellectual, who seeks to subvert or delegitimize the discipline within which he functions. Foucaultian criticism succeeds, if it succeeds at all, only locally, in the immediate institutional setting, at a particular point in the power network. What exactly the critic does, however, and what it means to succeed, remains unclear. Foucault's writings, his example too, suggest something more like a series of discrete provocations than a coherent set of linked activities—or, as a recent critic of Foucault argues, something more like insubordination than political dissent.[33] There isn't any stable reference to moral ideas or any sustained commitment to people or institutions by which outcomes might be measured. That is why Foucault cannot distinguish between different regimes, not at the "general" level of the state and not at the "specific" level of the prison either. His detachment makes for disability; when critical distance stretches into infinity, the critical enterprise collapses.

But ordinary men and women—citizens and prisoners too—are entirely capable of making the necessary distinctions. In those prison revolts with which we might rightly sympathize, for example, the prisoners don't in fact call into question the line between guilt and innocence or the truth value of jurisprudence or penology. Their "discourse" takes a very different form: they describe the brutality of the prison authorities or the inhumanity of prison conditions, and they complain of punishments that go far beyond those to which they were legally condemned. They denounce official arbitrariness, harassment, favoritism, and so on. They demand the introduction and enforcement of what we might best call the rule of law. It doesn't appear that Foucault, for all his sympathy, ever listened to any of this. And yet these descriptions, complaints, denunciations, and demands make an important point. Foucault is certainly right to say that the conventional truths of morality, law, medicine, and psychiatry are implicated in the exercise of power; that is a fact too easily forgotten by conventionally detached scientists, social scientists, and even philosophers. But those same truths also regulate the exercise of power. They set limits on what can rightly be done, and they give shape and conviction to the arguments the prisoners make. The limits are important even if they are in some sense arbitrary. They aren't entirely arbitrary, however, insofar as they are intrinsic to the particular disciplines (in both senses of the word). It is the truths of jurisprudence and penology, for example, that distinguish punishment from preventive detention. It is the truths of psychiatry that distinguish the internment of madmen from the internment of political dissidents. And it is the commitment to truth itself, even if it is only local truth, that distinguishes the education of citizens from ideological drill.

A liberal or social democratic state is one that maintains the limits of its constituent disciplines and disciplinary institutions and that enforces their intrinsic principles. Authoritarian and totalitarian states, by contrast, override those limits, turning education into indoctrination, punishment into repression, asylums into prisons, and prisons into concentration camps. These are crude definitions, but they can easily be elaborated or amended. They indicate, in any case, the enormous importance of the political regime, the sovereign state. For the state is the agency through which society acts upon itself. It is the state that establishes the general framework within which all other disciplinary institutions operate. It is the state that holds open or radically shuts down the possibility of local resistance.* The agents of every disciplinary institution strive, of course, to extend their reach and augment their discretionary power. In the long run, only political action and state power can stop them. Every act of local resistance is an appeal for political or legal intervention from the center. Consider, for example, the factory revolts of the 1930s that led (in the United States) to the establishment of collective bargining and grievance procedures, critical restraints on scientific management, which is one of Foucault's disciplines, though one that he alludes to only occasionally. Success required not only the solidarity of the workers but also the support of the liberal and democratic state. And success was functional not to any state but to a state of that sort; we can easily imagine other "social wholes" that would require other kinds of factory discipline.

A genealogical account of this discipline would be fascinating and valuable, and it would undoubtedly overlap with Foucault's accounts of prisons and hospitals. But if it were complete, it would have to include a genealogy of grievance procedures too, and this would overlap with an account that Foucault doesn't provide, of the liberal state and the rule of law. Here is a kind of knowledge—let's call it political theory or philosophical jurisprudence— that regulates disciplinary arrangements across our society. It arises

* Compare the argument of Stuart Hall with reference to Gramsci's "war of position": "This does not mean, as some people read Gramsci, that . . . the state doesn't matter anymore. The state is . . . absolutely central in articulating the different areas of contestation, the different points of antagonism, into a regime of rule. The moment when you can get sufficient power in the state to organize a central political project is decisive, for then you can use the state to plan, urge, incite, solicit, and punish" (Stuart Hall, "Gramsci and Us," *Marxism Today* [London], June 1987, p. 20).

within one set of power relations and extends toward the others; it offers a critical perspective on all the networks of constraint. The possibility of knowledge of this sort, specific to institutions and political cultures rather than to "points" in the power network, suggests that we still require (I don't mean that society requires, or capitalism or even socialism requires, but you and I require) Foucault's general intellectuals. We need men and women who tell us when state power is corrupted or systematically misused, who cry out that something is rotten, and who reiterate the regulative principles with which we might set things right. General intellectuals don't inhabit a realm of pure value, such as Benda described; Foucault is right to insist that there is no such place, no value untouched by power. They stand among us, in this place, here and now, and they find in our laws and norms reasons for argument. But Foucault stands nowhere and finds no reasons. Angrily, he rattles the bars of the iron cage.[34] But he has no plans or projects for turning the cage into something more like a human home.

But I don't want to end on this note. I don't want to ask Foucault to be uplifting. That is not the task he has set himself. The point is rather that one can't even be downcast, angry, grim, indignant, sullen, or embittered *with reason*, one can't be critical, unless one inhabits some social setting and adopts, however tentatively, its codes and categories. Or unless, and this is much harder, one constructs (along with other men and women) a new setting and works out new codes and categories. Foucault refuses to do either of these things, and that refusal, which makes his genealogies so relentless, is also the catastrophic weakness of his political theory and his social criticism.

12

Breyten Breytenbach: The Critic in Exile

Living at a Distance

Foucault's "disciplinary society" is Breyten Breytenbach's refuge from a real disciplinary society: a South African prison. Since 1983, Breytenbach has been a naturalized French citizen, living in Paris, grateful for France's "tolerance of political dissidents," free to travel wherever he likes (though not to his homeland), free to write as he pleases, even "to castigate [his] adopted *patria* if the need arose. (As it would.)"[1] Mostly, however, he has continued to castigate his native South Africa. He cannot live there; he is an exile or, as he now says, an emigré, but he is also the most brilliant of South African social critics. And the most self-conscious: he writes with extraordinary sharpness, intensity, and pain about the difficulty of writing from a distance—as he has had to do for most of his life—without daily contact, out of hearing of his own language. His language is Afrikaans, and he is said to be one of the finest poets ever to write in Afrikaans, though the greater number of his poems have been written in foreign countries, out of hearing.[2] Perhaps poetry is easier than criticism, for the poet listens with his inner ear, while the critic depends upon an actual dialogue. "Of course, you do take your language with you wherever you go—but it is rather like carrying the bones of your ancestors with you in a bag: they are white with silence, they do not talk back."[3]

Exile is a hard place. But it may, even so, be a good place for social critics—especially for critics whose people have placed themselves, as Breytenbach believes of his own people, on the wrong side of history. In France, he says, he is freed from his roots, detribalized. Shouldn't he be able, then, to write about the Afrikaners and the state they have made with detachment and objectivity? It's not impossible, I suppose, though no one who has read very far in the literature of exile will think that those are its chief qualities. Nor are they the chief qualities of Breytenbach's books and essays. He is himself very restrained in describing the advantages that exile offers to the social critic. "Being in another country may broaden his horizon. He may identify with other intellectuals and . . . hit the international circuit. Or he may—through his exile and because of his politics—identify with . . . oppressed classes [throughout the world]. But that is likely to be a one-way identification. It is rather like a dog loving the moon."[4] Like lovers, critics require some response to their pleas of engagement and concern. To rage at a distant people, to throw daggers at a map: these are not sustaining activities.

No one in his right mind, Breytenbach concludes, would choose exile, would prefer "to live away from intimate communication with his own people." If he had a choice. If he could attend to his preferences. People don't leave South Africa, he says, to find a better climate or to make more money. They leave because of political repression; they choose exile over prison.[5] In exile, they struggle to maintain the broken tie to the homeland, to resist the deadly silence—"at least as concerns the central problems of your country"—that is the exile's ultimate fate. Writing is one means of resistance, and I want to use Breytenbach's books to explore what the critic can say when he writes from exile and what kind of ties he can maintain to a people whose politics and society he has, more radically than any resident, rejected. Breytenbach is a special case, because he did go back to South Africa, not as a critic but as an underground militant, silently, with forged papers. Now, however, after seven years in prison, he seems (sometimes) resigned to his exile:

Do you see yourself as French?

I live in France.

And South Africa? Do you think you'll ever return there?

No. I could be rhetorical, smart-arsed, and say: *I am there*. But no.[6]

Exile and Clandestine Politics

Breytenbach's original departure was not politically motivated; he left South Africa when he was twenty for three years of wandering, odd jobs, writing, and painting. In 1962, he settled in Paris, more a bohemian expatriate than a political exile, and there he met and married a Vietnamese woman, Yolande Ngo Thi Hoang Lien. His first volume of poetry was published in South Africa in 1964; three more followed in the next six years, and the power of his writing was almost immediately recognized by his fellow Afrikaners who seem ready, perhaps too ready, to value their poets—as if the nationalist cause were served by any genuinely poetic use of the national language, whatever the poems actually say. (This became a source of considerable anxiety for the poet later on.) But when Breytenbach wanted to return to South Africa and receive in person various literary prizes that had been awarded to him, his wife was refused a visa and he was threatened with arrest under the Immorality Act—for living with a woman of a different race. It was then, strictly speaking, that his exile began. Long opposed to apartheid, he now began to write about it and to construct a political position.

As a wandering poet (painter too) and a Parisian expatriate, Breytenbach had already made a decisive break with Afrikaner society—an artist's version of the philosopher's escape:

> To the best of my powers, I oppose
> my people: cave dwellers.[7]

But the more he wrote about politics, the more clear it became that he had not really escaped the cave; he carried with him a terrible burden of guilt and rage. In the work of the later sixties and early seventies, this is often expressed in passionate diatribe—sometimes contained within, sometimes exploding, sometimes just replacing his poetry. He doesn't write in the language of the sun when he denounces the cave dwellers. Despite the reiterated theme of his prose fantasy, *Om te vlieg* (*To Fly* [1971]), "white is dead," Breytenbach's deepest feelings are still engaged with his "whitish" Afrikaner countrymen, who are very much alive. His politics reflect this engagement, as do his repeated attempts, personal and political in motivation, to return to what he describes alternately as the land of death and the garden of paradise.

In 1973, the authorities relented (they would soon have reasons to regret that decision) and issued visas to Breytenbach and his wife for a ninety-day visit. He spent the time talking with family and friends and showing the country to his wife. But he also spoke at a conference on Afrikaner literature, drawing a large crowd of enthusiastic students, and denouncing the apartheid regime. Throughout his visit, he was shadowed by security agents and, in a series of bizarre interviews, invited to spy on exiled dissidents when he returned to Paris. Instead, he wrote *A Season in Paradise*, a strange and beautiful book, haunting poetry and brilliantly inventive prose, intimate memoir, travel diary, political argument, a song of love and hate for his country and its people. The book somehow survived the censorship and was published five years later in South Africa, in Afrikaans, with only minor deletions, at a time when Breytenbach himself was in prison.[8]

Back in Paris in the middle seventies, he had organized a small political grouping more or less parallel in orientation to the Black Consciousness movement of Steve Biko—and opposed to the official line of the African National Congress (ANC), which was dominated, Breytenbach thought, by the Communist party. Though he advocated a unitary and democratic state in which the black majority would come into its own, he thought it necessary for white militants to work independently among their own people. "Just as I respect the black man trying to improve the dispensation of his . . . people, just so, I believe, will the black man respect me only to the extent that I am prepared to work for the transformation of my community—and not if I attempt to tell him what he ought to do."[9] This is another example of what I have been calling reiterative morality, and it is meant to contrast with the false universalism of the Communists, who were busy "papering over the real problems of cultural awareness" (and telling everybody, black and white, what to do). The Communists knew in detail the necessary course of the historical process and the necessary endpoint of the liberation movement. Breytenbach had ideas, mostly, about the immediate struggle. These were, however, Leninist ideas—"to regroup the progressive elements . . . into a revolutionary avant-garde"—and they pressed Breytenbach toward a politics as secretive and elitist as that of the party.[10]

In 1975, he returned to South Africa under a false name, with forged documents, on a clandestine mission. Exactly what he was supposed to do there had not been very carefully thought out; nor was he trained for the secret life—though this hardly seems an excuse for the extraordinary ineptness of his conduct. His fellow Afrikaner André Brink has suggested that he actually sought arrest in order to expiate his guilt at the hands of his own people.[11] I suspect that he was in headlong flight from his exile. Writing about apartheid from the safety of Paris must have seemed to him morally inadequate, inauthentic, risk free, and impotent. Breytenbach was one more critic reaching for heroism and unwilling, perhaps rightly, to make exile itself a heroic act. In any case, his tiny group had been penetrated by the South African police, and he was followed from his arrival in Johannesburg and arrested as he was leaving, along with most of the people he had managed to meet.

I shall not rehearse the details of his two trials and seven-year imprisonment (at the end of which he had something to teach prison reformers like Foucault about the value of humane detention).* More important here are his later reflections on clandestine political action. Though its protagonists try very hard to get inside the society they mean to change, clandestinity in politics is oddly similar to detachment in social criticism. Breytenbach describes the purity of thinking, heightened political consciousness, rigorous discipline, and intense loyalty of the band of secret militants. Like exile, clandestinity liberates the dedicated few from their parochial connections. "The very fact of having opted for [clandestine] action usually implies that one has established a certain distance between yourself and the traditional, overt political groupings in your country. You are thus less bound by the nationalist symptoms that these groups may manifest." Set loose from family and friends, from churches, parties, and mass movements, the militants can make their own way, guided only by their private understandings of truth and justice.

* There has been considerable controversy about Breytenbach's behavior at his first trial where, under pressure from his family and perhaps disoriented by months of solitary confinement, he appeared apologetic and compliant. For a hostile account, see Martin Garbus, *Traitors and Heroes: A Lawyer's Memoir* (New York: Atheneum, 1987), pp. 3–31. Breytenbach's own account can be found in *The True Confessions of an Albino Terrorist* (New York: Farrar, Straus and Giroux, 1985).

But this is the romanticism of the secret life, and Breytenbach has a seamier story to tell: "How the means corrupt the men, how [clandestine] groups become a law unto themselves, so infatuated with their own analysis, so turned in upon themselves, and so cornered when these analyses prove to be incorrect, that the only way out seems to be [more and more] vigorous forms of terrorism." Has this kind of politics ever been successful, he asks, "apart from, in some instances, making it possible for the clandestine activist to come to power?"[12]

Out of prison, Breytenbach renounced secret politics, criticized life in the clandestine cells (which he called "colonies of grave dwellers"—more restrictive, even, than the cave), confined his own activism to his writing. His view of apartheid was unchanged, but he had a new understanding of strategy and tactics. If you had to work in your own community, blacks among blacks, whites among whites, then you had also to attend to the actually existing consciousness of the community and not only to the heightened consciousness of your own small group. "Maybe," he wrote in 1983,

> we ought to settle for the slower processes; maybe we must, very paradoxically, extend our confidence to the people and whatever mass organizations the people may throw up. Ah, but that means that we have to accommodate the notion that our way . . . may be diluted or changed completely . . . since we shall be losing control over the evolution that we become part of. Isn't that what "power to the people" implies?[13]

One might say that the most important mass organization thrown up by the Afrikaner people is the National party—and Breytenbach certainly does not mean to defer to the Nationalists. He is only arguing that intellectuals with their correct doctrines ought not to preempt the opposition to nationalism; they should participate in oppositional politics, say their piece, and not worry about losing control.

Breytenbach is in any case an unlikely advocate of correct doctrines. His mind is too quick, critical, playful, ironic; his pen writes zigzag; his arguments are always provisional. "There is in fact no Truth," he told the Dutch PEN chapter a few months after his release from prison. "We are too fragile and volatile for that; we work with too many uncertainties. There is rather the continual shaping of something resembling, poorly, provisionally, 'truth.' "[14] No doubt, many of the PEN members were looking for something more absolute from a man who had just emerged from one of the modernist versions of hell. From suffering comes certainty. But if this is a standard expectation, Breytenbach is committed to defeating it. He is bound, indeed, to the cause of black political power and ready (today) to recognize the ANC as the mass organization that best represents that cause. But the cause is not in any simple sense "correct," his bond is by no means unconditional; he is still a critic, though he no longer occupies a clear-cut ideological position. His view of his own people, of the Afrikaners, is even more "fragile and volatile." Love and hate, identification and rejection are raised to such a pitch of intensity that A *Season in Paradise* seems now, looking back, an almost gentle book (by any objective standard it isn't gentle at all). Breytenbach is living through, and writing about, the hardest experiences of the social critic: exile, alienation, and defeat. How does the critic "settle for the slower processes" when "slower" is infinitely slow? How does he sustain a tie to people, country, and culture when all three are hopelessly implicated in an abominable politics?

The Critic and His Tribe

One of the repeated themes of Breytenbach's writing since his release from prison is a simple rejection of his own identity: "I am not an Afrikaner."[15] In A *Season in Paradise*, he had still used first-person pronouns, even in his harshest sentences. "We whiter ones," he wrote, "are the scum of a civilization based upon injustices."[16] Now he insists that the injustices are built into the identity; to use the name is to make a political statement; to reject the name is to reject the politics. At one point, briefly, he seems to have thought it necessary to reject Afrikaans too, as if nothing could be said in that language that did not carry oppressive meanings. But any such view involves a perverse judgment of his own poetry, which clearly carries different meanings: anger, reproach, guilt, and, more rarely, hope for the future. Indeed, South Africa today is far closer than the America that Marcuse described in 1964 to a totalitarian society in which "language tends to coagulate into a . . . manipulated and indoctrinated universe."[17] But Afrikaans is nonetheless not Newspeak; it can still be put to liberating use (and to other uses too: it is "our lithe language of love"), and Breytenbach has in fact continued to use it, describing himself now, whimsically, as the only Afrikaans-writing French poet.

That isn't quite right either. Breytenbach's critical strategy—which reflects, I think, his deepest feelings—has been to forge a new identity, not Afrikaner, certainly not French (though, as he says, he "lives in France"), and not alienated and detached either, not yielding to the conditions of exile (though for some writers, he says, "exile can be a country to explore"). His new identity is South African. He describes himself again—for the critic's identity, his self-naming, is an issue that must be settled if the critical enterprise is to move forward—as "a whitish Afrikaans-speaking South African African."[18] And speaking as one of *them*, Breytenbach makes the claim that Camus made for his own people. "South African Whites are African; they are there [he is writing from Paris] to stay." But he adds a proviso that has no Camusian equivalent: the problem of their staying can only be solved "within a Black socio-cultural field of reference."[19] Breytenbach is African in a way that Camus never was Algerian, and this identity is no mere construct, worked up for the critical occasion, a poetic invention. It is a real historical product; the Afrikaners have become one of the African tribes, hybrid like all the others; and Afrikaans is a creole language, seventeenth-century Dutch, radically simplified, with Malay and African additions—nothing like Camus's French. It is a language that the Afrikaners share with the coloreds (people of mixed race), who probably played the larger part in its development: a language that belongs now to Africa rather than to Europe and that invites its speakers to attempt a similar belonging.

Breytenbach's critique follows from his new identity. Apartheid, he argues, is "an effort to curb the forming of a South African nation—politically, economically, culturally, and therefore also racially—which should be one of the most normal things on earth given our interdependence and mutually hybrid origins."[20] The effort succeeds, apartheid works, but only by cutting the Afrikaner off from the people of his own country and from "the South African in himself." It is *his* identity that is artificial, the creation of political willfulness, so that today "the tribal ethos of the Afrikaners consists of negation, suppression, withdrawal, and reaction."[21] To say no to all that is not to abuse or reject oneself; it is more like self-knowledge than self-hate. And, similarly, to reject apartheid is not an act of treason, though it will be called that by the rulers of the state—who are themselves at war with the great majority of (what Breytenbach calls) their own people. "I'm not for one moment attempting to deny the South Africanness, the *Africanité* of those now ruling; I am, however, saying that the opposition is patriotic, coming from within, in the name of the healing of the South African nation."[22]

A South African patriot, yes; but still with reference to his own tribe Breytenbach is marginal, dissident, subversive. He acknowledges his responsibility and therefore his connection: "What exists in this country has been perpetrated in our—in my—name, in our—in my—language. Although, therefore, I am no one's delegate but my own and that of my fleas, I cannot and will not dissociate myself from this mess."[23] But connection of this sort is a perpetual torture, and to dissociate oneself, to make the most of one's marginality, is a permanent temptation. The temptation takes many different forms, and Breytenbach, one feels, has worked his way through all of them. Writing in 1985, in the "End Notes" to his *End Papers* (a book that has to be read simultaneously from both ends), he describes the most common form of political escape: "Many of us projected our . . . local marginalism on to a romantic, potentially revolutionary 'elsewhere.' " This is a description, though only a partial one, of his own politics in the early 1970s in which third world radicals play surrogates for himself and his comrades. Now he asserts what I take to be the central theme of his criticism, of his poetry too: "*The essential is not elsewhere.*"[24] The line that I quoted in my introduction, "Poetry is mainstream," makes the same point, perhaps a little desperately, since it seems to insist upon what is obviously (by all the rules of common sense) untrue. But this is Breytenbach's poetic truth. The poet/critic speaks to the heart of his people, provides "sense-making interpretations" of the social realities of his country. He cannot dissociate himself; he cannot choose some other, more suitable country (though he "lives in France"). If he is marginal to the world that apartheid has made, he nonetheless declares himself to be in the mainstream of his own history and his national culture.

The "mainstream" poet/critic has two tasks, Breytenbach argued in 1983: "He is the questioner and the implacable critic of the mores and attitudes and myths of his society . . . he is also the exponent of the aspirations of his people."[25] Ten years earlier, when he wrote *A Season in Paradise*, Breytenbach managed to perform both these tasks, not easily, to be sure, not without radical shifts of emphasis and tone, but without overt self-contradiction. For he found in the Afrikaner community of the heartland, among farming families far away from the cities, aspirations that he could honestly expound: toward unity and harmony with the land and people of Africa. He found, or he thought he found, the South African in the Afrikaner, and he interpreted this as a kind of pre-Nationalist humanism, which a critic attuned to his people might still retrieve—though the time for retrieval was fast running out. Today the task remains but it isn't clear that time remains. Who is it, after all, who supports apartheid? Whose interests are served by the ideology of separation? Once one has finished a critique of Afrikaner "attitudes," is there anything left to hope for from Afrikaner "aspirations?" Critics of Breytenbach have compared him to Camus, unable to make the final break, to give up on his tribe, to recognize, as one of them writes, that "history has passed Afrikaner humanism by."[26]

Certainly, there have been Afrikaner humanists, and there also exists a tradition of *volkskritiek* within which Breytenbach may well belong, if only as an extreme case. *Volkskritiek* will only work, according to the earlier Afrikaner poet N. P. van Wyk Louw, if the critic is closely connected to his people and "prepared to share its shame."[27] I think that Breytenbach does in fact share the shame, willy-nilly, prepared or not. But it is clear from his writing since his imprisonment that he resents the sharing; perhaps he feels that the years in prison burned the shame out of him. Even more important, he now denies his own guilt—and repudiates every kind of guilt-ridden politics: "Guilt and all . . . [the] breast-beating sentimentalism engendered by guilt—these are out. Leave that to the judges and the preachers. Don't be a preacher or a judge."[28] If he was once sentimental about (some of) his own tribe, he at least won't transfer the sentimentality to the tribes his own tribe oppresses. Does that make him a distanced and objective critic of all the African *volke*, liberated from the shame and guilt of personal membership? Not quite; for when he says, "I am not an Afrikaner," he says it to his fellow Afrikaners; he isn't trying to establish his credentials among the other tribes or with some international audience. He wants his own people to repeat the repudiation; he wants them to *become* Afrikaners according to a new understanding of the name.

Hanging in There

From the beginning of his political involvement, Breytenbach called himself a revolutionary; he did not believe that apartheid could be reformed, humanized, liberalized, or made more flexible. Small victories of that sort only strengthened the system as a whole. South Africa would not be a decent place until "the present power structures are broken down by destroying the very foundations on which they rest."[29] The *Sestigers*, the South African avant-garde of the sixties, only lent legitimacy to the regime, he insisted, by their literary protests. Reformers were secret supporters of apartheid. Breytenbach denounced them in a poem written in 1969, at the height of his own radical fervor—his muse in this case deserting him entirely:

> many-tongued arse-lickers of the bourgeois.[30]

But this sort of thing was merely the ugly reflection of an internal struggle; the adjective and the noun of Breytenbach's identity (as it then was) were at war with one another: *Afrikaner radical*. Even a minimalist commitment to the adjective seemed to deny the seriousness of the noun.

A decade and a half later, Breytenbach expressed the dilemma in a prose more lively and inventive than his 1969 poem:

> I could argue—well, yes, I must blow them out of the bathtub, see, I'm trying to yeast Afrikaner sensibilities from within and therefore I start with the bread we break together, even if only via the basic complicity of the common mumbo-jumbo, I mean, language, I mean, *taal*. How else could I have a say-so? Ah, but how do I avoid the twisting and the bending, the kneeling and the back-stabbing, the compromises, the ethical corruption, in my attempts to "hang in there?"[31]

A serious writer trying to work *from within* (this double preposition is common in Breytenbach's essays) a people on the wrong side of history can hardly escape self-doubt. If he is censored or banned, how can he reach the men and women he needs to reach? And if he is uncensored, unbanned, isn't that a sign that he has compromised himself, that he is being used? "You will then have to decide whether your opposition, which you have adapted in order to survive, now permitted to exist, is not . . . making the totalitarian state stronger by giving it a lark mirror of internal flexibility."[32] Breytenbach has made his own decision: his books, poems, essays are published in South Africa (I cannot find many signs of adaptation). Though he doesn't live there, he "hangs in there."

It is also a sign of "hanging in," I think, that Breytenbach is critical of black revolutionaries as well as of white reformers. I don't mean that he is looking now for some small piece of middle ground, equidistant from revolution and reform. The middle isn't, in his view, a matter of intellectual discovery; it is a difficult political creation. And he seems to believe, sometimes, that the time for creation is long gone. Consider the tenses of the verbs in the following lines: "A political 'middle ground' . . . could have been established only were there to be, by now, say two or three thousand White political prisoners."[33]* As it is, whites, even white radicals, have made themselves irrelevant to revolutionary politics. So he says, sometimes; and yet he is himself involved, if not in revolutionary politics anymore, then in a politics of some sort, the politics of culture, Gramsci's war of position ("yeasting the sensibilities")—and he is determined to be involved on his own terms, responsible for his own actions. "Responsibility implies the freedom to be critical. Few positions are as demeaning as that of the 'fellow-traveller.' "[34] And again, in the same essay, "Black on White," in which he asserts the irrelevancy of white radicalism: "I cannot allow my involvement to be decided by the acceptance or the rejection, the appreciation or the disregard, of my Black compatriots."[35]

Camusian again: "I cannot act differently from what I am." He is one of the whitish South Africans, part of the problem, but nevertheless "there to stay," "a minority whose position will have to be accommodated beyond [the Black] takeover."[36] The takeover seems to him inevitable, the accommodation not so—though he does seem convinced that black rule, whatever its character, will not produce a new apartheid, a mirror image of the present system. "It is conceivable," he wrote in 1983 in an appendix to his prison memoirs, "that the present totalitarian state will be replaced by one which may be totalitarian in a different way, and intolerant of alternative revolutionary schools of thought, more hegemonic [since it will have majority support] but minus the racism."[37] It is not difficult to imagine the criticism the critic has reaped for that sentence. From the left, he is accused of red-baiting—as if "totalitarianism" is a word that must never be spoken by a leftist critic—while writers just to his right, *Sestigers*, reformers, liberals, worry that he is too eager to rush into this different totalitarianism (as he once rushed into prison?). Perhaps he should insist more on the details of "accommodation": how will whites be protected in the new regime? It is clear enough that he wants them to be protected; he insists on their place in any future South African state. But he also insists that they can only

* This is what distinguishes Breytenbach's exile from Silone's: in fascist Italy, thousands of Silone's comrades were in prison—including, in 1929, his own brother. Breytenbach's brother, by contrast, is a high-ranking officer in the South African army. Silone had suffered a political defeat, but he could imagine a continuing struggle; for Breytenbach politics itself is deeply problematic.

claim their place in the course of a political struggle whose aim must be to undermine and subvert the place they now occupy. If there is no struggle, there is no claim: the Afrikaner will have to "trust his black nanny to hold him and not drop him."[38]

That last line (from a 1986 interview) is more a joke and a warning than an argument. As Camus understood, even people in the wrong have rights and can rightly lay claim to a secure future. But, Breytenbach argues, it would be a kind of indecency to focus on white rights and white security while the apartheid regime still stands and blacks are

> taken into custody, Shattered
> Stoned
> Hanged
> Lashed
> Used
> Tortured
> Crucified
> Interrogated
> Placed under house arrest
> Made to slave their guts out
> Banished to obscure islands till the end of their days.[39]

The critic must strive instead to create a new awareness among his own people of what is being done in their name. Not merely *for* them (as might have been said of the *pieds noirs* in Algeria, the largely passive beneficiaries of French dominion), but *by* them. The Afrikaners are the agents of their own mastery, and the task of the critic is to overmaster the master in their collective self-understanding, to create a new Afrikaner consciousness. But he won't try to do this with lies; he won't bind himself to the orthodoxies of the oppressed; he won't paint pretty pictures of a liberal and democratic future. In fact, the future is radically uncertain, and the longer the apartheid regime lasts, the more likely it is to be bloody. Perhaps a new oppression will follow upon the old. The old must be dismantled in any case. "There is no other way."[40]

Breyten Breytenbach: The Critic in Exile

Criticism and Exile

Can one wage the Afrikaner war of position from Paris? Isn't Breytenbach, despite the sentimental insistence that he is "wedded forever to the cause of the South African people," the most extreme case of an alienated intellectual? The vector of all his contradictory impulses is exile, and in exile he finds himself at the end of his rope, a dangling man. We can place him in a series: first Marcuse and Foucault give up whatever hopes they may once have had for the working class—and for themselves as movement or party intellectuals, connected to the forces of social change. And then Breytenbach gives up whatever hopes he may once have had for the nation (as a replacement for the working class)—not only his own but the other too: Afrikaner and African alike fall victim to his bitter realism, and he too surrenders his ambition for an activist role. All the gods have failed; the critic is reconciled at last to a complete atheism. He lives in exile in Paris where he is comfortable only because anyone can be comfortable in Paris, the city that refugees and expatriates claim as their own: "La France aux Français; Paris est à nous!"[41]

This sketch captures something of Breytenbach's mood (I mean, the mood of his writing), but it misses the commitment that lies, improbably, somewhere beyond atheism. Why does he sit in Paris and write *about South Africa*?

> To get through with it. To break through to clarity. Also to continue the struggle. I know power structures are practically immutable and when broken down they're more likely than not to be replaced by others which are as exclusive and manipulative. . . . But I must hang in there, hoping to help set off some alarms somewhere. . . . I know, don't I, that I need not believe or trust in the possibility of attaining the objective in order to keep moving. . . . Besides, continued commitment may just succeed in being perceived as a form of solidarity and support—by those in . . . transit areas and prisons who need to feel *some* human concern in order to survive.[42]

He is kept alive as a critic by the very extremity of his situation. He can't fall silent, as Camus did, for his people are still the masters of their fate—which is also to say that there are policemen, torturers, oppressors, who act in his name, though he does what he can to distance himself: "I am not an Afrikaner." He can't live in South Africa; he can't give up the hope that his own South African tribe (the one whose language is his "heart-language") will find some way to make its peace with the other tribes. If he is disappointed again and again by his people's failure to produce a specifically Afrikaner resistance, he still can't walk away from them; he can't stop his anger even if he also can't acknowledge the hope that anger implies. Nor, again, can he sign up with the organized opponents of Afrikaner oppression, for though he supports their struggle, he does so without the illusions that they require from their supporters. Anyway, he is one of the whitish ones, painfully aware of "the problems of cultural awareness." In Breytenbach connection has become desperate. He knows that the critic can only be effective when he speaks "in his language, in his land," and there he sits at ease in Paris, talking French.[43] Nevertheless, he hasn't accepted his exile and substituted a more general and abstract commitment for the particular one that he can only barely sustain—"like a dog loving the moon." What else can a critic-in-exile do? "He must force himself to maintain a dialogue with the inside. . . . He must bark all along the borders."[44]

13

Conclusion: Criticism Today

Dealing with Defeat

I could have chosen eleven other social critics. Every friend that I consulted suggested a different list. But any list of critics involved in one or another of the movements covered by Ortega y Gasset's phrase, "the revolt of the masses," would raise the same issues as those I have addressed, in roughly the same form. The only way to understand these issues, it seems to me, is to study the engaged intellectuals, one after another—men and women who let the revolt shape their lives, though without surrendering to its organizers and new officials.

The portraits I have sketched don't often match the stereotype of a leftist social critic. The actual critics don't measure up, most of them, to the conception of heroism that has dominated, not the history, but the ideology of the left. I have alluded to this conception again and again, mostly by way of contrast. Consider it once more, for the last time.[1] The stereotypical leftist critic breaks loose from his local and familial world (bourgeois, petty-bourgeois, conformist, religious, sheltered, provincial, and so on), escapes with much attendant drama, detaches himself from all emotional ties, steps back so as to see the world with absolute clarity, studies what he sees (scientifically, in accordance with the most advanced views), discovers universal values as if for the first time, finds these values embodied in the movement of the oppressed (class, nation, gender, his own or the other—so long as the "finding" is objective, it doesn't matter), decides to support the movement and to criticize its enemies, who are very often people such as he once was. The critic attaches himself to the popular revolt, sometimes negotiating, sometimes not, about the terms of the attachment. Mostly, so the stereotype suggests, the terms are not negotiated in any detail; Sartre's unconditional championship of the Algerian FLN is a typical example. Since the oppressed represent universality or, alternatively, the social order of the future, what would be the point of conditions?

This description isn't silly; it wouldn't be stereotypical if it did not touch the type, at least at a few places. But it has the air of a theoretical account, not a life story; it reads like a set of instructions: if you want to be a social critic, do this and this. Most social critics, if they are any good at all, live without a handbook, and what they do, what happens to them, is more complicated and interesting than the stereotype suggests. It is unusual to find someone whom it really fits—like Rosa Luxemburg, when she writes in a letter to her friend Mathilde Wurm that she has no special place in her heart for the sorrows of the Jews.[2] I am sure that she wrote those words with pride, for she was claiming that she had made the required break with her own past and her own people; now her heart was equally open to everyone's sorrows. But imagine Ignazio Silone writing a sentence like that about the peasants of the Abruzzi or Orwell about the English or Camus about the *pieds noirs* or even Breytenbach about his Afrikaner "tribe." However intense their quarrels with their past and people, few critics get all that far from the place where they begin. They travel across oceans and continents; they measure geographical distance in hundreds and thousands of miles. But critical distance is still measured in inches, and every inch is worried, agonized over, the subject of intense thought and afterthought.

Strict objectivity is a goal that is never in fact achieved; the critic is partisan from the beginning. His mind and heart are partial, particular; he never quite stands free and freely chooses his commitments, but struggles instead to sort out the commitments he already has. Nor is universality waiting to be found where he expects to find it. While there may well be (as I believe) universal value in opposing oppression, the oppressed themselves have their own values, their own interests too—and their values and interests are often in conflict. Oppressed men and women are not the appointed agents of world-historical transformation; they are not waiting breathlessly to fulfill the mission the critic sets for them. The movements they create, heroic in their origins, turn out later on to be lethargic, bureaucratic, corruptible. The victories they win are incomplete and compromised; and often they don't win. If the masses can be mobilized, they can also be demobilized and dominated. And, what is most striking, they can be demobilized and dominated by militant elites acting in their own name—though also in the name of detachment, science, and a false universalism. In the best of cases, neither national liberation nor socialist revolution meets the standards of the social critic; and sometimes the new regimes are as bad as the old; sometimes they are far worse. What does the critic do then? How does he deal, as every twentieth-century critic has had to deal, with defeat and disappointment?

One response is to cease to be a critical intellectual, to become an apologist instead, defending with eyes resolutely closed what can no longer be defended with eyes open. I have not tried here to describe the various forms of critical capitulation, of which Stalinism is by far the most important in the politics of the left. Criticism has its swan songs and fag ends as well as its heroic beginnings. There are indeed intellectual betrayals, though these only rarely match Benda's description; they are guided more often by considerations of place and power than by ties of affection. But capitulation and betrayal are subjects for another book (even if they are also subjects for social criticism—at the hands, for example, of East European dissidents).[3]

Another response, more interesting to me because it is the more obvious conclusion of detachment and universalist pretension, is to generalize one's criticism, to become a critic-at-large surveying the whole world, critical of modernity, popular culture, mass society, bureaucracy, science and technology, the welfare state, and anything else that turns up. Herbert Marcuse comes close to this sort of thing (and there are many other examples to be found among "critical theorists," leftist admirers of Greece and Rome, latter-day Rousseauians—as well as, what one would more readily expect, among conservative communitarians and religious fundamentalists). The tone of such work suggests a collectivist version of misanthropy, though it is only what modern man, mass man, has wrought that is condemned. Disillusioned with popular revolt, and without much feeling for the daily life of the people, critics-at-large make a virtue of necessity and return to an earlier understanding of the critical enterprise: Benda's and before. They seize the heights and, as if they had never been there, disdain the cave. If they aren't perfectly detached and objective, they are at any rate fairly undiscriminating in the reach of their dislike.

A third response, recommended but not exemplified by Foucault, is to become a critic-in-the-small, accepting as the price of defeat a radical localization of critical activity. The Foucaultian intellectual would like to play at least a minor role in Gramsci's "war of position," but he has given up any hope for social cooperation or political alliance. He is not so much a professional critic as a critic in the little world of his profession, and the likely profession these days is academic: hence the critical wars of the 1980s, which have no echo outside the academy since the critics have no material ties to people or parties or movements outside. Academic criticism under these circumstances tends steadily toward hermeticism and gnostic obscurity; even the critic's students barely understand him.[4]

From disconnection to connection and then back again: the free-floating social critic attaches himself to popular causes and historic struggles, and after a time, defeated and unhappy, he floats free again. Is this the course of criticism in the twentieth century? Benda stands at the beginning, high-toned and optimistic; Gramsci and Silone, Buber and Camus, wrestle inconclusively with the dilemmas of commitment; Marcuse stands near the end, high-toned and grim. In one of his more resigned-to-exile pieces, Breyten Breytenbach captures the mood of endings, the elegy in reverse:

> The world is becoming greyer, smoother, less textured. . . . The patterns have set. There are of course the obvious examples: the digitalization, the ordinormalization, the computerization of the human and her world. The getting accustomed to living by balance of terror. The acceptance that survival can be assured only by fabricating and selling death-doing instruments. Existing with the necessity of torture and wipe-outs. Wiping the mouth and voting. Having the WC fixed, buying polyester shirts. Drip-dry minds.[5]

This is the palaver of the critic-at-large. It has its point (and it isn't obscure), but it lacks the specificity and force of an older social criticism; it compares badly with the wonderfully tactile, almost caressive, prose with which Breytenbach describes his own South Africa. Are we condemned to palaver? Is that what disappointed social critics come to, at the end?

But the end seems to me, like all the beginnings, something less than inevitable. Only the ideological tie between the critic and the people has been broken, the doctrinal confidence in the historic mission of this or that class or nation. No doubt, this break leaves some critics floating free, disappointed and disconnected. But that's not a necessary outcome, for the moral tie isn't broken; or it need not break; or it can be renewed; or one can just hold on, "hang in there." Social criticism does not depend on a positive identification of historical agency—as if Marcuse's discovery that there are no social forces of which we can say with certainty that they are liberating forces signifies the end of criticism, the last critical word, after which the small talk begins. I see no reason to accept the claim that criticism is hostage to theory, let alone to a particular theory like Marxism, so vulnerable to historical disproof. It helps, of course, to have a theory, to have some grasp on the forces at work in society, some more or less systematic set of expectations about the future. But when theory crashes, we can still rely, as Silone says, on our moral sense as a "guide to knowledge." When I first read that sentence, I assumed that Silone meant to say, a guide to moral knowledge. I now think that he was more ambitious: the moral sense is also a guide to social and political knowledge and perhaps a better guide than the crashed theory ever was—if only because it is more widely shared. It is a faculty of perception and understanding, if not, like theoretical Reason, of mastery; it makes intelligent participation possible, if not rational control. Liberty, justice, democracy, domination, oppression, exploitation, cruelty, violence, terror, mass murder, totalitarian rule—this is the language of politics in the twentieth century, a time of large hopes, high risk, desperate efforts, fearful culminations. Who can doubt that this language is better employed by a person of moral sensitivity without a theory than by a morally obtuse person with the grandest possible theory? In any case, the sensitive critic, still tied to his fellows, can "hang in there," though he may hurt while he is hanging in; moral sensitivity is the armor of critical survival.

Hamlet's Glass

The tasks of the critic, thus armored, are nicely set out by Breytenbach: to question relentlessly the platitudes and myths of his society and to express the aspirations of his people. The second of these isn't possible, obviously, unless the people actually have aspirations that reach beyond or clash with the social order in which they live. If the masses are entirely satisfied, as Marcuse argues, then the critic is left with the thankless task of criticizing their satisfaction, which he hopes to replace with his own unfulfilled aspirations, the products of detachment and solitary reflection. But why should anyone accept the replacement? And what can the critic do when it is refused? These are difficult questions for the critic-at-large, but they need not call into doubt the critical enterprise itself. Imagine a critic who isn't detached, free-floating, or alienated. He understands himself instead as a social being, "a man of a certain region, a certain class, and a certain time" (Silone), critical of "his own world" (Bourne). His values, even his universal values, are first of all the values of a particular person, and they are shared with a particular set of other people: "average values" (Camus). Even if he has a personal version of the average values, it won't be entirely unfamiliar. So he can presume on his fellowship and express his own aspirations for the collective life in which he shares. Though he starts with himself, he speaks in the first person plural. This is what we value and want, he says, and don't yet have. This is how we mean to live and don't yet live.

We criticize our society just as we criticize our friends, on the assumption that the terms of the critique, the moral references, are common. The writer, says Breytenbach again, "holds his words up to us like mirrors." Why is this a critical activity? Because we don't see in the writer's mirror what we want to see. Consider the famous case of Hamlet and his mother. "You go not till I set you up a glass," Hamlet says, "Where you may see the inmost part of you." Hamlet's glass is the most powerful of critical instruments. And its critical power doesn't depend upon any utopian view of marriage or motherhood; no radically innovative theory about a wife's or a mother's duties is necessary. Hamlet counts on the fact of moral agreement: his mother's view of how she should behave is the same as his view.

> . . . Sit you down,
> And let me wring your heart, for so I shall
> If it be made of penetrable stuff;
> If damnéd custom have not brazed it so
> That it be proof and bulwark against sense.[6]

"Custom" refers here to everyday behavior, the appearances that we keep up, the veneer of respectability that we see or hope to see when we peer into our own mirrors. And "sense" means feeling and emotion, but also moral sense and common sense, which give shape and purpose to our feelings. In Hamlet's glass, his mother sees simultaneously what she (really) is, and what she most deeply wishes to be:

> Thou turn'st my eyes into my very soul.[7]

The social critic similarly turns our eyes into our very souls—a superfluous activity, again, if we are collectively or individually soulless, morally insentient and obtuse. He assumes that we have souls more or less like his own; he starts from there, and given that starting point his own mirror is as effective as Hamlet's.* With it he fulfills Breytenbach's two tasks. First, he shows us to ourselves as we really are, all pretense shattered, stripped of our moral makeup, naked. Here he is like those reforming photographers of the Progressive and New Deal eras, Lewis Hine and Walker Evans, for example, who played such a central role in the exposure of child labor, slum housing, and rural poverty, "ripping aside . . . the veil that disguised and mystified the brutal system of production."[8] Once the veil is gone, the system *seen*, no further commentary is necessary. But the critic is also a commentator, providing, second, an account or interpretation of what, in our very souls, we would like to be: all our high hopes and ideal images of self and society. I said of Hamlet and his mother that their shared understanding of marriage and motherhood had nothing utopian about it. But I don't mean to exclude utopia from social criticism, only to stress that the hopes and ideals have an actual location—in our "souls," in our everyday consciousness of the moral world. It is only the social order within which hopes are realized and ideals acted out that is located "nowhere." The point of holding up the mirror is to demonstrate that the ideal order is not here, or that we're not there. The stories that we tell ourselves about the realization of freedom and equality are untrue: one has only to look in the glass and see.

The critic looks first and then he forces the rest of us to look: "Go not till I set you up a glass." We need no other eyes than our own to see what has to be seen; we stand where we are standing. It is a mistake, in social criticism as in moral philosophy, to suppose that we must escape our situation in order to describe it accurately. If he aims at objectivity, writes the phi-

* Someone is sure to ask: but what if the critic is talking to a committed Nazi who looks in the mirror and admires the image of himself in boots and swastika, arrogant and cruel? Such a person stands outside the world of moral agreement. Criticism has no grip on him; with him there is little use talking, more use fighting. The critic speaks instead to all those other men and women, by far the greater number, who are uneasy with the mirror image.

losopher/theologian Franz Rosenzweig (a coworker of Buber's and here in complete agreement with him),

> the thinker must proceed boldly from his own subjective situation. The single condition imposed upon us by objectivity is that we survey the entire horizon; but we are not obliged to make this survey from any position other than the one in which we are, nor are we obliged to make it from no position at all. Our eyes are, indeed, only our own eyes; yet it would be folly to imagine that we must pluck them out in order to see straight.[9]

"The entire horizon," in my mirror metaphor, refers to the picture presented in the glass: all the moral disfigurements must be acknowledged—but also, lest objectivity be lost, whatever there is of beauty. Mirrors presumably don't lie, but people learn how to look in a mirror so as to see only what they want to see. The critic points to the rest.

There are as many mirrors as there are social critics and as many mirror images as there are people willing to look into the glass. Every mirror, every image has its proper name or possessive pronoun. Hamlet's glass might serve for all of Denmark (and show what's rotten in the state), but only if he could persuade the Danes to confront their collective reflection, and only if he could read the image in the light of Danish aspirations. Whenever it points to particular images and expresses particular aspirations, criticism is a pluralizing activity. Because of this pluralism, critics have a third task to add to Breytenbach's two: they must fight against the propensity of their fellows, their fellow critics also, to think that when they look in the mirror they see the entire world. Their own blemishes reveal everyone else's; their aspirations are universal ends; their very soul is the world-soul. I think that it has been the single greatest sin of leftist social criticism to insist that one mirror image properly read, one theoretical account of social life, can tell the whole story of human society. It is possible, I suppose, to see the world in a grain of sand—at least, one can "see" all the other grains of sand. It is not possible to study one group of people, even a highly "advanced" group, and see all the others. For this reason, the critic is bound to imagine other people peering into other mirrors, even though he cannot see what they see; he must acknowledge the endless reiteration of his own critical activity.

These, then, are the three tasks of criticism: the critic exposes the false appearances of his own society; he gives expression to his people's deepest sense of how they ought to live; and he insists that there are other forms of falseness and other, equally legitimate, hopes and aspirations. I don't mean that every hope and aspiration has the same legitimacy. That is far too relaxed a view of the world; no social critic could possibly accept it. Nor is the meaning of critical exposure always a local and particular meaning. If what is rotten in the state of Denmark includes murder and betrayal, then all of us can recognize the rottenness. For some purposes, we all stand in front of the same mirror. But only for some purposes: the critic who forgets the importance of "his own language, his own land" (Breytenbach) won't write strong or persuasive criticism. Neither his exposure of ugliness nor his expression of value will ring true. Nor will he be able to acknowledge the otherness of other people.

National-Popular Criticism

I won't pretend that this Hamlet-model of social criticism is proof against critical failure or that it is a sovereign remedy for the pathologies of disconnection. In the world of criticism, there is neither proof nor sovereignty. The model suggests a way of carrying on after the gods of communism and nationalism have failed. Critical philosophers today can find no human instruments designated in Heaven or instructed by History to act out their critique; the card-carrying intellectual can't count on the agency that issues his card. But ordinary men and women continue to hope for a better life than the one they have, and political leaders continue to justify themselves in ideal terms, claiming to serve the people's hopes. The critic elaborates the hopes, interprets the ideals, holds both against his mirror image of social reality. The contrast is intended to set people in motion. Only rarely can critics ally themselves with people already in motion, "social forces," as they are commonly called, marching—but never like an army under orders—toward the critical objective. Critics are not generals. They are only critics, and they must find satisfaction in an activity that is more often morally irritating than materially effective.

Still, they hope to be effective; it is the natural form of their ambition. Effectiveness is most likely, it seems to me, when the critic operates in what Gramsci calls the "national-popular" mode. I take this to mean, national in form, popular in content, or better, national in idiom, popular in argument. The ideal critic in this mode is loyal to men and women in trouble—

oppressed, exploited, impoverished, forgotten—but he sees these people and their troubles and the possible solution to their troubles within the framework of national history and culture. Nation, not class, is the relevant unit, even when the critic is most closely attuned to the injuries of class. He can express working-class aspiration, for example, only if he realizes that full membership in the national community is what most workers aspire to. The pull of the common culture is powerful, and here criticism does not require resistance. On the contrary: the critic must speak the language of the country, ordinary language; and whatever his own sophistication and learning, he must maintain some continuity with the traditions of common complaint. National-popular criticism is inclusive, very much like W. H. Auden's conception of literature:

> The pious fable and the dirty story
> Share in the total literary glory.[10]

So with criticism: glory doesn't belong only to the critical equivalent of the epic or the tragic poet. If the critic is to speak for his fellows, he must also speak with them, and when what he says sounds unpatriotic, he has to insist upon his own deeper patriotism. "A movement that does not honor a society's constant values," writes the Polish critic Adam Michnik about the labor union Solidarity, "is not sufficiently mature to undertake the reshaping of that society."[11] If we take this standard seriously, we have to acknowledge that a large number of immature men and women—often very learned and philosophically talented men and women—have written social criticism in the twentieth century. They have failed to pay a decent respect to the opinions of their fellows; they have been too quick to insist upon the virtues of heroic loneliness and solitary wisdom.

Sometimes, of course, the critic must stand alone—as Silone did when he broke with his comrades in the party or as Orwell did when he struggled to sustain a leftist politics against the standard apologies for Stalinism or as de Beauvoir did when she condemned the participation of women in their own subjection or as Breytenbach does today, in exile, unable to live under the apartheid regime. But the values that make this stand possible are not the private values of the social critic. Or, better, when they are his private values, they set him against his own people in a more radical sense than criticism requires (or than "mature" criticism allows); they amount to a declaration of war. "Every ethic conceived in solitude," writes Camus in

The Rebel, "implies the exercise of power."[12] Solitary conceptions make for cruel deliveries. When the critic tries to act out his new ethic, he finds himself without sufficient popular support or even understanding; he can impose his ideas only by force. Perhaps he speaks an esoteric language. Perhaps his ideas are too distant from the culture of the people to whom they are addressed. This kind of loneliness is likely to be willful; there are very few critics in the long history of social criticism who have been driven, protesting helplessly, into incomprehensibility. More often, incomprehensibility is chosen for the sake of its compensations: individual heroism and sectarian rectitude.

By contrast, the national-popular intellectual speaks the common language. He has what Breytenbach calls an "uncivil tongue," but he is not uncultured or antisocial; he attacks only the false civility, the polite conventions, that hide the injuries of class or race or gender and that turn values into ideologies. The form of his attack will vary with the character of his culture, but he is likely to pay close attention to national history, finding in his people's past (its literature and art as well as its politics) a warrant for criticism in the present. In this sense, the biblical prophet was a national-popular intellectual: he spoke to the hearts of his people even when he was most harshly critical of their behavior, reminding them of Egypt, Sinai, the covenant—the sacred events, ritually celebrated, that made them a *people.* He upheld the cause of the poor and the oppressed without pretending that they had no share in the common life. And, for all his rage, he maintained his own connection too—indeed, rage was his connection: it was only his own people whose conduct enraged him.[13] I don't mean to suggest that this kind of criticism is necessarily or always or even often successful. The success of the prophets was mostly of the sort called today "critical success," which is to say that they impressed other critics. But their books were read and reread among the people; they touched the hearts they spoke to, even if they did not alter the behavior they criticized. Criticism in the national-popular mode is potentially effective. And, what is equally important, it does not depend for its effectiveness upon the use of force.

But we are more accustomed, perhaps, to national-popular apologetics. How is it possible to guarantee the critical character of arguments in this mode? There is no guarantee, of course; nor is there any guarantee for arguments in the mode of distance and solitude. The solitary or alienated critic, committed, as Camus suggests, to the exercise of power, is likely to lose his critical grasp on the instruments of power—like Marxist intellectuals with regard to the Communist party. National-popular critics face similar dangers (I leave aside the danger of sentimentalism, for which distance is a genuine remedy; but the danger is of relatively minor intellectual significance). They too can become the prisoners of instrumentality: uncritical of the state that fortifies the nation or of the movement or party that defends the people. These failures of criticism are the result of what Silone calls the fascist mentality, which values the handkerchief while degrading the nose.

It is often said that loyalty to nation or party turns the intellectual from criticism to apologetics, and so loyalty itself is made a critical target. Thus Philip Rieff in a sharp attack, written in the 1950s, on the conformism of American intellectuals: today, he writes, it is "loyalty, not truth, [that] provides the social condition by which the intellectual discovers his environment." The result is a steady drift from social criticism to policy science, from "the New School [for Social Research] to the Rand Corporation."[14] Perhaps Rieff catches the drift, though it has to be said that the two institutions, some thirty years later, still coexist—as they or their equivalents, barring totalitarian repression, always have. But loyalty/truth is a bad dichotomy. As I argued in the introduction, truth by itself has never been the animating passion of the social critic. Even Molière's misanthrope, despite his classic defense of critical truth-telling, is differently driven. Nor is criticism possible as a social practice in the absence of loyalty. The intellectuals who founded the New School had, to be sure, been accused of disloyalty during the First World War. But we have no reason to repeat the accusation. These were reformers in a long American tradition.[15] Committed (like Randolph Bourne) to social uplift, whose society were they trying to lift up?

It is the authorities who call the critic disloyal. And they are right at least in this respect: that no state, regime, leader, party, movement, or central committee commands his unquestioning loyalty. Ideally, the critic is a masterless man, a masterless woman, who refuses to pay homage to the powers-that-be. Critical distance is established by this refusal, and no further refusals are necessary for the sake of criticism. Painful breaks with family and friends, so common in the lives of social critics, are the result, not the prerequisite, of their critical activity. The case is the same with exile: the critic does not give up his country in order to find the truth; he gives it up so as to live by the truth he has already found. At the very moment he leaves, he accuses the men and women he leaves behind of desertion: they, not he, have abandoned the constant values of their society. Critical distance in the relevant sense is less a matter of intellectual perspective or personal circumstance than of political position. What is crucial is the critic's independence, his freedom from governmental responsibility, religious authority, corporate power, party discipline.

He is an oppositional figure, and he must remain independent if he is to sustain his opposition. But I don't think that it is useful to describe the critical posture, in Sartrean style, as one of absolute opposition, undifferentiated antagonism—the writer writing "against all readers." This description carries over into the world of social criticism the self-understanding of the literary avant-garde: "The man of letters," wrote Baudelaire, "is the enemy of the world."[16] But Sartre was an enemy of the world only in France; he surrendered his enmity all too quickly when he visited Cuba or China or wrote about Algeria. Absolute opposition is a kind of bad faith. Similarly, the overgeneralized argument of a writer like Marcuse is a kind of bad theory, intellectually inauthentic in much the same way as the Sartrean posture is morally inauthentic. It fails to acknowledge or come to grips with those aspects of our world that are still open, workable, valued by our fellow citizens. The maxim that guides the critic must be more qualified: when the fish stinks, say that it stinks; and when it doesn't stink, don't say that it does.

The political meaning of absolute opposition is precisely expressed in a manifesto by the Sartrean epigone, Philippe Sollers: "The intellectuals are in opposition. By definition. Out of principle. From physical necessity. . . . They are opposed to all majorities as also to all oppositions hoping to become the majority." To which Breytenbach, sitting in Parisian exile, has made exactly the right response: Sollers's argument shows, he says, "an inability to distinguish between different types of political regimes. Besides, it is arrogant."[17] The arrogance of power here finds its secret ally in the arrogance of opposition. For criticism will never shake the world unless it is directed against specific features of the world that other people besides the critic recognize as wrongful, oppressive, brutal, or unjust. So the critic must be loyal to the others, to all those men and women for whom a different regime will make a difference. He cannot disregard their interests any more than he can, simply, grossly, repudiate their values. He is in opposition here, and here, and here; he is never in absolute opposition.

But this partial, differentiated critique is not any easier—I think it is much harder—than absolutism is. The critical intellectual climbs toward an absolutist position the way a child climbs a tree, without any sense that he will ever have to come down; it is a pure adventure. The critic who refuses absolutism refuses also the exhilaration of the heights. He stands among the people; he feels, as Gramsci says he should, their "elementary passions." But he *takes* stands different from theirs, for they are often guided by the ideologists of the state or the party, and he is not. His independence distances him from ordinary men and women as well as from bureaucrats and officials. He inches away from the people-nation, in order to criticize what the majority of his fellows find worthy of praise. Sometimes, persecuted by the regime and without strong support among the people, he must go into exile. But even in exile, he cannot embrace the pleasures of absolutism. He is a critic of the regime, not of the people; or of some of the people, not others; or of the people in one sense, not in another. His exile is a physical, not a moral condition—which is to say of him what Michnik says of the Polish exiles of the 1950s: they did not by leaving "place themselves outside the nation."[18] Why not? Because they continued to identify with the nation, to defend its interests, to interpret its values; and because distance for them was more pain than glory.

Despair and Hope

Writing about Silone, I argued against the idea that his "return" to the heretical Christianity he first learned in his native village was an act of despair. But despair would hardly be an inappropriate response to the politics of the twentieth century. In a sense, of course, this politics opens the way to critical success: there is so much to criticize, so many ugly regimes, corrupted parties and movements, failed leaders, false ideologies. Social criticism today is a genre rich in possibility and rich in achievement too. Some of the greatest achievements I have discussed here, but think of the books that I have omitted: Czeslaw Milosz's *Captive Mind*, Milovan Djilas's *New Class*, C.Wright Mills's *White Collar*, Jürgen Habermas's *Legitimation Crisis*, and many other strong and negative accounts of the societies we inhabit, the lives we live. But all these are critical, not material successes; they make the world visible, they don't make it over. The hope that was so vibrant only a few decades ago, that criticism would control and shape the revolt of the masses, seems dead and gone today. In fact, this hope has died many deaths: in the twenties and early thirties, with the rise of fascism; at the end of the thirties, with the coming of the war; in the fifties, with the (belated) exposure of Stalinism; at the end of the sixties, with the self-destruction of the New Left. Who can count the defeats or estimate the extent of the disillusion? In the last year before the Second World War, the novelist E. M. Forster argued in favor of despair: "There is nothing disgraceful in despair. In 1938–39 the more despair a man can take on board without sinking, the more completely is he alive."[19] We have to worry, though, about the quality of his life.

The important thing is not to sink—and how else does one keep afloat except by criticizing what is going on in the surrounding waters? "Always, in every situation," wrote Martin Buber, "it is possible to do *something*."[20] I would be inclined to say, almost always; criticism is never without reasons and warrants, but there may be terrible moments when it has no point. In any case, it was only two years after Forster's argument for despair that Orwell wrote his pamphlet, *The Lion and the Unicorn*, looking toward an English revolution and a Labor government; only six years later that Silone returned to Italy and joined the Socialist party; only nine years later that Buber confronted the radically unexpected fact of Israel's independence. Critical occasions, which is also to say, occasions for hope, arise even in the worst of times. So it behooves the critic to be ready and waiting, maintaining his independence, keeping in touch with common complaint, polishing his glass. He is like a commuter watching expectantly for a train (but there is no schedule).

It isn't only world wars or revolutionary crises or liberation struggles that make for critical occasions. We don't always operate on such a grand scale; nor, for obvious reasons, should we want to. Local insurgencies, reformist campaigns, economic strikes, electoral battles—these are not necessarily less important or less hopeful than revolutions. They are only less dangerous, and far more frequent. Now the critic must work to connect the small event to a larger vision and to hold the protagonists to their own putative idealism. He functions in a role that Foucault claims has been superseded but that never in fact will be superseded: he is a "general intellectual," critical of the power structures that inhibit popular participation in political life (including the power structures of popular parties and movements). He has a sense (it isn't his alone) of how society as a whole ought to look. But the general intellectual doesn't stand on a mountaintop, master of all he surveys; he claims no authority, issues no commands. Himself a participant, he works at a certain difficult distance, balancing "solidarity" and "service." He is, whenever he can be, the enemy of disconnection. To find one's way in the litile battles as well as the big ones, to be faithful to the hopes of popular revolt, to outlast the defeats, to sustain a form of criticism internal to, relevant to, loyal to democratic politics—that is courage in social criticism.

NOTES

1. Introduction: The Practice of Social Criticism

1. In the discussion that follows, I rely chiefly on conversations with friendly social critics but also on the literature of Marxism, "critical theory," and the avant-garde. See Max Horkheimer, *Critical Theory*, trans. Matthew J. O'Connell and others (New York: Herder and Herder, 1972), esp. the essay "Traditional and Critical Theory"; and Renato Poggioli, *The Theory of the Avant Garde*, trans. Gerald Fitzgerald (Cambridge, Mass.: Harvard University Press, 1968), esp. chaps. 6, "The State of Alienation," and 7, "Avant-Garde Criticism."
2. Amos 5:21.
3. Plato, *The Last Days of Socrates*, trans. Hugh Tredennick (London: Penguin Books, 1954), pp. 36–37 (Apology 30–31).
4. Hosea 9:14.
5. Plato, *Last Days*, p. 38 (Apology 32).
6. Karl Marx, *Capital: A Critique of Political Economy*, trans. Samuel Moore and Edward Aveling, ed. Frederick Engels (New York: International Publishers, 1967), 1:10.
7. See Mark Curtis, "The Alienated Intellectuals of Early Stuart England," *Past and Present*, no. 23 (November 1962):25–43.
8. Alasdair MacIntyre, *Herbert Marcuse: An Exposition and a Polemic* (New York: Viking, 1970), p. 102.
9. Jerrold Seigel, *Bohemian Paris: Culture, Politics, and the Boundaries of Bourgeois Life, 1830–1930* (New York: Viking, 1986), pp. 10, 11.
10. Charles Russell, *Poets, Prophets, and Revolutionaries: The Literary Avant-Garde from Rimbaud Through Postmodernism* (New York: Oxford University Press, 1985), pp. 29–30.
11. Karl Marx, "Contribution to the Critique of Hegel's Philosophy of Right: Introduction," in *Early Writings*, trans. and ed. T. B. Bottomore (London: Watts, 1963), p. 52.
12. On the language and style of the *Manifesto*, see Marshall Berman, *All That Is Solid Melts into Air: The Experience of Modernity* (New York: Simon and Schuster, 1982), chap. 2.
13. Herbert Marcuse, *One-Dimensional Man: Studies in the Ideology of Advanced Industrial Society* (Boston: Beacon Press, 1964), esp. chap. 7.
14. Edmund Wilson, *The Dead Sea Scrolls: 1947–1969* (New York: Oxford University Press, 1969).
15. Breyten Breytenbach, *End Papers: Essays, Letters, Articles of Faith, Workbook Notes* (New York: Farrar, Straus and Giroux, 1986), p. 154.
16. Amos 7:16–17.
17. Plato, *Last Days*, pp. 33, 43 (Apology 28, 36).
18. Ibid., p. 35 (Apology 30); Amos 3:2.
19. St. Matthew 10:34–36.
20. Simone de Beauvoir, *The Second Sex*, trans. and ed. H. M. Parshley (New York: Alfred A. Knopf, 1953), pp. 63–64.
21. I owe this image to Irving Howe.
22. Martin Buber, *A Land of Two Peoples: Martin Buber on Jews and Arabs*, ed. Paul R. Mendes-Flohr (Oxford: Oxford University Press, 1983), pp. 20–21.
23. On the difficult question of Marx's moral views, see Steven Lukes, *Marxism and Morality* (Oxford: Oxford University Press, 1985).
24. Cf. Seyla Benhabib, *Critique, Norm and Utopia: A Study of the Foundations of Critical Theory* (New York: Columbia University Press, 1986).

25. *Hamlet*, III.iv.178.
26. Christopher Lasch, *The New Radicalism in America, 1889–1963: The Intellectual as a Social Type* (New York: Vintage Books, 1967), p. 256.
27. Ibid., p. xv.
28. See the first version of *The Social Contract*, in Jean-Jacques Rousseau, *Oeuvres Complètes* (Paris: Pléiade, 1964), 3:287.
29. Bertolt Brecht explored these issues in the late 1920s and early 1930s in a series of plays, the best known of which is *The Measures Taken*. See the discussion in Russell, *Poets, Prophets*, pp. 219–21.
30. José Ortega y Gasset, *The Revolt of the Masses* (New York: Mentor, 1950).
31. Quoted in Joseph Frank, *Dostoevsky: The Stir of Liberation, 1860–1865* (Princeton: Princeton University Press, 1986), p. 175.
32. Marx, "Contribution to the Critique," pp. 53, 59.

2. Julien Benda and Intellectual Treason

1. Julien Benda, *The Betrayal of the Intellectuals*, trans. R. Aldington (Boston: Beacon Press, 1955).
2. Ibid., p. 111.
3. Ibid., p. 153.
4. J. Dillenberger, *Martin Luther: Selections from His Writings* (Garden City, N.Y.: Doubleday, Anchor, 1961), p. 380.
5. Benda, *Betrayal*, pp. 30, 53, 122.
6. Ibid., p. 48.
7. Ibid., p. 77n.
8. Ibid., p. 171.
9. Ibid., p. 43.
10. Ibid., pp. 30–31.
11. Ibid., p. 85.
12. Ibid.
13. Ibid., pp. 127–28, 129n.
14. Ibid., pp. 18–21.
15. Ibid., p. 74.
16. Ibid., pp. 36n, 149.
17. Reported in Ray Nichols, *Treason, Tradition, and the Intellectuals* (Lawrence: University of Kansas Press, 1978), p. 81.
18. Benda, *Betrayal*, p. 36.
19. Ibid., p. 152.
20. Ibid., p. 94.
21. Quoted in Nichols, *Treason*, p. 90.
22. Benda, *Betrayal*, pp. 149–50.
23. Quoted in Nichols, *Treason*, p. 164.
24. Benda, *Exercice d'un enterré vif* (*Juin 1940–Août 1944*) (Geneva: Editions des Trois Collines, 1944), p. 174.
25. Benda, *Betrayal*, pp. 8–9.
26. Ibid., p. 129.
27. Isaiah Berlin, *Personal Impressions*, ed. H. Hardy (New York: Viking Press, 1980), p. 151.
28. Ibid., pp. 147, 149.
29. Nichols, *Treason*, p. 128.
30. Benda, *Exercice*, p. 175.
31. Paul Nizan, *The Watchdog: Philosophers of the Established Order*, trans. P. Fittingoff (New York: Monthly Review Press, 1971), p. 67.
32. Nichols, *Treason*, p. 137; see also D. L. Schalk, *The Spectrum of Political Engagement; Mounier, Benda, Nizan, Brasillach, Sartre* (Princeton: Princeton University Press, 1979), pp. 40–41.
33. Benda, *Un régulier dans le siècle* (Paris: Gallimard, 1937), p. 198.
34. Benda, *Exercice*, p. 172.
35. L. A. Coser, *Men of Ideas* (New York: The Free Press, 1965), p. 360.

36. Benda, *Betrayal*, pp. 81–82.
37. *Ethics of the Talmud* (*Pirke Avot*), 1:10.
38. Benda, *Betrayal*, p. 127.

3. The War and Randolph Bourne

1. Christoper Lasch, *The New Radicalism in America, 1889–1963: The Intellectual as a Social Type* (New York: Vintage Books, 1967), pp. 101, 256.
2. Letter to Alyse Gregory, quoted in Lillian Schlissel, ed., *The World of Randolph Bourne* (New York: E. P. Dutton, 1965), p. xxxi.
3. Letter to Prudence Winterroud, in Schlissel, ed., *World of Randolph Bourne*, p. 298.
4. Bruce Clayton, *Forgotten Prophet: The Life of Randolph Bourne* (Baton Rouge: Louisiana State University Press, 1984), p. 24.
5. "The Social Order of an American Town," quoted in Clayton, *Forgotten Prophet*, p. 80.
6. Randolph Bourne, "This Older Generation," in his *The Radical Will: Selected Writings 1911–1918*, ed. Olaf Hansen (New York: Urizen Books, 1977), pp. 162–63. This is the most complete collection of Bourne's essays and articles (it includes no letters), and I will cite it whenever I can.
7. Ibid., p. 166.
8. Randolph Bourne, "A Moral Equivalent for Universal Military Service," in his *History of a Literary Radical*, ed. Van Wyck Brooks (New York: B. W. Huebsch, 1920), pp. 193, 194.
9. Randolph Bourne, "Youth," in *Radical Will*, p. 104.
10. Bourne, "This Older Generation," pp. 167–68.
11. Randolph Bourne, "The Life of Irony," in *Radical Will*, pp. 142–43.
12. Letter to Prudence Winterroud, quoted in Schlissel, ed., *World of Randolph Bourne*, p. xix.
13. Randolph Bourne, "Traps for the Unwary," in *Radical Will*, p. 483.
14. Randolph Bourne, "The Art of Theodore Dreiser," in *Radical Will*, p. 465.
15. Randolph Bourne, "Trans-National America," in *Radical Will*, pp. 248–64.
16. Randolph Bourne, "The Jew and Trans-National America," in his *War and the Intellectuals*, ed. Carl Resak (New York: Harper and Row, 1964), p. 132.
17. Bourne, "Trans-National America," p. 249.
18. Ibid., p. 255.
19. Bourne, "Traps for the Unwary," p. 483.
20. Raymond Williams, *Culture and Society, 1780–1950* (New York: Columbia University Press, 1958), pp. 325–26, 328.
21. Randolph Bourne, "The Price of Radicalism," in *Radical Will*, p. 299.
22. Lenin, *What the "Friends of the People" Are* (1894; reprint, Moscow: Foreign Languages Publishing House, 1951), p. 286.
23. Bourne, "Traps for the Unwary," p. 483.
24. Bourne, "The Life of Irony," p. 144.
25. Lasch, *New Radicalism*, p. 256.
26. Quoted in Charles Forcey, *The Crossroads of Liberalism: Croly, Weyl, Lippmann and the Progressive Era, 1900–1925* (New York: Oxford University Press, 1961), p. 273.
27. Randolph Bourne, "The Collapse of American Strategy," in Schlissel, ed., *World of Randolph Bourne*, p. 168.
28. Randolph Bourne, "The War and the Intellectuals" and "A War Diary," in *Radical Will*, pp. 313, 327.
29. Randolph Bourne, "Twilight of Idols," in *Radical Will*, p. 343.
30. Bourne, "A War Diary," p. 324.
31. Bourne, "The War and the Intellectuals," p. 307.
32. Bourne, "Twilight of Idols," p. 342.
33. Ibid., p. 343.
34. Ibid., p. 345.
35. Floyd Dell, quoted in Forcey, *Crossroads*, p. 275.
36. Quoted in Clayton, *Forgotten Prophet*, p. 215.
37. Bourne, "The War and the Intellectuals," p. 315.
38. Bourne, "Twilight of Idols," p. 346.
39. Bourne, "A War Diary," p. 329.

40. Letter to Van Wyck Brooks, in Schlissel, ed., *World of Randolph Bourne*, p. 320.
41. Randolph Bourne, "The State," in *Radical Will*, pp. 359, 361.
42. Ibid., p. 365.
43. Randolph Bourne, "Old Tyrannies," in *Radical Will*, p. 171.
44. Ibid., p. 173.
45. Letter to Sara Bourne, in Schlissel, ed., *World of Randolph Bourne*, p. 326.

4. Martin Buber's Search for Zion

1. Martin Buber, *I and Thou*, trans. Walter Kaufmann (New York: Charles Scribner's Sons, 1970). See also the contributions of Nathan Rotenstreich, Maurice Friedman, Malcolm Diamond, and Emmanuel Levinas in *The Philosophy of Martin Buber*, ed. Paul Arthur Schilpp and Maurice Friedman (La Salle, Ill.: Open Court, 1967).
2. The story was told to me by Dr. Uri Simon, son of Ernst Akiva Simon, one of Buber's closest friends.
3. Martin Buber, A *Land of Two Peoples: Martin Buber on Jews and Arabs*, ed. Paul R. Mendes-Flohr (Oxford: Oxford University Press, 1983).
4. Quoted in Maurice Friedman, *Martin Buber's Life and Work: The Later Years, 1945–1965* (New York: E. P. Dutton, 1983), p. 345.
5. Ibid., p. 365.
6. Martin Buber, *Israel and the World: Essays in a Time of Crisis* (New York: Schocken, 1963), pp. 217–28. ("Nationalism" is translated by Olga Marx.)
7. Ibid., p. 225.
8. Ibid., p. 216.
9. *Sanhedrin* 74a. The quotation does not appear in Buber's text; I have used it to illustrate his meaning.
10. Buber, *Israel and the World*, p. 221.
11. Buber, *Land of Two Peoples*, p. 91.
12. Ibid., p. 87.
13. Amos 9:7; Buber, *Israel and the World*, p. 224.
14. Buber, *Land of Two Peoples*, p. 85.
15. Buber, *Israel and the World*, p. 248.
16. Buber, *Land of Two Peoples*, p. 80.
17. Buber, *Israel and the World*, pp. 234–35.
18. Quoted in Mendes-Flohr's introduction, Buber, *Land of Two Peoples*, p. 20.
19. Buber, *Land of Two Peoples*, p. 140.
20. See, for example, Buber, *Land of Two Peoples*, pp. 166 and 199.
21. Buber, *Israel and the World*, p. 255. On Buber in the 1940s, see Idit Zertal, "The Poisoned Heart: The Jews of Palestine and the Holocaust," *Tikkun* 2, no. 2 (1987):120.
22. Buber, *Land of Two Peoples*, p. 35.
23. Ibid., p. 221.
24. Ibid., p. 170.
25. Ibid., p. 129.
26. Ibid., p. 174.
27. Ibid., pp. 176, 178.
28. Buber, *Israel and the World*, p. 111 (emphasis in original). A more complete version of the inaugural lecture can be found in Martin Buber, *Pointing the Way*, trans. Maurice Friedman (New York: Schocken, 1974), pp. 177–91.
29. Buber, *Land of Two Peoples*, p. 210.
30. Buber, *Israel and the World*, p. 255.
31. Buber, *Land of Two Peoples*, p. 223.
32. Ibid., p. 162.
33. Ibid., p. 292.
34. Ibid., p. 223. The translator has "like that of any other Israeli," but I doubt that Buber meant so quickly to identify himself with the new state. "Israelite" would be a literal translation; "Jew" probably best expresses his meaning.
35. Ibid., p. 245.

36. Buber, *Israel and the World*, p. 257.
37. Buber, *Land of Two Peoples*, p. 304.
38. Buber, *Israel and the World*, p. 261; cf. Buber, *Land of Two Peoples*, p. 255.
39. Buber, *Israel and the World*, p. 258; on this theme, see Bernard Susser, *Existence and Utopia: The Social and Political Thought of Martin Buber* (Rutherford, N.J.: Fairleigh Dickinson University Press, 1981), pp. 147–52.
40. Buber, *Land of Two Peoples*, p. 250.
41. Ibid., p. 255.
42. Buber, *Pointing the Way*, p. 217; Buber, *Land of Two Peoples*, p. 244.
43. Buber, *Israel and the World*, p. 111.

5. Antonio Gramsci's Commitment

1. See, for example, *Marxism and Democracy*, ed. Alan Hunt (London: Lawrence and Wishart, 1980).
2. Antonio Gramsci, *Selections from the Prison Notebooks*, ed. and trans. Quinton Hoare and Geoffrey Nowell Smith (New York: International Publishers, 1971), p. 238. This selection has established the authoritative text for English-speaking Gramscians; it is well introduced and helpfully annotated; but Hoare and Smith tell their readers nothing about their principles of selection. What have they left out, and why?
3. Ibid., p. 239.
4. Ibid., pp. 132–33.
5. Ibid., p. 453.
6. Frank Parkin, *Marxism and Class Theory: A Bourgeois Critique* (New York: Columbia University Press, 1979), p. 81.
7. Gramsci, *Prison Notebooks*, p. 9; cf. also p. 323.
8. Ibid., p. 324.
9. Ibid., p. 327; cf. p. 333 on the "contradictory consciousness" of ordinary people.
10. Ibid., p. 326n.
11. Karl Marx and Friedrich Engels, *The German Ideology*, ed. R. Pascal (New York: International Publishers, 1947), p. 39.
12. Ibid., pp. 40–41.
13. Gramsci, *Prison Notebooks*, pp. 181–82.
14. Quoted in Chantal Mouffe, "Hegemony and Ideology in Gramsci," in *Gramsci and Marxist Theory*, ed. Chantal Mouffe (London: Routledge and Kegan Paul, 1979), p. 181. In my view, this is the best account of what Gramsci might have meant by "hegemony."
15. Gramsci, *Prison Notebooks*, p. 395.
16. Ibid., pp. 324, 333.
17. Ibid., p. 350.
18. Antonio Gramsci, "The Southern Question," in his *The Modern Prince and Other Writings*, trans. Louis Marks (London: Lawrence and Wishart, 1957), p. 50.
19. Quoted in John Cammett, *Antonio Gramsci and the Origins of Italian Communism* (Stanford: Stanford University Press, 1967), p. 78. On the Turin years, see also Martin Clark, *Antonio Gramsci and the Revolution That Failed* (New Haven: Yale University Press, 1977), and Gwyn Williams, *Proletarian Order: Antonio Gramsci, Factory Councils and the Origins of Communism in Italy, 1911–1921* (London: Pluto Press, 1980).
20. Cammett, *Antonio Gramsci*, p. 88.
21. Lenin, *What the "Friends of the People" Are* (1894; reprint, Moscow: Foreign Languages Publishing House, 1951), p. 286.
22. Gramsci, *Prison Notebooks*, p. 334.
23. Ibid., p. 334.
24. On "sitting still," see ibid., p. 42.
25. Ibid., p. 334.
26. Ibid., p. 197.
27. Quoted in James Joll, *Antonio Gramsci* (Harmondsworth: Penguin, 1978), p. 53.
28. Quoted in Harold Entwistle, *Antonio Gramsci: Conservative Schooling for Radical Politics*

(London: Routledge and Kegan Paul, 1979), p. 72. This is an extremely useful book, which breaks loose from some of the pieties of contemporary Gramscians.

29. Gramsci, *Prison Notebooks*, p. 186.

30. Ibid., pp. 330–31.

31. Ibid., pp. 331, 418.

32. Ibid., p. 398.

33. Ibid., p. 37.

34. Ibid., p. 40.

35. Ibid., pp. 35–36 (emphasis added). The "character" of a party member, Gramsci wrote (in *Prison Notebooks*, p. 268), is revealed by his "resistance to the pressures of surpassed cultures."

36. Gramsci, *Prison Notebooks*, p. 43.

37. Cammett, *Antonio Gramsci*, p. 12.

38. Alastair Davidson, *Antonio Gramsci: Towards an Intellectual Biography* (London: Merlin Press, 1977), provides a good account of Gramsci's Sardinian years.

39. Gramsci, *Prison Notebooks*, p. 418.

40. Quoted in Davidson, *Intellectual Biography*, p. 181.

41. Gramsci, *Prison Notebooks*, pp. 19, 20.

42. Ibid., pp. 77–79.

43. Ibid., p. 195.

6. Ignazio Silone: "The Natural"

1. Arthur Koestler, *Arrow in the Blue* (New York: Stein and Day, 1984), p. 317.

2. Ignazio Silone, *Emergency Exit* (1965), trans. Harvey Fergusson (London: Victor Gollancz, 1969), p. 63.

3. Ibid., pp. 63–64.

4. Ibid., p. 64.

5. Ignazio Silone, *Fontamara*, trans. Gwenda David and Eric Mosbacher (Harmondsworth: Penguin Books, 1934), p. 240.

6. Ignazio Silone, *Bread and Wine*, trans. Gwenda David and Eric Mosbacher (New York: Harper and Brothers, 1937), pp. 148–49.

7. Ibid., pp. 157–58.

8. Ignazio Silone, "On the Place of the Intellect and the Pretensions of the Intellectual," in George de Huszar, ed., *The Intellectuals: A Controversial Portrait* (Glencoe, Ill.: Free Press, 1960) pp. 262–63.

9. Silone, *Emergency Exit*, p. 65.

10. Ibid., pp. 117–18. For this essay, I have used the translation by Darina Silone, "The Choice of Comrades," in *Voices of Dissent* (New York: Grove Press, 1958), p. 328.

11. Silone, "Choice of Comrades," p. 329.

12. Ibid.

13. Silone, *Emergency Exit*, p. 65.

14. George Mosse used this phrase to characterize Silone at a seminar at The Hebrew University in Jerusalem (May 1987), where I read an earlier version of this chapter.

15. Silone, *Emergency Exit*, p. 66.

16. Silone, *Bread and Wine*, p. 291.

17. Silone, "On the Place of the Intellect," p. 261.

18. Ignazio Silone, *The Seed Beneath the Snow*, trans. Francis Frenaye (New York: Harper and Brothers, 1942), p. 172.

19. Silone, *Emergency Exit*, p. 85.

20. Silone, *Bread and Wine*, p. 129.

21. Silone, *Seed Beneath the Snow*, p. 29.

22. Silone, *Bread and Wine*, pp. 80–81.

23. Silone, *Seed Beneath the Snow*, pp. 300–301.

24. Henri Troyat, *Tolstoy*, trans. Nancy Amphoux (Garden City, N.Y.: Doubleday, 1967), p. 531.

25. Nicola Chiaromonte, "Silone the Rustic," *Survey* 26, no. 2 (Spring 1982):44.

26. Thorstein Veblen, "The Intellectual Pre-eminence of Jews in Modern Europe," in his *Essays in Our Changing Order* (New York: Viking Press, 1934), p. 227.

27. Silone, *Bread and Wine*, p. 29.
28. Ignazio Silone, A *Handful of Blackberries*, trans. Darina Silone (New York: Harper and Brothers, 1953), p. 120.
29. Michael Harrington, *The Accidental Century* (Baltimore: Penguin, 1966), p. 201.
30. Silone, *Bread and Wine*, p. 290.
31. Silone, *Emergency Exit*, p. 1.
32. Silone, "Choice of Comrades," p. 333.
33. Silone, *Emergency Exit*, pp. 108, 98.
34. Ibid., p. 109.
35. Silone, "Choice of Comrades," p. 334.
36. Chiaromonte, "Silone the Rustic," p. 44.
37. Silone, *Seed Beneath the Snow*, p. 280.
38. Ibid., p. 111.
39. Silone, "Choice of Comrades," p. 335.

7. George Orwell's England

1. Raymond Williams, *George Orwell* (New York: Columbia University Press, 1981). Reading Williams on Orwell, I have been helped by Paul Thomas's lively and perceptive essay, "Mixed Feelings: Raymond Williams and George Orwell," *Theory and Society* 14, no. 4 (July 1985):419–44.
2. George Orwell, *Homage to Catalonia*, intro. Lionel Trilling (Boston: Beacon Press, 1955), p. 5.
3. Raymond Williams, *Politics and Letters: Interviews with New Left Review* (London: Verso, 1981), pp. 384–92. The phrase "social patriotism" is first used in the interview by the *NLR* editor, but it is adopted by Williams (see p. 386).
4. Williams, *George Orwell*, pp. 12, 24.
5. George Orwell, "Inside the Whale," in *The Collected Essays, Journalism and Letters of George Orwell*, ed. Sonia Orwell and Ian Angus (New York: Harcourt, Brace, and World, 1968), 1:515.
6. I have quoted the poem as Orwell quotes it in "Inside the Whale." Auden revised the poem sometime in 1939, dropping the line about "necessary murder." For the revised version, see *The English Auden: Poems, Essays and Dramatic Writings: 1927–1939*, ed. Edward Mendelson (New York: Random House, 1977), pp. 210–12; the changes are described by Mendelson on pp. 424–25.
7. Orwell, "Inside the Whale," 1:516.
8. Orwell, "The Proletarian Writer," in *Collected Essays*, 2:38.
9. Orwell, *The Road to Wigan Pier* (New York: Harcourt, Brace and Company, 1958), p. 261.
10. Ibid., pp. 179–80.
11. Ibid., p. 180.
12. Orwell, *Homage to Catalonia*, p. 232.
13. Williams, *George Orwell*, p. 91.
14. Orwell, *Wigan Pier*, p. 180.
15. Orwell, *Keep the Aspidistra Flying* (New York: Popular Library, 1957), p. 219.
16. Trilling, "Introduction," in Orwell, *Homage to Catalonia*, p. xv.
17. George Orwell, *1984* (New York: Signet, 1950), pp. 8, 74, 106, 109.
18. Trilling, "Introduction," p. xviii.
19. George Orwell, *The Lion and the Unicorn*, in *Collected Essays* 2:97.
20. Ibid., 2:57 (emphasis in original).
21. Orwell, "My Country Right or Left," *Collected Essays*, 1:539; repeated in *Lion and Unicorn*, 2:103.
22. Orwell, *Lion and Unicorn*, 2:109.
23. George Orwell, "Notes on Nationalism," in *Collected Essays*, 3:362.
24. Orwell, *Lion and Unicorn*, 2:68.
25. Williams, *Politics and Letters*, p. 391.
26. Orwell, *Lion and Unicorn*, 2:95.
27. See Williams's appreciation of this point in *George Orwell*, p. 87.
28. Alex Zwerdling, *Orwell and the Left* (New Haven: Yale University Press, 1974), p. 16.
29. Richard Wollhiem, "Orwell Reconsidered," *Partisan Review* 27, no. 1 (Winter 1960):95–96.
30. Zwerdling, *Orwell and the Left*, pp. 9–10; see also George Orwell and Reginald Reynolds, eds. *British Pamphleteers*, vol. 1, intro. George Orwell (London: A. Wingate, 1948).

31. Orwell, *Lion and Unicorn*, 2:96.
32. See George Orwell, "James Burnham and the Managerial Revolution," in *Collected Essays*, 4: 160–81.
33. George Orwell, "Rudyard Kipling," in *Collected Essays*, 2:195.
34. Zwerdling, *Orwell and the Left*, p. 13.
35. Orwell, *Wigan Pier*, p. 212.
36. George Orwell, "Charles Dickens," in *Collected Essays*, 1:459.
37. George Orwell, "Arthur Koestler," in *Collected Essays*, 3:235.
38. Williams, *Politics and Letters*, pp. 391–92.
39. George Orwell, "Preface to the Ukrainian Edition of *Animal Farm*," in *Collected Essays*, 3: 404–5.
40. George Orwell, "As I Please," in *Collected Essays*, 3:226.
41. See the useful reading in George Woodcock, *The Crystal Spirit: A Study of George Orwell* (New York: Schocken Books, 1984), pp. 217–19.
42. Orwell, "Koestler," 3:236.
43. Orwell, *1984*, p. 62.
44. Irving Howe, *Politics and the Novel* (New York: Meridian Books, 1957), p. 236.

8. Albert Camus's Algerian War

1. Herbert R. Lottman, *Albert Camus: A Biography* (Garden City, N.Y.: Doubleday, 1979).
2. Simone de Beauvoir, *Force of Circumstance*, trans. Richard Howard (Harmondsworth: Penguin, 1968), p. 497; Conor Cruise O'Brien, *Albert Camus of Europe and Africa* (New York: Viking Press, 1970), pp. 88–92. O'Brien goes on to suggest a redeeming, though it seems to me implausible, interpretation of *The Fall.*
3. Albert Camus, *Notebooks: 1942–1951*, trans. Justin O'Brien (New York: Harcourt Brace Jovanovich, 1978), p. 182.
4. Camus, *Notebooks*, p. 250.
5. De Beauvoir, *Force of Circumstance*, p. 362.
6. Camus, *Notebooks*, p. 13.
7. Ibid., p. 54.
8. Jean-Paul Sartre, "A Plea for Intellectuals," in his *Between Existentialism and Marxism*, trans. John Mathews (New York: Pantheon, 1975), p. 260.
9. De Beauvoir, *Force of Circumstance*, p. 467.
10. Ibid., pp. 381, 397.
11. Sartre, "Plea for Intellectuals," p. 261.
12. De Beauvoir, *Force of Circumstance*, p. 472.
13. Quoted in Philip Thody, *Albert Camus: 1913–1960* (London: Hamish Hamilton, 1961), p. 212.
14. Franz Fanon, *Toward the African Revolution: Political Essays*, trans. Haakon Chevalier (New York: Grove Press, n.d.), p. 81.
15. Jules Roy, *The War in Algeria*, trans. Richard Howard (New York: Grove Press, 1961), p. 122.
16. Albert Camus, "Misère de la Kabylie," in *Actuelles III: Chronique Algérienne 1939–1958* (Paris: Gallimard, 1958), pp. 33–90.
17. Quoted in Ray Nichols, *Treason, Tradition, and the Intellectual* (Lawrence: University of Kansas Press, 1978), p. 164.
18. Camus, *Notebooks*, p. 78.
19. Ibid., p. 144.
20. Albert Camus, "Crise en Algérie," in *Actuelles III*, p. 122.
21. Quoted in Lottman, *Albert Camus*, p. 618.
22. Albert Camus, "Lettre à un militant algérien," in *Actuelles III*, pp. 126–27; reprinted in Albert Camus, *Resistance, Rebellion, and Death*, trans. Justin O'Brien (New York: Alfred A. Knopf, 1961), p. 127.
23. Albert Camus, "Avant-propos," in *Actuelles III*, p. 14; Camus, *Resistance*, p. 113.
24. O'Brien, *Camus of Europe and Africa*, p. 102.
25. Camus, "Avant-propos," p. 25; Camus, *Resistance*, p. 121.
26. Camus, "Avant-propos," p. 17; Camus, *Resistance*, p. 116.
27. Camus, *Notebooks*, p. 176.

28. Camus, "Avant-propos," p. 19; Camus, *Resistance*, p. 117.
29. Camus, "Avant-propos," p. 14; Camus, *Resistance*, pp. 113–14.
30. Albert Camus, "Algérie 1958," in *Actuelles III*, p. 200; Camus, *Resistance*, p. 144.
31. Camus, "*Crise en Algérie*," p. 95.
32. Camus, "Avant-propos," p. 20; Camus, *Resistance*, p. 118.
33. Albert Camus, "Appel pour une trève civile," in *Actuelles III*, p. 176; Camus, *Resistance*, p. 136.
34. Camus, "Avant-propos," p. 27; Camus, *Resistance*, p. 123.
35. Roy, *War in Algeria*, p. 123.
36. Camus, "Avant-propos," p. 15; Camus, *Resistance*, p. 114.
37. Roy, *War in Algeria*, p. 122.
38. O'Brien, *Camus of Europe and Africa*, p. 105.
39. Camus, "The Artist and His Time," in his *The Myth of Sisyphus, and Other Essays*, trans. Justin O'Brien (New York: Vintage, n.d.), pp. 147–48.
40. Camus, "Appel pour une trève civile," p. 183; Camus, *Resistance*, p. 141.
41. Thody, *Albert Camus*, p. 210.

9. Simone de Beauvoir and the Assimilated Woman

1. See Michel le Doeuff, "Simone de Beauvoir and Existentialism," *Feminist Studies* 6, no. 2 (1980): 277–89, and Linda Singer, "Interpretation and Retrieval: Rereading Beauvoir," *Hypatia: A Journal of Feminist Philosophy*, no. 3 (1985):231–38.
2. Simone de Beauvoir, *The Prime of Life*, trans. Peter Green (New York: Lancer Books, 1966), p. 516.
3. Simone de Beauvoir, *Force of Circumstance*, trans. Richard Howard (Harmondsworth: Penguin Books, 1968), p. 195.
4. This is the argument of an unpublished essay by Sonia Kruks on de Beauvoir and "the weight of situations," which Dr. Kruks has kindly allowed me to read.
5. Simone de Beauvoir, *The Second Sex*, trans. and ed. H. M. Parshley (New York: Alfred A. Knopf, 1953), p. xxix.
6. Alice Schwarzer, *After The Second Sex: Conversations with Simone de Beauvoir*, trans. Marianne Howarth (New York: Pantheon, 1984), p. 36; cf. p. 70.
7. De Beauvoir, *Second Sex*, pp. 24, 57, 64.
8. Ibid., pp. 27, 22.
9. Ibid., p. 63.
10. Ibid., p. 451.
11. Ibid., p. 50.
12. Ibid., p. 386.
13. Ibid., p. 495.
14. Ibid., p. 65.
15. Ibid., p. 32.
16. Schwarzer, *After the Second Sex*, p. 43.
17. De Beauvoir, *Second Sex*, p. 121.
18. Ibid., pp. 58, 140.
19. Ibid., p. 128. See Mary Evans's argument that Beauvoir's analysis points to "the reproduction by women, through an essentially bourgeois emancipation, of much that de Beauvoir finds least acceptable in Western Society," in *Simone de Beauvoir: A Feminist Mandarin* (London: Tavistock, 1985), pp. 124–25.
20. De Beauvoir, *Second Sex*, p. xxxvii.
21. Schwarzer, *After the Second Sex*, p. 45.
22. De Beauvoir, *Second Sex*, p. 133.
23. Ibid., p. 718.
24. Ibid., p. 603.
25. Ibid., p. 627.
26. Ibid., p. 604.
27. Ibid., p. 131. Roughly thirty years later, de Beauvoir described herself in the 1940s as a woman who had "abdicated, in some crucial respects at least, my womanhood. If I put it in economic terms . . . I had become a class collaborationist" (quoted by Carol Ascher, *Simone de Beauvoir: A Life of Freedom*

[Boston: Beacon Press, 1981], p. 129). But at the time collaboration was described more like camaraderie: she was more at home among men than among women.

28. Schwarzer, *After the Second Sex*, p. 46.

29. Jean Bethke Elshtain, *Public Man, Private Woman: Women in Social and Political Thought* (Princeton: Princeton University Press, 1981), pp. 306–10; Mary O'Brien, *The Politics of Reproduction* (Boston: Routledge and Kegan Paul, 1983), pp. 65–76. The best review and critique of recent arguments about female values is Jean Grimshaw, *Philosophy and Feminist Thinking* (Minneapolis: University of Minnesota Press, 1986).

30. De Beauvoir, *Second Sex*, p. 146.

31. O'Brien, *Politics of Reproduction*, p. 75.

32. De Beauvoir *Second Sex*, p. 617.

33. Iris Marion Young, "Humanism, Gynocentrism, and Feminist Politics," *Hypatia: A Journal of Feminist Philosophy*, no. 3 (1985): 176. For some evidence of the existence of a "counter-universe," see Patricia Meyer Spacks, *Gossip* (Chicago: University of Chicago Press, 1986).

34. Young, "Humanism," p. 176 (she is not reporting her own views); for a more balanced, though no less categorical, account of moral differences between men and women, see Carol Gilligan, *In a Different Voice: Psychological Theory and Women's Development* (Cambridge, Mass.: Harvard University Press, 1982).

35. Young, "Humanism," p. 180.

36. Schwarzer, *After the Second Sex*, p. 78.

37. Kate Soper, "The Qualities of Simone de Beauvoir," *New Left Review*, no. 156 (March–April 1986):128.

38. Schwarzer, *After the Second Sex*, pp. 116–17.

39. Ibid., p. 78.

10. Herbert Marcuse's America

1. R. D. Laing, review of *One-Dimensional Man* in *New Left Review* 26 (July–August 1964):80.

2. Herbert Marcuse, *One-Dimensional Man* (Boston: Beacon Press, 1966), p. xvii.

3. Ibid., p. 254.

4. Ibid., p. xii.

5. Ibid., pp. 256–57.

6. Ibid., pp. 4, 76.

7. Ibid., pp. 9, 12.

8. Ibid., pp. 1–2.

9. Ibid., p. 1.

10. Ibid., p. 32.

11. Ibid., p. 3.

12. Ibid., pp. 50–52.

13. Cf. John Stuart Mill, "Utilitarianism," in *The Philosophy of John Stuart Mill*, ed. Marshall Cohen (New York: Modern Library, 1961), p. 333.

14. The story has many "right-wing" versions; for the first of its "left-wing" versions, see Jean-Jacques Rousseau's *Discourse on the Origins of Inequality*.

15. Marcuse, *One-Dimensional Man*, p. 6.

16. Ibid., p. 7.

17. Ibid., p. 6.

18. Ibid., p. 49.

19. Ibid., p. 242.

20. Quoted in ibid., p. 80, from an article in *Nouvelle Révue Française*, July 1956.

21. Marcuse, *One-Dimensional Man*, p. 3.

22. C. Wright Mills, *The Power Elite* (New York: Oxford University Press, 1956).

23. Marcuse, *One-Dimensional Man*, pp. 31, 57.

24. Randolph Bourne, "Traps for the Unwary," in his *The Radical Will: Selected Writings, 1911–1918*, ed. Olaf Hansen (New York: Urizen Books, 1977), p. 483.

25. Marcuse, *One-Dimensional Man*, p. 61.

26. Ibid., p. 64.

27. Ibid., pp. 64–65.

28. Ibid., p. 71.
29. Ibid., p. 245.
30. Ibid., p. 250.
31. See Marcuse's essay, "Repressive Tolerance," in Herbert Marcuse, Barrington Moore, Jr., and Robert Paul Wolff, A *Critique of Pure Tolerance* (Boston: Beacon Press, 1965).
32. Marcuse, *One-Dimensional Man*, pp. 174, 199, 194, but cf. p. 86, where Marcuse makes a very different and probably more accurate claim: "Society expresses its requirements directly in the linguistic material but not without opposition; the popular language strikes with spiteful and defiant humor at the official and semi-official discourse." But his dominant note is suggested by the quotations in my text.
33. Ibid., p. 103.
34. Allen Graubard, "One-Dimensional Pessimism: A Critique of Herbert Marcuse's Theories," in *Beyond the New Left*, ed. Irving Howe (New York: McCall Publishing Company, 1970), p. 161.
35. Marcuse, *One-Dimensional Man*, p. 178.
36. Marcuse, *An Essay on Liberation* (Boston: Beacon Press, 1969), p. 47.
37. Marcuse, *One-Dimensional Man*, p. 192.
38. Ibid., p. 72.
39. Ibid., p. 134.
40. Ibid., pp. 123–24.
41. Ibid., pp. 231–32 (emphasis in original).
42. Ibid., p. 232.
43. Ibid., p. 251.
44. Ibid., pp. 40–42.
45. Ibid., p. 41.
46. Ibid., p. 215 (emphasis added).

11. The Lonely Politics of Michel Foucault

1. Michel Foucault, *Power/Knowledge: Selected Interviews and Other Writings, 1972–1977*, ed. Colin Gordon (New York: Pantheon, 1980), p. 145.
2. Ibid., p. 193.
3. Ibid., p. 133.
4. See Foucault on Borges's encyclopedia, *The Order of Things*, trans. A. S. London (New York: Pantheon, 1970), p. xv.
5. Foucault, *Power/Knowledge*, p. 102.
6. Ibid., p. 188.
7. Ibid., p. 187.
8. See the argument in Peter Bachrach and Morton S. Baratz, "The Two Faces of Power," *American Political Science Review* 56 (1962):947–52.
9. Michel Foucault, *The History of Sexuality*, vol. 1: *An Introduction*, trans. Robert Hurley (New York: Vintage, 1980), p. 94.
10. Michel Foucault, *Power, Truth, Strategy*, ed. Meaghan Morris and Paul Patton (Sydney: Feral Publications, 1979), p. 60.
11. Foucault, *Power/Knowledge*, p. 98.
12. Foucault, *Power, Truth, Strategy*, p. 126.
13. Foucault, *History of Sexuality*, p. 96.
14. Foucault, *Power/Knowledge*, p. 96.
15. Michael Walzer, "Dissatisfaction in the Welfare State" (1967), in *Radical Principles: Reflections of an Unreconstructed Democrat* (New York: Basic Books, 1980), p. 33.
16. Foucault, *Power/Knowledge*, p. 62.
17. Michel Foucault, *Discipline and Punish: The Birth of the Prison*, trans. Alan Sheridan (New York: Vintage, 1979), p. 271.
18. Foucault, *History of Sexuality*, pp. 140–41.
19. Foucault, *Power/Knowledge*, p. 142.
20. On the meaning of *episteme*, see Foucault, *Order of Things*, pp. xx–xxiv.
21. Foucault, *Discipline and Punish*, p. 223.
22. Michel Foucault, *Language, Counter-memory, Practice: Selected Essays and Interviews*, ed. Donald F. Bouchard (Ithaca: Cornell University Press, 1977), p. 230.

23. Foucault, *Language*, p. 231.
24. Ibid., p. 227.
25. For a somewhat similar critique of Foucault's anarchism, see J. G. Merquior, *Foucault* (London: Fontana, 1985), chap. 10.
26. Foucault, *Power/Knowledge*, p. 130.
27. Ibid., pp. 134, 136–37.
28. Paul Patton, "Of Power and Prisons," in Foucault, *Power, Truth, Strategy*, p. 126.
29. Foucault, *History of Sexuality*, p. 94.
30. Foucault, *Power/Knowledge*, pp. 126ff.
31. Ibid., p. 131.
32. Charles Taylor, "Foucault on Freedom and Truth," *Political Theory* 12 (1984):179–80.
33. Jim Merod, *The Political Responsibility of the Critic* (Ithaca: Cornell University Press, 1987), p. 158.
34. I owe this image to Clifford Geertz.

12. Breyten Breytenbach: The Critic in Exile

1. Breyten Breytenbach, *End Papers: Essays, Letters, Articles of Faith, Workbook Notes* (New York: Farrar, Straus and Giroux, 1986), p. 20.
2. For English translations of selected poems, see *In Africa Even the Flies Are Happy*, trans. Denis Hirson (London: John Calder, 1978).
3. Breytenbach, *End Papers*, p. 74.
4. Ibid., p. 75.
5. Ibid., pp. 209, 74.
6. Ibid., p. 228.
7. Quoted in Jack Cope, *The Adversary Within: Dissident Writers in Afrikaans* (Cape Town: David Philip, 1982), p. 168.
8. Breyten Breytenbach, *A Season in Paradise*, trans. Rike Vaughan, intro. André Brink (London: Faber and Faber, 1980). I have taken many biographical details from Brink's introduction. Breytenbach's conference talk, titled "A View from Outside," appears on pp. 151–60.
9. Breytenbach, *Season in Paradise*, p. 154; Breytenbach's analysis of the ANC can be found in *The True Confessions of an Albino Terrorist* (New York: Farrar, Straus and Giroux, 1985), pp. 74–78.
10. Breytenbach, *End Papers*, p. 69.
11. Cope, *The Adversary Within*, p. 178.
12. Breytenbach, *True Confessions*, pp. 81–86.
13. Ibid., p. 86.
14. Breytenbach, *End Papers*, p. 100.
15. Breytenbach, *True Confessions*, p. 280; Breytenbach, *End Papers*, p. 94.
16. Breytenbach, *Season in Paradise*, p. 203.
17. Herbert Marcuse, *One-Dimensional Man* (Boston: Beacon Press, 1966), p. 199.
18. Breytenbach, *End Papers*, p. 34.
19. Ibid., p. 237.
20. Ibid., p. 41.
21. Ibid., p. 56.
22. Ibid., p. 190; cf. p. 20.
23. Breytenbach, *Season in Paradise*, p. 154.
24. Breytenbach, *End Papers*, p. 247 (an end note commenting on an essay written in 1971).
25. Ibid., p. 99.
26. Neil Lazarus, "Longing, Radicalism, Sentimentality: Reflections on Breyten Breytenbach's *A Season in Paradise*," *Journal of Southern African Studies* 12, no. 2 (April 1986):177.
27. N. P. van Wyk Louw, *Lojale Verset*, in *Versamelde Prosa*, 1:166–68. I owe this reference to Hermann Giliomee.
28. Breytenbach, *True Confessions*, p. 360.
29. Quoted in Cope, *The Adversary Within*, p. 173.
30. Quoted in ibid., p. 172.
31. Breytenbach, *End Papers*, p. 205.
32. Ibid., p. 16.

33. Ibid., p. 204; cf. Cope, *The Adversary Within*, p. 166.
34. Breytenbach, *End Papers*, p. 104.
35. Ibid., p. 205.
36. Ibid., p. 204.
37. Breytenbach, *True Confessions*, p. 359.
38. Quoted in Hermann Giliomee, "Apartheid and the Afrikaner Literary Tradition of 'Loyal Resistance,'" paper for a conference on South African politics and writing, Montpellier, France, May 1987, p. 27.
39. Breyten Breytenbach, "breyten prays for himself," in *In Africa Even the Flies Are Happy*, p. 6.
40. Breytenbach, *True Confessions*, p. 359.
41. Breytenbach, *End Papers*, pp. 19, 207.
42. Ibid., p. 32.
43. The phrase "in jou taal, in jou land" is from a speech Breytenbach gave at Stellenbosch University in April 1986—his only visit to South Africa after he was released from prison (he has been refused a visa ever since). The text can be found in *Die Suid-Afrikaan*, Fall 1986, p. 12.
44. Breytenbach, *End Papers*, p. 76.

13. Conclusion: Criticism Today

1. The best single source is Jean-Paul Sartre, "A Plea for Intellectuals," in his *Between Existentialism and Marxism*, trans. John Mathews (New York: Pantheon, 1975), pp. 228–85. See my discussion in chapter 8.
2. Quoted in Walter Laqueur, *A History of Zionism* (New York: Holt, Rinehart and Winston, 1972), p. 435; my criticism of these lines also follows Laqueur's.
3. The classic account of critical capitulation is Czeslaw Milosz, *The Captive Mind*, trans. Jane Zielonko (New York: Vintage, 1955).
4. A useful critique of Foucault and the academic work he has inspired can be found in Jim Merod, *The Political Responsibility of the Critic* (Ithaca: Cornell University Press, 1987), esp. chap. 7.
5. Breyten Breytenbach, *End Papers: Essays, Letters, Articles of Faith, Workbook Notes* (New York: Farrar, Straus and Giroux, 1986), p. 29.
6. *Hamlet*, III. iv. 34–38.
7. *Hamlet*, III. iv. 89.
8. Alan Trachtenberg, "Ever—the Human Document," in *America and Lewis Hine*, ed. Walter and Naomi Rosenblum (New York: Aperture, 1977), p. 129; quoted in Robert Westbrook, "Lewis Hine and the Ethics of Progressive Camerawork," *Tikkun* 2, no. 2 (1987):25.
9. *Franz Rosenzweig: His Life and Thought*, ed. Nahum Glatzer (New York: Schocken, 1961), p. 179.
10. *The English Auden: Poems, Essays, and Dramatic Writings, 1927–1939*, ed. Edward Mendelson (New York: Random House, 1977), p. 183.
11. Adam Michnik, *Letters from Prison*, trans. Maya Latynski (Berkeley: University of California Press, 1985), p. 198.
12. Albert Camus, *The Rebel: An Essay on Man in Revolt*, trans. Anthony Bower (New York: Vintage, 1956), p. 36.
13. See my discussion of the prophet Amos in Michael Walzer, *Interpretation and Social Criticism* (Cambridge, Mass.: Harvard University Press, 1987), chap. 3.
14. Quoted in Irving Howe, "This Age of Conformity," in his *A World More Attractive: A View of Modern Literature and Politics* (New York: Horizon, 1963), p. 259.
15. See Peter M. Rutkoff and William B. Scott, *New School: A History of the New School for Social Research* (New York: Free Press, 1986), chap. 1.
16. Baudelaire and Sartre are quoted in Renato Poggioli, *The Theory of the Avant-Garde*, trans. Gerald Fitzgerald (Cambridge, Mass.: Harvard University Press, 1968), pp. 111, 126.
17. Breytenbach, *End Papers*, p. 145.
18. Michnik, *Letters from Prison*, p. 20.
19. Quoted in Samuel Hynes, *The Auden Generation: Literature and Politics in England in the 1930s* (Princeton: Princeton University Press, 1982), pp. 338–39.
20. Martin Buber, *A Land of Two Peoples: Martin Buber on Jews and Arabs*, ed. Paul R. Mendes-Flohr (Oxford: Oxford University Press, 1983), p. 138.

INDEX

Index

Index

Index